THE

Curriculum

Also by Stanley Bing

Biz Words

Crazy Bosses

What Would Machiavelli Do?

Throwing the Elephant: Zen and the Art of Managing Up

Sun Tzu Was a Sissy

The Big Bing

Executricks, Or How to Retire While You're Still Working

100 Bullshit Jobs . . . And How to Get Them

Rome, Inc.

Bingsop's Fables

NOVELS

Lloyd: What Happened

You Look Nice Today

THE
Curriculum

Everything You Need

to Know to Be a

Master of Business Arts

Stanley Bing

HARPER
BUSINESS

An Imprint of HarperCollinsPublishers
www.harpercollins.com

FIRST EDITION

Background image of paper texture courtesy of Red Koala/Shutterstock, Inc.
Head/brain silhouette courtesy of Itlada/Shutterstock, Inc.

Library of Congress Cataloging-in-Publication Data has been applied for.

ISBN: 978-0-06-199853-9

14 15 16 17 18 ov/rrd 10 9 8 7 6 5 4 3 2 1

To Dick and Jane and Burt and Bill and Peter and Mel and of course Les.

Thanks for the memories.

A man may say full sooth in game and play.

—Geoffrey Chaucer, 1390

CONTENTS

The Curriculum

001.

Preface

This core curriculum and extensive elective courses are based not on ivory tower musings but on actual workplace experience augmented by as much research as seems necessary to back it up. The course is comprehensive but will certainly not take anywhere near the two years and up to $250,000 involved in those offered by well-established, time-consuming and tedious ivy-covered institutions stocked with professors who would be eaten for lunch by most serious business executives.

The course is designed for those who want to play by a different game plan than those who go from A to B and are content to stop at C. You will not be stopping at C. You will go all the way to Z and even beyond, if you've got the will and nerve—and aren't too sentimental. It's business, after all. It's not personal.

Supporting our conclusions will be the trove of research and speculation made available by the National Association for Serious Studies, a research organization and think tank established by this author.

002.

A Note on the National Association for Serious Studies

The National Association for Serious Studies is a national organization dedicated to a number of serious studies. It was conceived at the beginning of the century to establish credibility for the conclusions reached by the faculty of the Association on a variety of subjects, and as such is in essence no different than any other institution now providing intellectual weight to a variety of concerns of different philosophical, political, or commercial stripe. All conclusions and associated graphics are based on serious research and extensive anecdotal and direct observation by senior members of the Association, who, as is common in many research enterprises, have based their findings on what they discovered once they knew what they wanted to find.

The work of the National Association is overseen by its senior management, which is guided by a board of directors, each of whom is highly distinguished in his or her chosen field. Unlike other boards, however, board members of the National Association for Serious Studies are not compensated, except perhaps at the occasional social function at which somebody else picks up the check.

All data, analysis, conjecture, and graphical interpretations offered in this Curriculum by the National Association for Serious Studies are proprietary, and adhere to the highest standards of Internet journalism.

003. CURRICULUM OVERVIEW:
The Road to Power

This book is divided into four major sections:

- The Core Curriculum
- The Advanced Curriculum
- Tutorials and Electives
- Glossary of Key Vocabulary

It is structured like a solar system, with the red-hot, primal magma in the center and the cooler, more evolved planets revolving around it at a safe distance. Like this:

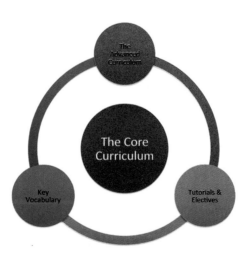

The inquiring student may have some questions at this point. Let's get to those now.

Q: Can I really skip the expense and aggravation of getting an MBA by studying this Curriculum instead?

A: Yes and no. If you want to inhabit the exciting world of finance, an MBA is a nice thing to have. It takes out vast portions of your brain and replaces them with a certain kind of thinking that is useful in business. And that kind of knowledge, as valuable as it is in the construction of mortgage-based security instruments and acquiring assets with debt, is useless in daily life. On the other hand, a traditional MBA does not provide you with a seminar on how to use an expense account as an effective strategic instrument, or how to bullshit your way through a difficult situation. That is because MBAs are generally taught by people who assume that business, particularly Big Business, is a serious occupation where grim, gray operatives ply their trade and the irreverent, irrational, or subversive need not apply. They are right, to a certain extent. But they are also profoundly wrong in a way that will slow them down and make them vulnerable to those who are operating in a more intuitive, hedonistic, and personality-driven way.

We must also consider the terrible cost in financial and human terms that the traditional MBA exacts on its recipients and those around them. People go into business school as recognizable human beings. Only some emerge intact. The rest come out bland, or gnarled, or super-smug, or reptilian, or in a kind of daze they only wake up from when it's too late, usually around age forty-five.

Throughout this Curriculum, a high value will be placed on retaining the basic nugget of yourself, so you won't have to spend the rest of your adult life wandering in an emotional and intellectual wilderness of your own making.

Q: Do people ever really make it to the top without an MBA?

A: Excuse me? Here's a list of people who never got an MBA:

- **Steve Jobs,** the Mozart of the twentieth century, cofounder of Apple and Pixar;
- **Walt Disney,** builder of worlds, the Steve Jobs of his day;
- **Muriel Siebert,** scrappy, tough, the first woman to be elected to the New York Stock Exchange, defied the glass ceiling virtually alone for decades;
- **Richard Branson,** adventurer and billionaire founder of Virgin;
- **Mary Kay Ash,** the founder of Mary Kay Cosmetics, started with nothing and ended up

building a multibillion-dollar enterprise; the leading female entrepreneur in U.S. history;

- **Sergey Brin**, billionaire cofounder of Google, now working on inventing an edible hamburger made entirely of bovine stem cells;
- **Larry Page,** billionaire cofounder of Google who now runs the company;
- **Michael Dell**, billionaire founder of Dell Computers, which at this writing is not doing all that well. But he is;
- **Oprah Winfrey**, billionaire entrepreneur CEO of her own production company, Harpo (Oprah spelled backward) and cited by many as the most influential woman in the world;
- **Larry Ellison**, mega-billionaire cofounder of Oracle software company, owner of the entire Hawaiian Island of Lanai and new proprietor of the America's Cup, which he has turned from an international sporting event into a corporate celebration of himself;
- **Steve Wozniak,** billionaire cofounder of Apple;
- **Mark Zuckerberg**, deeply odd founder of Facebook, billionaire in a hoodie;
- **Sara Blakeley**, founder of Spanx undergarments and the world's youngest self-made female billionaire;
- **Ron Popeil**, the genius behind the marketing of the pocket fisherman, the Ginzu knife, and so many other products that would never have occurred to you.

Did we mention Bill Gates? Founder of Microsoft? He's on the list, too.

None of these people went to business school. Most (except for Winfrey and Blakeley) never graduated from college. Who else is on our list of MBA-free titans?

- **CEOs** galore. Warren Buffett did attend Wharton, but he left after two years. He complained that he knew more than his teachers. Perhaps he was kidding. Warren is a big kidder. Great sense of humor. Plays the ukulele. After departing Wharton, he got his degree from the far less swanky University of Nebraska–Lincoln, going on to earn a master's of science in economics from the Columbia Business School. But look, Ma, no MBA.
- **Big corporate nabobs (BCN)**. Names will be redacted to protect these excessively affluent individuals, but they are there, hidden for the most part in the fine woodwork of every major corporation.
- **Moguls:** They're a very special breed. It's hard to say what separates the Barry Dillers* or Bonos from the recondite CEOs and BCNs. Whatever it is, they didn't learn it in

---

* Dropped out of UCLA after one semester.

business school. For while the big domes on Wall Street, who arguably caused the collapse of our economic system, have MBAs, these guys often don't.

◦ **Cheese artisans:** Just one of many jobs that involve skills unrelated to business schooling and at which people can make a living and be very happy. That could be you.

Q: Well, okay. But I'm sure a lot of terrific business people *have* their MBAs.

A: Here, for instance, are some graduates of just one institution. The Wharton School of the University of Pennsylvania:

◦ **Dennis Levine,** one of the great financial criminals of the 1980s, the branded mascot of the Greed Is Good guys. He has since benefited from the general cultural amnesia of our day to emerge as a highly regarded pundit, philosopher, and lecturer on a wide range of interesting subjects, including business ethics.

◦ **Ron Perelman,** hugely successful raider in his day, now a major investor, groomer of mergers and acquisitions, and philanthropist.*

◦ **Michael Milken,** crucial in the development of the idea that you could buy a valuable asset with little more than your reputation in your pocket. Inventor of the junk bond. Indicted on ninety-eight counts of racketeering and securities fraud in 1989, he pleaded guilty to six securities and reporting violations. He was sentenced to ten years but only served two after testifying against his former associates. A huge philanthropist now, he has positioned himself as a business philosopher of sorts. Has his own think tank, which holds a big get-together of moguls, senior upper middle managers, hangers-on, bloggers, and reporters who get together once a year in Los Angeles to posit on the future of the business world and scratch each other where they itch.†

◦ **Raj Rajaratnam,** convicted in 2012 of insider trading and was sentenced to the longest term for that crime in history, fourteen years.

---

* The relationship between odious behavior in early business life and subsequent philanthropy will be explored later.

† Think tanks don't really hit the big time until they have an associated conference. The First Annual Symposium on the Future of Everything, held by the National Association for Serious Studies and a sponsor to be named later, is now being mapped out.

Of course, I'm stacking the deck. There are hundreds and hundreds of wonderful people who went to Wharton, and many jerks who went to lesser business schools, or greater ones. Bernard Madoff, perpetrator of the greatest financial crime in American history, a stone-cold Fagin who stole $40 billion from his unsuspecting victims, an individual who makes the lowest insect look like a noble creature, never got an MBA. On the bright side, he did serve as nonexecutive chairman of the NASDAQ stock exchange and a consultant to the Securities and Exchange Commission before he was busted, so you can't say that he let his lack of education hurt him none.*

And now, as Father William said, "I have answered three questions, and that is enough." Let's look at how *The Curriculum* is built:

The Four Levels

First, the **core curriculum** will teach you the fundamentals of the real world. After that, there is a hefty dose of **advanced material** that tries to help you get granular and muscular as you deal with the daily world that right now you may be ill prepared to encounter. Then a host of **tutorials and electives** will be offered for advanced study. This is followed by a comprehensive **glossary of business terms** to help you build your vocabulary. A good vocabulary is necessary for those who wish to appear more intelligent than they really are. No business career can take off without it. For those who wish, a **Final Exam**, to be graded by the faculty of the National Association, will be available on its website. For those who are into such things, **a diploma suitable for framing** is included at the end of this book.

Power: The Ultimate Payoff

In the end, business is like ballet. Some have a talent for it. Those who do never stop taking classes, practicing, working out their muscles and sinews, even when they sleep. The art of learning the dance is never done. One layer builds on another, conveying the one true coin of the realm. Power.

---

* Paul Simon, "Kodachrome," 1973.

The Curriculum = Power

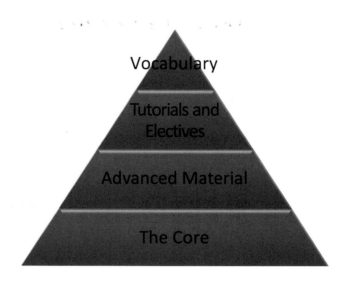

These four elements will build your personal power over time, each contributing to different degrees as you move through your career. The following graphic expresses the shifting importance of each element of the Curriculum.

Contribution to Personal Power

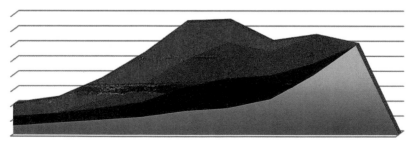

- The Core (*in blue*) will be valuable throughout your time on Planet Business, actually growing as you progress until it is overwhelmingly the most useful phalanx of tools in your arsenal;

- The Advanced Curriculum (*in red*) is critical as well, but most essential in the middle years of your quest, since it is primarily with the *management of issues* that this portion of the Curriculum is concerned.

- Your **Tutorials and Electives** (*in green*) are key as you hone your craft, and are never truly completed, as new issues emerge and old ones fade in your continual pursuit to *master the form* of daily workplace life.

- Finally, the question of *how you express yourself* is very important in the beginning and middle years, dwindling a bit as you attain the pinnacles of power. Nobody cares if the top dog is articulate, has a good **Vocabulary** (*in purple*) or makes much sense. That's one of the perks that come with a perch at the top.

The goal is power. The Curriculum is the way. Let's begin.

100.

The Core

THE CORE

The Core Curriculum establishes a common language and foundation upon which a real-world business career can be mounted. Courses include:

101: Not Appearing Stupid
102: Fabricating a Business Personality
103: Selling, Marketing, and Negotiating
104: Managing
105: Group Interaction
106: Fundaments of Power

While the core is not in itself sufficient for mastery in the business arts, it must be completed before more sophisticated development is possible. Those who ignore the core and proceed directly to the helter-skelter world of daily business are essentially in the same position as monkeys given the assignment to type on a keyboard until they achieve *Hamlet*. There's always a chance it may work out well, but if it does it will be by accident, and only after an unacceptable length of time.

All elements in the Core are of virtually equal importance, although the role of both management of others and group interaction is somewhat less critical to the armature of the whole. We begin with a first step that may seem simple but in fact makes all other steps possible. A trip on the way out of the starting gate has disqualified more than one runner on his or her way to glory.

Elements of the Core (%)

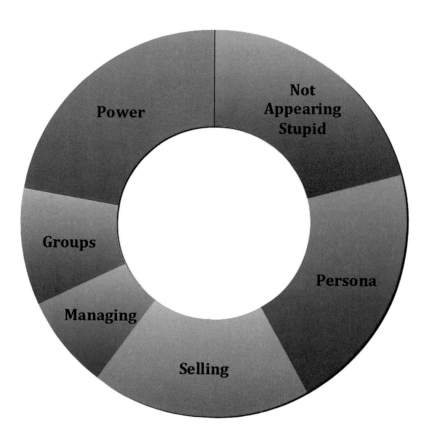

COURSE 101: Not Appearing Stupid

The workplace is accepting of all kinds of people, but not those who appear to be stupid. Looking stupid is almost always an impediment to success, and in certain fields it is a virtual roadblock. In this, the first layer of the Core, we will examine the implications of looking stupid and develop a clear strategy to avoid it.

First, let's look at how the appearance of being stupid can affect your chance of success. The following chart, based on proprietary data from a number of credible sources, illustrates dramatically how the appearance of stupidity has an impact on how one does in one's chosen field. Each color bar represents the "chance of success" a man or woman may possess while demonstrating intelligence or the demonstrable lack of it. What is clear is that in all cases, the appearance of intelligence is an asset, and the inverse not so much.

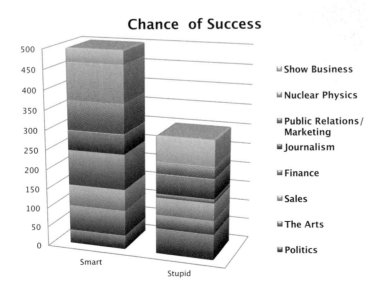

Notes, working vertically downward in the bar:

- ◦ In show business, perhaps more than any other field (shown in the pink bar at the top of the stack), the appearance of stupidity may not only be more readily accepted (most clearly among the beautiful) but may in fact build one's chance of advancement, particularly if the appearance of stupidity is married to an aggressive, obnoxious personality;
- ◦ The appearance of stupidity all but wipes out the chance of success in nuclear physics (in light blue) but does not eradicate it entirely, thanks to the popularity of various nonsensical flavors of string theory;
- ◦ Interesting recent developments seem to indicate that the appearance of intelligence is more important in the field of public relations (burnt umber) than it is in journalism (aqua), thanks to advances made possible by the Internet;
- ◦ In finance, sales, and the arts, stupidity is a definite undesirable, although perhaps less so in sales, where enough people are drunk after noon to obscure the issue;
- ◦ In politics, the appearance of stupidity actually proves to be an asset in a measurable number of cases.

The punishment or reward for visible stupidity helps to shape the makeup of each of the professions examined above. This concept emerges quite clearly when the same data employed above is expressed as a function of profession. Here, in the first such review of its type, is a general breakdown of the mix between apparently stupid people and demonstrably smart people in these same businesses and vocations:*

---

* National Association for Serious Studies, © 2013.

Smart vs. Stupid: Key Professions

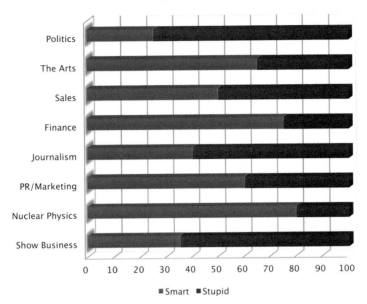

Smart ▪ Stupid

Some interesting themes develop here. At the top, the impact on our political system is clearly evident from the makeup of those who have no problem evincing considerable stupidity. On the other hand, in the field of nuclear physics only the most evolved eggheads can abandon rational thought altogether and secure a spot on a PBS documentary. The remainder of practitioners must look smart, albeit not socially.* The percentages in show business are somewhat skewed by the presence in the sample of talent agents.

The most important conclusion we reach from this data is that those who wish to succeed in the higher levels of business life—generally occupied by those in ultra-senior management as well as the upper regions of finance, sales, and communications (PR/marketing)—must appear to be the least stupid. While they most often are not smarter than anybody else, those who prosper and advance under the big tent are clearly more adept at *appearing not stupid* than the rest of us, not only in everyday life but, perhaps more important, in crucial business situations as well.

---

* See *The Big Bang Theory*, Chuck Lorre/Bill Prady, CBS Television Network, 2007–.

The punishment for the appearance of stupidity is immediate and irrevocable, and can undo a life of appearing relatively sentient. Some examples for further study:

- Marc Antony: Fabulous soldier, great orator, sexiest man alive circa 50 BC. Falls in love with Cleopatra, who then leads him around by his phallus for the rest of his life. At the Battle of Actium, he spends most of the engagement out of harm's way on Cleopatra's barge, looking stupid.

- Martha Stewart, one of the smartest and most aggressive self-marketers in history, with a fortune of her own and a multimillion-dollar empire built on selling her sagacity and taste, fiddles around with a small investment and is nabbed for it by the feds. Cornered, she fails to listen to her most loyal and intelligent advisors, hires new advisors who are stupid, and then tries to lie her way out of the situation and ends up going to jail. A stupid story all the way around, all the more stupid because it appears so stupid.

- And let's not even talk about what the obviously most stupid merger in history, that of Time Warner with AOL, did to the reputations of everybody involved, but probably most disastrously to arguably one of the smartest men in media, Gerald Levin.

Ironically, the most harm comes to the most intelligent people when they do stupid things. Most recently, that phenomenon—people who are so smart they're effectively stupid—was widespread among the group of pseudoscientists in the field of economics, where stupidity seems to be conferred on the formerly intelligent along with the diploma.

It's difficult to appear nonstupid in the world of business. There are for certain many, many challenges, roadblocks, and disincentives along the way, including:

Too Many Topics: How can one appear informed, acute, and prepared to opine on the wide variety of subjects that arise in a business day?

- ✔ Personnel issues
- ✔ Financial matters
- ✔ Strategic and tactical conundrums
- ✔ Menu selections in the presence of highly opinionated oenophiles and gustatory hedonists
- ✔ Moral enigmas
- ✔ Unplanned and unforeseen subjects that pop up with regularity—perhaps the most

frightening eventuality of all, particularly in the tech sector, where the crazy blizzard of buzzwords, fancies, rumors, and blather associated with the constant, roiling sea of trends is all but insurmountable.

Too Many Agendas: The plethora of those more senior than you who utter stupid things to which you might be forced to give the appearance of agreement;

Not Enough Knowledge: Then there's your own lack of training in the art of expressing yourself in an on-point and cogent way even when you have nothing to say and no means of expressing it.

This last issue—how to not get caught being stupid in all contexts—is what we now intend to address.

Mastering the Elements of Nonstupid Discourse

Fortunately, one does not have to be a genius to grasp and then successfully employ the tenets of excellent business discourse both written and verbal. A smattering of knowledge and the ability to exude confidence is key. Simple fundamentals and a battery of practice should help any student attain skills in this area that are completely appropriate in virtually any business context.

Here are the makings of the crucial foundation upon which the appearance of nonstupidity may be built:

A. *Reading and writing basic business English.* Further discussion on e-mail and texting technique is provided in later chapters in this Curriculum, but the basics of decent business writing, analog and digital, are relatively simple. Master these very few rules and you will distinguish yourself as, quite literally, among the 5 percent who don't appear to be stupid when required to commit a thought to paper:

1. Say what you mean. Don't be afraid to do so, within reason. Of course, "what you mean" may, in fact, be a reiteration of what someone else means, that is up to you, but don't make people read a bunch of gibberish to finally ascertain what you intend to communicate. Possible "what you mean" statements include:

    a. "I agree with Lenny."

    b. "I don't agree with Lenny."

    c. "Okay by me."

    d. "There are three reasons I don't like this. It's against policy. It will annoy Mr. Roover. It will be hard to accomplish. Let's talk about this in person."

The thing that distinguishes all these utterances is that 1) they are clear, 2) they are in declarative form, and 3) you don't have to be a genius to get it. That's good writing.

    2. Adhere to common forms of English. There is such a thing as an English sentence. It is made up of some very basic fundaments:

    a. A subject

    b. A verb

    c. An occasional object

    d. A reason for its existence

It's amazing how few people can construct a sentence from these building blocks. For instance, this is not a sentence: "After Mr. Roover and us are coordinating the Toledo meeting is key." Likewise: "Get with Karen and coordinate interstitial SMATPE defibrillation in Zone 6 operations" says nothing and takes time to do it. Here are some good business sentences that will help you appear intelligent:

    a. "Chuck can do it."

    b. "Let's not go crazy on this thing."

    c. "Talk to Karen about it and get back to me."

    d. "There is absolutely no research to support that. Show me some research and maybe we can formulate further strategic alternatives."

This last, obviously, is a more complex sentence. But it says what it means and also puts off definitive action for a later date. That's a good sentence. It does, however, utilize *jargon*, which may be defined as a business-specific term that implies knowledge of the subject and also injects unnecessary complexity into the utterance for the purpose of 1) obfuscation and 2) showing off. Prime practitioners of jargon may be found at this writing in the bullshit fields of digital/social media and finance, where such mystification is sometimes necessary.

Rotten writing is often employed in business by those trying too hard to appear not stupid. Consider this short excerpt, found while perusing the website of the *Harvard Business Review*:

> Furthermore, organizations that focus their strategy on digital transactions based on automating and substituting physical resources for digital will only feel digital. Such digital substitution strategies create virtual copies of the real world, creating e-channels, e-stores and other e-surrogates for physical processes. An e-store, for example, still uses the same basic business model and business processes of its brick-and-mortar equivalent. That may be more efficient, but it's also easy to duplicate. The result is greater commoditization via price transparency and a reliance on advertising or "free" revenue models few companies can profitably support.

Yes, the structure of each sentence is adequate. The cumulative effect of the whole, however, may help explain the large percentage of MBAs and business professionals who need a couple of drinks after work.

Beyond coherent written expression, the effort to avoid the appearance of stupidity also mandates . . . an *ability to conceal that which you do not know.* Many smart people are, for instance, scared of economics. They think that if they talk about it, they will look stupid. Such is not necessarily the case. The truth is, nobody knows anything about economics. As an exact discipline or predictive enterprise, it's about as scientific as phrenology, the study of bumps on the human head. Let us put it more simply: You don't need to know anything about economics to talk about it. Just stay out of it and your risk of seeming stupid will be cut roughly in half. When the moment comes when you must speak about such matters, do not be intimidated. There are a host of things you can do to acquit yourself without apparent stupidity:

Appearance of Stupidity

Statements to Avoid

- I won't be available over the weekend. Call me Monday.

- My voice mail is full.

- Whose fucking idea was *that*?

- Screw shareholder value!

- What's EPS?

- Can you believe Mr. Baroslawski's new toupee?

- Twitter is for morons.

- Facebook is worthless as a marketing tool.

- The honest approach: "Really? I have no idea who's right. Opinions are like start-up ideas. Everybody's got one."

- The judicious approach: "Look, I don't think we're going to solve anything here if nobody in the entire field can agree. Let's move on to something we can actually sink our teeth into. Like that croissant over there."

- The wise idiot: "I have absolutely no idea what you're talking about, but frankly, it's above my pay grade, isn't it?"

- Nodding: We will explore the vast variations and enormous value of professional nodding in a later tutorial. But a good nodding never hurt anyone.

At times, however, certain simple financial issues cannot be simply avoided without some stupidity exposure. This is particularly true of core financial subjects that affect your colleagues and superiors directly, like:

➤ *The behavior of the stock market.* When the market is up, you may chuckle and say, "More buyers than sellers!" When it is down, you may likewise shake your head and observe, "More sellers than buyers." These two comments, incredibly, seem to fall within the radius of acceptable stupidity in such discussions. If the market is acting unusually weird, as it does so often these days, you may also, when others are discussing the matter and your comment seems advisable in some way, simple look amused, amazed, or disconcerted and say, "Fucking Europe," or, if the geopolitical news is leaning to the East, "Fucking China."

➤ *Stock grants and stock options.* If your senior colleagues are gloating about their holdings, as they will, won't they, you may listen politely for a while and then say, "It's a good thing we're not in this for the money." They will laugh. You may also, if you know them well and are comfortable with them, observe, "Let me know when there's another seat on the gravy train." Expressions of greed are never out of line, and actually hint at vast layers of intelligence they perhaps never knew you had.

➤ *The "size" of your company.* This is an objective, precise fact that you should know. It is known as the "market cap," and it may be roughly calculated daily by the number of shares of your company held by the public (in common stock) times the price of each individual share. You may also want to keep abreast of your company's annual revenue, and its relative position compared with a number of your direct industry competitors, which you should also know. If you are asked about any of these subjects and are caught with nothing but your tongue hanging out, people will suspect that you are stupider than they thought you were, and you probably are.

➤ *A rough understanding of mergers and acquisitions (and their potential implications to you and all you know and love).* We will discuss this issue more later. All you must master to avoid the appearance of stupidity are the following three rules:

> 1. **Companies are either buyers or sellers.** If your company is out to acquire others, that's a good thing for you. If you are for sale, you might want to keep your resume up to date.
> 2. **Discussions of M&A matters are most often secret.** A fancy term for something that is secret is "proprietary." Using the word *proprietary* makes you appear smart and discreet.*
> 3. **There is no such thing as a merger.** There are only buyers and sellers. Those who are bought are in danger when they have to bend over to pick up the soap. That's good to know.

➤ *Utilization of the term "leverage."* I believe that overuse of this term immediately designates the person using it as a potential stupidhead. The only time you should use it is when you are discussing the possibility of purchasing something with debt. Beyond that, recognize those who lever everything all the time as big fakers who are trying to impress others and conceal the fact that they don't know what's going on.

We will further delve into the topic of Faking Financial Literacy once we depart from the Core, but at this juncture all that the serious but jejune student requires is mastery of the following essential terms:

◦ GAAP, an acronym that means "Generally Accepted Accounting Principles." GAAP numbers are generally found buried in a company's quarterly earnings statements after adjustments, charges, positioning, and other tricky ways of displaying the firm's performance. GAAP numbers give you a genuine look at how a company is doing, all kidding

---

* National Association for Serious Studies, © 2012; all information proprietary.

aside, and are therefore often considered by senior management to be a very annoying topic.

○ EBITDA or OIBIDA: A non-GAAP expression that means Earnings Before Interest, Taxes, Depreciation, and Amortization, or, for OIBIDA, Operating Income Before Interest, Depreciation, and Amortization. Forget the terms themselves. Don't freeze up! This is just a way of looking at financial performance that excludes a lot of nasty, inconvenient measurements that depress perception of a company's success. Now, if *you* could ignore all the interest you have to pay on your loans, all the federal, state, and local taxes you have to pay, and the depreciation and amortization by which your assets are devalued, your financial picture would look awesome, too.

○ EPS: Earnings Per Share. A GAAP measurement that is widely useful and respected by all parties—Wall Street, the business media analysts, and even your mother, if she knew anything about it. A company's EPS is one of the solid factors that go into the determination of its stock price. Recently, corporations have discovered how to jack up their EPS by purchasing vast blocks of their own stock. Some hate that, because it obscures what's really going on by producing higher EPS without any real underlying business improvement. Others love it for the exact same reason.

○ Margin: A margin is how much of an operation's revenue it gets to keep as profit. There are operating margins and profit margins and other kinds of margins, and so on and so forth, but the bottom line is that if you make a dollar in revenue and pay 45 cents in expenses, you have a 55 percent margin. Wall Street likes you to grow your margins, which is why they get all hot and sticky when they hear that a company is about to fire a bunch of people to boost their margins.

One must also be able to look at a spreadsheet without blanching or puking all over it in fear. This involves a twofold strategy:

1. *Sagacious nodding*: Never is this more important than when you're looking at a page of gobbledygook that might as well be the Rosetta Stone. Respectful, silent inclination of the head over the holy object is always appropriate, and much better than something like "Does there have to be so *many* numbers?"
2. *One pointed question*: If you feel that being silent for an entire meeting is detrimental to your image, select a very specific cell of the spreadsheet, plant your finger on it, and po-

litely inquire, "What's this? I don't follow exactly." This will imply that you know what the rest of the spreadsheet is all about, and will encourage the finance person who is being asked to explain the thing to you. They love to do that.

A final point on this, our first foray into the Core. At this early stage of your career, be very, very careful in your usage of humor. Jokes are rarely funny in all circumstances and some are not funny at all. In fact, most jokes are not funny. The joke is often actually an expression of repressed sexual or social anxiety* or desires that are unacceptable to recognize in a business context. And unless it is formulated by a professional in full working knowledge of his or her audience and personal context for such humor, it is likely to bomb and make you look extremely stupid for trying to tell a joke at all. Humorous witticisms may be appropriate for those who can manage them, but they, too, are dangerous in the extreme for the neophyte. Further tutelage will be available later in this Curriculum, but in any consideration of stupidity avoidance, extreme reticence in this area is advised.

Concluding Thought

Finally, there is this: The best way to avoid looking stupid is simple—but very difficult to accomplish if you are, in fact, either stupid or prone to error, due to lust, pride, or even good intentions. And the best absolute inoculation against the appearance of stupidity is this:

Don't do stupid things.

How painfully basic! And yet . . . every day, in every walk of life, in government, the military, academic establishments, and, of course, the world of business, smart people are doing stupid things. There would be no tabloid newspaper industry without the constant stupidity of normally intelligent people. Most of these goings-on you can see in your morning blog scan:

- Mergers and acquisitions that generate massive write-downs[†]
- Dishonest shortcuts that destroy national reputations[‡]
- Sexual indiscretions among consenting adults who should know better[§]

---

* See *Wit and Its Relation to the Unconscious*, by Sigmund Freud and A. A. Brill (Vienna, 1905).

† See Hewlett-Packard's acquisition of Autonomy, which resulted in a $5 billion charge.

‡ See "Toxic Toothpaste Made in China Is Found in the U.S.," *New York Times*, June 2, 2007.

§ See Petraeus, Clinton, Weiner, Spitzer, et al.

- ◦ Embarrassing public tirades that make the individual look like a moron*
- ◦ Financial bumbles of one kind or another†
- ◦ Fashion or hair decisions that create challenges to personal credibility‡
- ◦ Tweets and Facebook postings that lead to apologies, embarrassment, etc.§

Try to stay away from this kind of behavior and those who indulge in it. And if you cannot, make sure that you are well compensated and have a nice network of contacts upon whom you can draw when the inevitable outcome hits the fan.

And when it does? Don't look stupid. That's right—I'm talking to you! Take that dumb, bewildered look off your face!

Exercises

1. From today's business section of either the *Wall Street Journal* or your local newspaper, select at least three examples of stupidity. Ascertain whether the action was taken by a person who is actually stupid or by a comparatively smart person who has done a stupid thing. Also ask yourself whether the action was indeed stupid or merely appeared so. Spend at least five minutes thinking about what you would do in his or her place.

2. Review your actions over the course of the last year. Note down at least three things that you have done that appeared stupid, and that could have been avoided.

3. Seek out a person in the finance department of your company and carefully make your way through a discussion of how the quarter is going. Find out whether the company will meet Wall Street expectations for revenue, EPS, and net income, and do this without revealing that you don't know what you're talking about.

---

* See Karl Rove, Donald Trump, et al.

† See Dick Fuld and the entire senior management of Lehman Brothers, now defunct.

‡ See Donald Trump again.

§ See Alec Baldwin.

Fabricating a Business Personality

Y ou will never move forward if you do not assume a working personality that supplants your own, at least in part, while you grow on the job. Those who do not have a functional business persona distinct from their "true" personality either go mad or become the CEO.

For the most part, the ability—and the right—to reveal one's true self grows over time, until you reach the highest levels of power, where people are unalterably and irrevocably authentic, gigantic, festering warts and all. Sometimes all that's left are the warts . . . and a lot of money.

Ample research conducted at a very high level reveals that the ability to express one's "true" self is directly driven by status and power, as expressed by Title:

Freedom to Express True Self

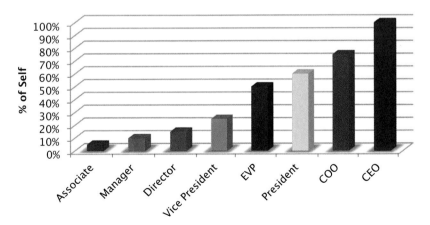

With power comes the right to be yourself, whatever that self might be.*

---

* Reservation of self may not only be a positive; it may also be a requisite for survival. The more of the actual self that

This relationship between self-expression and power may be calculated mathematically, employing a useful equation developed for this purpose by the authors of this Curriculum as part of an ongoing effort to quantify what has generally been considered unquantifiable. Extensive field testing has been conducted utilizing the following equation, and it has been found to be highly effective in predicting the amount of permissible self an individual may demonstrate within an organizational setting:

$$G = Px^2$$

In this formulation, permissible Genuine Personality (G) is a function of two things:

◦ An individual's Personal Power (P, on a scale of 1–10), multiplied by . . .
◦ the square of a certain indefinable and uncontainable quality that one cannot conceal. We will call that X, and measure it on a scale of 1–100.

In senior management, the expression of Genuine Personality (G) may be huge—a product not only of the Power (P) conferred by the rank and title, but also by the enormous size of that uncontainable, irrepressible X factor (X^2) that makes a George Washington the leader of his country and Bill Clinton the most charismatic guy in any restaurant he chooses to enter.*

---

is held back for home use, the less of the genuine self will end up being invaded by the daily vicissitudes of the job. Powerful people who employ no distinction between their business personalities and their genuine ones eventually lose themselves to the job and become gross distortions of the human being who once resided within them. You may decide that their fate need not be yours. If so, the fact that you have constructed a working personality as distinct from your genuine one will be a powerful tool in the retention of your integrity and sanity. Or, you may want to be the boss instead.

* There is only hearsay evidence in the case of Washington, but Bill Clinton's X factor is ascertainable by direct observation. In 2010, the author was having lunch at Michael's, a restaurant in midtown Manhattan that caters to the successful and self-important. At approximately 1 p.m., former president William Jefferson Clinton entered the establishment. The effect on the collected nabobs, billionaires, middle managers, agents, publishers, media executives, journalists, editors, bankers, politicians, and runway models could not have been more dramatic. People had a hard time maintaining control of their cutlery. Mouths dropped open. All the available air in the room rushed to encompass Mr. Clinton, leaving everyone else gasping. Women trembled. Men goggled. Clinton took his seat. It took more than five minutes before anybody in the place was capable of eating or indeed speaking above a whisper. I believe the former president had a salad. Nobody left as long as he remained at his table. There were several celeb-

Let's take a real-world example.

Your CEO-sized might carry a Power vector (P) of 9.5 out of 10 and an uncontainable expression of true self (X) of 92 out of 100. Top numbers are somewhat diminished by the assumption that the CEO in question is not an owner of the company or a completely mad, raving mogul. Still, the number achieved is:

$$\textit{Genuine Personality (G)} = 9.5 \ x \ (92x92) = 80{,}408$$

A very respectable Genuine Personality level indeed!

Now let's look at a fictional manager-level person, not at the very beginning of a lackluster career but perhaps a youngish player on the rise. Such a person might have a Power metric (P) of, say, 4.1 out of 10 and a permissible personal quantum (X) of, perhaps, 28, which is appropriate to a somewhat timid lower-middle executive who hasn't been given the freedom to fly his or her freak flag very proudly just quite yet. Thus:

$$G = 4.1 \ x \ (28x28) = 3{,}214$$

Not impressive, is it? Less than 5 percent of his or her boss's freedom to express Genuine Personality. Best be careful how you manage yourself, young woman or man. At least for now.

As you go along, however, a low X factor obviously will mean a very diminished ability to express whatever genuine human being resides within you (G). This can be a very significant deterrent to job satisfaction. The answer lies in *building your X factor over time.* That is, the expression of true self is not only something to be feared, not only a danger to you. It also confers a tremendous power if properly understood and handled. Controlled and folded into a coherent business persona, this X factor, if properly managed, can provide a vast resource of individuality and dynamic energy to your persona.

---

rities lunching with him who might otherwise have created something of a stir. Nobody noticed them or cared who they were. Clinton had all the X factor in the place, more than nine years after he had relinquished the office that made him famous.

Happily, a variety of personal excesses and dysfunctions are valuable in the world of business. One of them may be yours. If so, rejoice, and begin carefully to develop it, because it will become the cornerstone of why people eventually come to fear you and possibly even respect you. Here are just a few who have demonstrated a close relationship with personal power and made their possessors a lot of money:

Personality Qualities That Build "X-Factor"

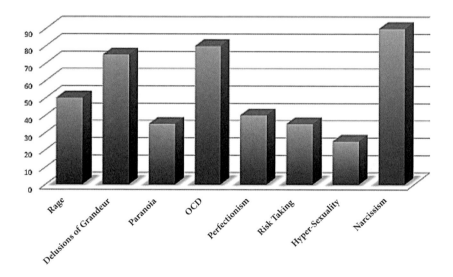

It is no coincidence that each of these so-called personality problems is also the signature style of many successful people. A few that I can think of right now possess not one or two, but *all* of them. These are the truly blessed, even if they aren't very happy.

Still, even factoring in the value of what would be considered mental disorders in any other context, only the very few, the very insane, or the very lucky can climb to great heights solely through employment of their actual selves and associated eccentricities from the get-go. Even Stalin had to listen to Lenin for a while. The great and near great must, at least for a time, craft who they are to the extent that they must interface with others, take orders without blanching, exercise their determination and creativity without running afoul of dangerous creatures, and more. Let's look at how you might go about assembling a business persona you can sustain over time, until you have the right, the title, the power, and the cadre of friends and supporters to let yourself run amok.

The Functional Business Personality

ach student will have to determine what kind of mix upon which he or she will settle, but the constituent parts of the whole are relatively immutable:

Elements of Business Personality

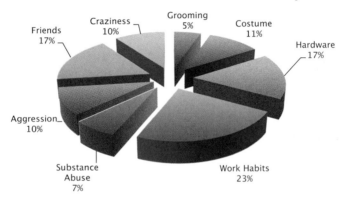

The chart above dissects the elements of personality, with each element expressed in a proportion as it displays itself in a relatively well-balanced individual. You, however, will have to make decisions on makeup and proportion for yourself. Before you do, let's look at the elements:

1. **Grooming (5%):** There are men who still use strong aftershave and women who travel in a cloud of seductive scent. Others (men, mostly) have facial hair. These things contribute mightily to one's definition of organizational self.

2. **Costume (11%):** For many years, everybody in China and at, say, Westinghouse dressed in the same blue suit. In China, they added a red scarf and a little blue cap sometimes, and in Pittsburgh men wore blue ties with little silver polka dots. Deviations from that norm made a statement. Today, I know of at least one individual who wears bow ties. This, too, goes a long way toward the construction of his persona, for better or worse.

3. **Choice of hardware (17%):** At this stage of history, the display of your hardware makes a powerful statement about you, particularly if the implement you fish out when the phone rings is a clamshell that belongs in the Smithsonian.

4. **Work habits (23%):** What does "on time" mean to you? Are you organized? Responsive? Available to do a conference call while attending your mother's funeral?

5. **Substance abuse (7%):** Alcohol and other stimulants and depressants play an enormous role in business, government, and the arts. You need to establish your positioning vis-à-vis this important issue, to ensure minimum destruction of your newly minted persona. This, like so many other things, is not only a personal but primarily a cultural issue. When the CFO hands you a Sambuca Romano at 2 a.m. as a nightcap after two cocktails and three bottles of wine, you'd better know how to drink it without calling Ralph on the Big White Phone.*

6. **Approach to aggression, rage, and violence (10%):** There are those, even when young, who operate on a short fuse. This gives the ones destined for greatness immediate and credible power—the power to scare people. Later, that develops into the power to kill people, sometimes literally. In the early stages of your career, that potential energy must be somewhat circumscribed, but if you are one of those lucky few who can get angry at a moment's notice and frighten even those older and more potent than you are, then good for you. The other kind of angry people are the ones you see picking up cigarette butts on the sidewalk and screaming about fluoride in their water. You'll want to apprehend the difference.

7. **Friends (17%):** We will delve into this issue in a later level of study, but an initial look at the role played by "friends" in the business universe is a key part of your Level 100 personality construct. Friends can sometimes, if not always, be counted upon as allies, which are more important than friends. An understanding of the nature of *friendship in context*, too, is important.

---

* Business life is jam-packed with a variety of nomenclature referring to the act of throwing up, possibly because everybody has done it at one point or another. In addition to the phrase above, those in common usage include:
  Barking at ants
  Doing a Technicolor yawn
  Huarking
  Laughing at the ground
  Worshipping at the porcelain shrine
  Recycling the Ragu

8. **Craziness (10%):** Each individual must wrangle his or her personal insanity and use it for the best business objectives. One must also learn to manage the insanity of others. Those who do not currently possess insanity are encouraged to acquire some.

Implementing Your Strategy

Now that we've named the key elements, let's spend some time ascertaining what choices will be right for you in each important regard.

1. Grooming

It's so easy to make fun of the way people groom themselves. We are not a dignified species. Those who do achieve dignity are in danger of looking equally ridiculous if they overgroom.

First: You want to smell good, but you don't want to smell too good.

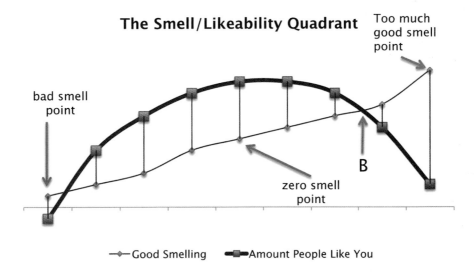

Conclusions to be drawn from this chart:

- Smelling bad renders an individual significantly less likable than other options;
- The smallest improvement in personal odor is rewarded with an immediate improvement in likability;
- Maximum likability is achieved in the neighborhood of the zero smell point, although high likability is sustained just short of that point and after it as well;
- There is, however, a crossover point (B) where an excess of good smell results in a cataclysmic decline in likability not dissimilar to the reaction that others have when in the presence of a bad smell point.

The takeaway here is very clear: Try to hover around the zero smell point where the entire issue of personal aromatic aura doesn't even arise. I would not even mention this, it seems so painfully obvious, except for the fact that every day it is possible to run into people who smell either too bad or too good. This is most particularly true in cubicle culture. It is truly remarkable how many offices have an individual who violates olfactory protocol. What does one say to such people? It's a huge question. Don't make people ask themselves that question.

Then there is the issue of hair. Only God knows why He or She blessed some of us and ignored the others. Those with decent hair do not have a grooming issue. Those with compromised hair must somehow deal with it. It's business. It's not personal. But until you solve the matter for yourself, it will feel goddamned personal.

Unfortunately, in our day men and women can no longer wear enormous wigs that solve the problem for everybody, like this:

Other solutions do avail themselves, although none is optimal. That may still be true. As people grapple with this question, the following options are most often under consideration:

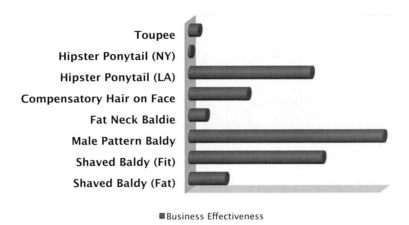

■Business Effectiveness

"Business effectiveness" as expressed in the X axis of this chart is driven primarily by several considerations:

1.   The amount that the issue of hair arises when in conversation with the individual in questions;
2.   Whether the hair or lack of hair is viewed as a negative or positive;
3.   Overall cultural determinations. A teeny-weeny ponytail in Los Angeles may qualify one as a savvy agent capable of bringing Brad Pitt over for cocktails; in New York it classifies its bearer as a shallow poser who doesn't have the courage to face life without a little projectile sticking out of the back of his head.

In that regard, the negative attitude toward toupees makes them difficult to wear in a business context. Hair transplants, too, have an unfortunate aspect of being a work in progress for quite some time. Businesspeople hate seeing unexpected things from those they expect to act expectedly, and a changing cranial landscape can be disconcerting.

It is tempting to advise those whose scalp is making inroads to simply forget about it and move on. It's good advice. Many, many great leaders from the past up to the present day have fought prodigious battles and won in every way but this one. The list is long and illustrious. A few examples:

- Julius Caesar, who wore a laurel wreath around all the time to disguise his receding hairline and quite literally invented the comb-over;
- Ben Franklin, John Adams, other Founding Fathers, who generally went for the bald-up-front-ponytail-in-the-back look and made it work for them;
- Mao Zedong, titan of twentieth-century male-pattern baldness;
- Jack Welch, former head of General Electric, now a ubiquitous poster boy for semi-retirement;
- Margaret Thatcher, who towered over a generation of British politicians with the help of her bouffant;
- Lloyd Blankfein, swaggering Czar of the Empire of Goldman Sachs
- Hillary Clinton, a perennial hairstyle flip-flopper;
- Barry Diller, who looks like he uses his proud, gleaming head as a battering ram;
- Donald Trump, whose bizarre hairstyle succeeds in making him look more bald than he would look if he actually shaved his head. Does he care? No!

At the same time, those who enjoyed terrific, bushy hair but are otherwise of questionable historical value include:

- Adolf Hitler/ young Justin Bieber (forehead combover)
- Kim Jong Il/comedian Marty Allen (tower of frizz)

The key to this, as in other critical business strategies, is to adopt an approach for yourself and then decline to vary from that personal norm.

One final grooming consideration: shaving. For women, at least on this part of Planet Business at this stage of the game, that means all public surfaces. For men also, in the opinion of many. While tidy mustaches and beards are commonplace, they often do little to add to one's luster unless they are planned out carefully, maintained as part of one's overall image, and worn with consistency until people view your hairy appendage as a reasonable part of your overall face.*

2. Costume

Every organization, every industry, has a look that speaks to power, self-control, and a certain amount of incongruity. The latter is important, except in insurance and all but the highest levels of accounting, where any level of self-expression might be viewed as freaky. At the current moment, it is possible for the student joining any sector of the workplace to ascertain within days what the prevailing expected costume might be, and where variation and personal statement are permissible. Consult the following table if you have any doubts:

ATTIRE: Men

INDUSTRY	SUIT	SHIRT	TIE	PERSONAL EXPRESSION
Entertainment	Snappy	Solid or light checked	Only at WME, otherwise no	Chest hair/stud in ear/nose

---

* Among male players under the age of thirty, in such fields as show business and tech on both coasts, the appearance of full-blown beards has been noted with interest by senior management, which is studying the situation to see if it has an impact on productivity. The carefully unshaven look is also now popular with individuals still sporting only one chin, but has only caught hold in the acting and fashion communities. Whether it spreads outward to other industries and beyond the blue coasts remains to be seen.

INDUSTRY	SUIT	SHIRT	TIE	PERSONAL EXPRESSION
Investment banking	Blue pinstripe	White (possible blue stripe)	Sumptuous ($250 minimum)	Black AmEx
Internet/Start-ups	Possible hoodie	Tee with heavy ironic content	As if	Body odor
Conglomerate	Gray pinstripe	White (short sleeve in summer)	Blue with gray polka dots or gray with blue polka dots	Cuff links and/or tie pin
Real estate	Loud jacket and slacks	Bold	Fat	Aftershave

Obviously, these are just guidelines. But they are useful guidelines. A real estate agent who dresses like an Internet start-up dude (or CEO) won't sell many houses, unless, of course, he's marketing homes in the hipster neighborhood of Brooklyn, New York, where every article of clothing is an ironic statement. When the author worked at Westinghouse in the later years of the twentieth century, a man in brown shoes might as well have been wearing a fez.*

For women in the workplace, research affirms the wisdom of knowing one's industry but not, as so many were forced to do in the 1980s and 1990s, pretending that you are simply another kind of vanilla businessman. Women costumed as boring old men went out with "dress for success" books. There are, of course, slightly different metrics than those for men.

---

* In fact, not long ago I attended a business dinner where one of the participants showed up in a brown suede suit. At a staff meeting not long after, one of the senior officers at the table commented invidiously on the young man's selection of suede as a fabric suitable for a business setting. There was a murmur of assent around the table, and then another senior officer added, "And it was brown." A short, respectful silence ensued, not dissimilar to the type one expects at a funeral service.

ATTIRE: *Women*

INDUSTRY	SUIT	BLOUSE	SCARF	PERSONAL EXPRESSION
Entertainment	Anything short of evening wear	Maybe a nice sweater	If you like, but it's not necessary	One extra button accidentally left undone
Investment banking	Blue pinstripe	White	Or a tie, slightly loosened	Cartier brooch
Internet/Start-ups	More businesslike than the men	Too busy to notice	Nah	Bottle of tequila in the credenza
Conglomerate	Gray very short skirt	Slinky	Hermès	The scent that launched a thousand meetings
Real estate	Market appropriate	Bold	Beautiful	Killer six-inch pumps

The issue of how each sex manipulates the other via the age-old vehicles of fantasy, lust, and frustration will be saved for a later segment of this Curriculum. Suffice it to say that clothing (as well as the prior subject of grooming) is part of a ubiquitous, albeit now largely verboten and unspoken realm of human interaction in the workplace. Those who are dubious about the impact that personal appearance and, for lack of a better term, sex appeal, can have on business success are encouraged to Google the phrase "attractive people do better" and then return to the rest of this chapter.

But enough about the shallow stuff. Let us now elevate the discussion by taking a look at the reputational implications of the hardware you carry with you that is now, or soon will be, an integrated part of your persona.

3. Hardware

As I write this, I am aware that by the time you read this it will be—at least pertaining to any specific implement or technology—at least slightly obsolete, even if the conclusions we reach are not. For instance, at this writing the BlackBerry appears to be dying. It's been dying, in fact, for longer than most start-ups stay in business. Somebody decided that physical buttons were a bad idea and now we all have to poke at screens with our greasy little fingers in order to send a simple e-mail. Most implements we carry around are better suited for sexting and listening to music than for business.

The fact remains, the tools you carry do have a significant impact on the way people see you and the way you feel about yourself, and are therefore an important factor in the fabricated persona you are creating for professional use. Right now, here is a snapshot of where we are in time.

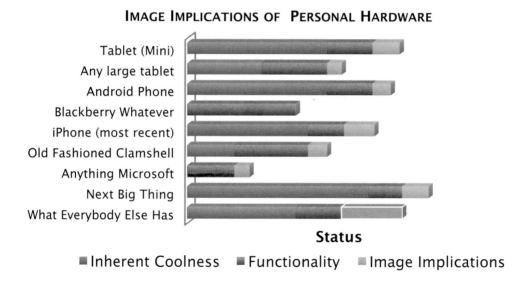

Several conclusions may be drawn from the data underlying this graphic.*

---

* Data accumulated via observation and polling of 12,540 business users of digital technology over a period of twenty-five years. Study is ongoing, all specific data proprietary. © 2014, National Association for Serious Studies.

1. Functionality is not the primary issue in the selection of hardware for those wishing to construct their helpful persona. If it were, the BlackBerry with the physical keyboard would still be around. Get something new. People will love you.

2. Apple does not have a stranglehold on the marketplace that it seemed to have for a while. A very credible and workable alternate universe exists among Androids. In fact, a significant number of bankers and IR people seem to be using the Samsungs with the big screens. Their spreadsheets look better on it.

3. Interestingly, the old-fashioned clamshell not-so-smartphone also carries with it a kind of "screw-you" aura for those who wish to appear just ever so slightly out of the hot zone of technology. There are a lot of people, some of them quite elderly and powerful, who hate the phenomenon of "everything new all the time," too. The clamshell speaks to them in an interesting way.

4. Microsoft remains the sixty-five-year-old guy with the goatee trying to pick up young girls at the party.

5. What everybody else has is always a good alternative.

Finally, a word about Bluetooth earpieces and their reputational impact:

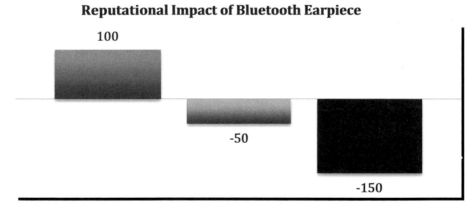

Reputational Impact of Bluetooth Earpiece

■ Before Noticed by Others
■ After Spotting
■ After People See That You Are Talking on It

4. Work habits

What *is* "good work"? While standards are shaped, as always, by the local and company culture, the truth is that "good work" is good work the world round. If the bridge one is building melts in the rain and dumps vehicles into the river, that is not good work, whether the road is in Istanbul or Newark. If the CEO's new palace develops a leaky roof, the fate of the architect would be the same whether the executive in question were named Augustus or Blankfein.

In some fields—particularly in the world of the sciences, like math, physics, and astrology—the sheer act of sitting for several years and covering a notebook with inexplicable squiggles may be considered "good work," even though what is produced is nugatory. Such an approach to labor, however, would be ill-received if the job at hand were the publication of a business book.*

The universal elements of what is considered "good work," in virtually all settings, professions, and cultures:

- The work conforms to or exceeds expectations;†
- It is produced in a timely manner;
- It falls within local and industry-wide standards for neatness;
- It is neither too long nor too short and may, if called for, recommend a solution or lay out all possible options;
- It may be transmitted electronically;
- Nobody in a senior position had to work too hard on it.

Conversely that which is not "good work" may be defined rather specifically as well:

- The work is not responsive to the stated assignment or the unspoken expectation;
- It is either too early or too late;‡
- It is presented in a manner that calls excessive attention to itself, either due to its finicky tidiness, ostentation, or unprofessional sloppiness;

---

* Research available upon request.

† See overall discussion of this point later in the chapter.

‡ Insufficient appreciation has been given to the obnoxious character of work that appears before the senior manager is prepared to engage with it. Proprietary studies reveal that early work is fully 67 percent as annoying as that which is tardy.

- It is too long to be read by the average contemporary individual with a one-minute, forty-five-second attention span, or, in the case of executives, full-blown adult attention deficit disorder;
- It is overly brief or shallow when brevity and shallowness were not part of the assignment;
- It is on paper and must be scanned to be read on a digital device, or sent in software that is not currently favored by the company;*
- It requires recasting, rethinking, editing, or significant further labor by the individual who assigned it before it may be passed on to the next level of management.

Within a corporate context, students should understand that all work assigned to them by their managers is given to them for a very simple reason: so that the person who has given you the work doesn't have to do it him or herself. This would seem to be a simple proposition. But it clearly is not. All too often, he or she who receives the work assignment makes critical errors in understanding not so much the nature of the assignment, but the nature of business work itself. This profound misunderstanding manifests itself in the following ways that are extremely irritating to the senior officer, the boss:

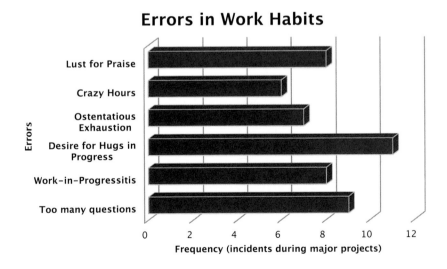

Errors in Work Habits

Errors (y-axis): Lust for Praise, Crazy Hours, Ostentatious Exhaustion, Desire for Hugs in Progress, Work-in-Progressitis, Too many questions

Frequency (incidents during major projects) (x-axis): 0, 2, 4, 6, 8, 10, 12

---

* N.B.: This author finds it increasingly irritating to receive long articles from lawyers written in the standard for that industry, WordPerfect. Nobody but lawyers write in WordPerfect, and documents received in that format, without associated PDF files, are impossible to open easily. The message conveyed by this practice, which is as inexplicable as it is widespread, is "we're lawyers and can use nonstandard software if we choose to, and if you don't like it, sue us."

Each one of these phenomena is deeply irksome to senior officers:

- **Lust for praise** telegraphs need and turns a businesslike assignment into an exercise in child care, where the child is *you*;
- **Crazy hours** are what people work when they do not know how to apportion their time, leading to . . .
- **Ostentatious exhaustion,** wherein the employee seeks pity for the burden of doing his or her job. This is especially aggravating for bosses who are at their wits' end with their own real work.
- The need baby also needs to receive **hugs in progress**, demanding love from an entity that is not really there to give it.
- At the same time, the now thoroughly obnoxious employee is displaying symptoms of **work in progressitis**, issuing updates, bragging about solutions, seeking guidance, and otherwise bothering the boss with a bunch of stuff that she or he thought they had succeeded in downloading.
- Finally, there are few things more grating than the idiot who is always at your door asking questions to which you have no answers. Each question is exponentially more exasperating than the one before.

All these gaffes are not only common, they are in fact commonplace, particularly the demand to be overpraised for the simple act of doing one's job. It is possible that the behavior of NFL players on the field has influenced younger players in the business sector, who seem to believe that the successful completion of an assignment is a legitimate occasion for chest bumps, preening dances in the end zone, and warm, teary speeches of congratulations from the coach. It isn't. You do your work. You make your money. You go home. Anything else is gravy. A great boss will praise you fully for the good stuff you do and not wear you out too badly when you fall short of expectations. There aren't many of those kinds of bosses around, so don't expect them. Learn to work without.

Let's complete our discussion of work habits with a little quiz:

Q: The individual who is meant to receive credit for the work done on a project is:

a. **You**, because you did all the work.

b. **You** and your team of people equally, who labored mightily over weeks and weeks with no help from senior management to get the job done.

c. **You**, your team of people, and all the folks in marketing, communications, research, and sales who put together the winning bid and reaped huge rewards for the entire corporation.

d. **Your boss**, who had nothing to do with any of it except during the five minutes he looked it over and said, "Okay."

If you answered 4, you are correct. Is that fair? Is that right? No. Does it make any sense? In fact, yes it does. Your job is to do great work and make your boss look good.* He or she will receive credit or sometimes, the blame, if he or she is honorable. If he or she is not, the subordinate must be willing to shoulder the pain of the whip in silence, short of total self-immolation. As the twentieth-century philosopher Hyman Roth once observed about a somewhat different business, "This is the life we have chosen." So suck it up.

Conversely, when the boss is destabilized by laziness, cluelessness, confusion, ineptitude, paranoia, or other operating difficulty, the worker is jeopardized as well. In fact, the less actual work done by one's boss, the more the executive comes to rely on those who are actually doing the labor that, as he or she matures, becomes increasingly odious for the boss to perform, as he strives to maintain the impression or illusion that he or she is up to bigger things. In addition, good work done by subordinates has a pervasive positive impact on fellow workers and, by extension, on the entire organization, conveying the sense that those who serve are the ones who are actually in charge.

In the end, all work habits, regardless of the particular assignment, should bring status and stability to the power structure that is supporting you and contributing to your power and well-being, and building the senior officer's reliance on the work you do. When performed correctly, that imperative translates as competence, honest ambition, and loyalty. In reality, while it may be all those things to some extent, the strategy is actually a pure expression of judicious self-interest.

And that is very "good work" indeed.

---

* In the later stages of the Hegelian master/slave relationship, the "master" may achieve stature by developing a powerful subordinate or subordinates who themselves accrue praise and credit for the work they do. In this case, the manager acquires status from the good work of those subordinates, earning praise from his bosses for his putative superior management skills. For our current purposes, let us assume that day is far away for you.

5. *Approach to Aggression, Rage, and Violence*

Those who aren't the least little bit dangerous aren't taken seriously in business. To succeed, the serious player must allow him or herself the strategic options of getting angry when necessary, or when they think, in a more calculated way, that it will do them some good.

Obviously, however, there are a lot of variables here. There is a big thick line between a young aspirant who possesses a fair quantity of admirable operating anger and a nutty guy who doesn't know the meaning of the word *insubordinate*, or a bully who makes smaller life-forms miserable. This is not to say that the latter types, commonly known in the business universe as "assholes," don't do well in corporate life. Of course they do. This Curriculum assumes that if you were one of those people, you wouldn't be taking this rigorous, measured, thoughtful, strategic approach to your career. You wouldn't be able to. Because you'd be an asshole, and assholes don't need a course to teach them how to be assholes.

At the same time, those who don't wield an ugly stick in an appropriate manner at an appropriate time are missing a key component of a sustainable business personality.

Research reveals that each level of the organization is allowed to display its own level of anger, with varying impact on the reputation of each. Those who do not display enough anger may be viewed as wimps. Too much may earn the angry operator the most unenviable title of all, one pertaining to the aforementioned sphincter.

Let's look at how the data shakes out and then offer some brief interpretations that you may find helpful in shaping the angry portion of yourself:

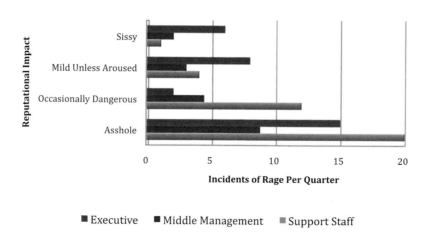

Reputational Impact Resulting from Displays of Anger

This data tells a rather complicated story, but one that is worth telling.*

- **Executive:** A certain amount of anger is expected from the senior ranks. Those who do not display sufficient rage when thwarted or frustrated are secretly judged lacking in some key component of classic executive chops. At just six displays per quarter, this particular executive is deemed something of a "sissy" in interviews conducted with peers and subordinates (top green line). A bit more pique, however, boosts the reputation of this senior officer into the highly respectable "Mild Unless Aroused" tier. A lot of good work goes on in that tier. Interestingly, an almost complete pullback to just two displays per quarter makes everybody very nervous. Suddenly, the boss is quiet . . . too quiet. This occasionally dangerous level is highly effective for those who seek to manage through fear—more effective, in fact, than yelling one's head off like the organizational rectum in Green Bar #4.

- **Middle management** has a much more difficult calibration to make: between Red Bar #1, where he or she is not drawing on enough reservoirs of unpleasantness and rage, and Red Bar #4, where in short order a little bit of yelling has tipped the scale over to the Asshole level. Middle management is perhaps the most constrained of all levels of business life. There is less margin for error, and every exercise of muscle must be executed with perfection and not overblown.

- Finally in this regard, is the insane metric that guides **support staff.** In those who work for weak people, or who are weak themselves, displays of irritation, ire, and wrath are rare, and nobody cares a bit what they say. They pass like wraiths through generations of corporate life unknown and unfeared. But as the role of the support staff grows, they attain the insane ability to be twice as scary and nasty as the people they work for. It is not that rare to find a support person who intimidates and frightens grown executives who themselves eat grenades for lunch, and the kind of Asshole they become (bottom blue bar) in fact runs the unelected government of the organization.

As for you, student, you should begin as a Sissy (top cluster of bars) and quickly aspire to become dangerous when aroused. As you grow, the amount of anger/rage you can display before you enter the Asshole zone grows. You should try never to enter that zone, but if you do, *never do so with anybody who won't forgive you.*

---

* Data based on extensive study of senior management, middle management, and support staff conducted 1982–2014, © National Association for Serious Studies. Private monograph available upon request.

An Anecdote from the Professor

I was once with a very senior mogul who had just enjoyed a $350 in-room massage in his suite overlooking the eighteenth green of the Pebble Beach golf course on the rugged, spectacular coast of the Pacific. He was, quite understandably, in a very good mood. We chatted affably for a while. The phone rang. "Yes?" he said, and his expression changed. His face turned purple. He listened for a moment, then he screamed into the phone, "WELL, BOB, IF YOU WANT TO GO TO WAR WITH US ON THIS I . . . WILL . . . CRUSH . . . YOU!! GO FUCK YOURSELF!!" He slammed the phone down. His face cleared instantly. His expression returned to benign pleasantness. "How was that?" he said to me with a naughty grin. "Pretty good, huh?" We shared a chuckle. Then he went out to play golf.

Exercise: Consider whether this mogul's strategy was more effective than a serious and polite discussion of the business issues. Were his gains short term, long term, or both? Then go out to a mall, airport, or other public location and scream at somebody who annoys you. Note the result.

In any event don't be a wimp. When you find out your boss has given the same assignment you have been working on for two weeks to another person as well because he believes in "the power of competition," when you've been kept waiting for hours for your boss to get off the phone and then discover he took the back way out to avoid you or simply because he or she doesn't feel like working, when you're the only one left in the office at 6 p.m. on a Friday and everybody else is out playing golf, when you realize there is a meeting on something that is in your bailiwick and you haven't been invited, when you submit a long report to your boss and his only response is to question how it has been formatted, when you are told there are no raises this year and then you find out that Bob next door just got one, probably because he is thin, with big pecs, and you are fat . . . There are as many reasons to get angry in a working day as there are working days.

There is one final consideration worth mentioning. Crazy people who are not expunged after a time earn a certain Teflon coating, rendering them impervious to some of the slings and arrows that those with more sanity are heir to. More on this later.

6. *Friends*

Friends in business are good to have. But they are not like friends in "real" life. In real life, a friendship is based on a balance of certain well-known qualities that make the friendship work. You have fun together. Your friend will help you when you need it, maybe lend you five bucks for a sandwich. Sometimes she says interesting things. And you just care about her, that's all, who's to say why? The affection was immediate, probably, and has grown over time. Here is the pie chart of an average friendship:

Real Life

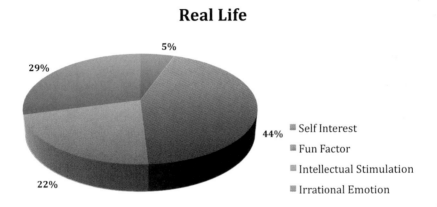

- Self Interest
- Fun Factor
- Intellectual Stimulation
- Irrational Emotion

So, while friendships in all phases of life may be heavily contextual, it is based on good, wholesome things that may even stand the test of time. The issue of self-interest barely enters into it in most cases.

In business, the mix is somewhat different:

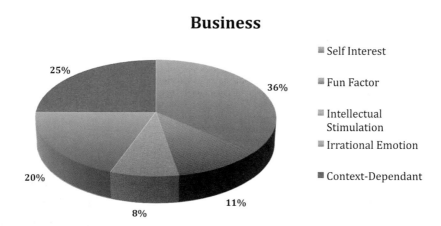

Business

- Self Interest
- Fun Factor
- Intellectual Stimulation
- Irrational Emotion
- Context-Dependant

25%   36%   20%   8%   11%

You will note the increased importance of both self-interest and a new category based wholly on context-dependent relations—business chatter, strategic discussions, review of open issues and challenges, etc., that take up so much of an average working friendship. Together, these two metrics add up to 61 percent of the whole, leaving less than half for the more traditional bases for working friendships—affection, intellectual stimulation, and fun. Even much of the intellectual stimulation and fun are context-based. In fact, if there were no alcohol involved in business, it is an open question whether the red segment of this chart would exist at all. The underlying engine of business friendship remains self-interest and work-related engagement, and, as in "real" friendships, a genuine emotional attachment that colleagues form for each other that generally lasts the length of their mutual employment.

May friends be counted upon to be allies, supporting you in your business goals and watching your back when danger is in the air? The answer is yes, sometimes. But not always.

There is a complex relationship between factors that make up the Level of Alliance by which a friend may be counted upon, in a business situation, to help another friend accomplish a goal or stave off a challenge. Components here include:

- *Affection:* a key component, but not the only one.

- *Self-interest:* Our friends very often are aligned with our business interests, but not invariably. It's unfair—in business as well as in "real" life—to demand total agreement on all points from one's friends, unless their self-interest aligns with ours.

- *Conflicts:* Our friends have conflicts that may either help or hurt us in a given situation. They may dislike someone who is working against us. Or they may like them. They may benefit from what you're trying to do, or be hurt by it. If a friend is with you, that's a good thing. But conversely, they may have good, solid reasons to oppose you, and you can't be a baby about these things.

The point is this: In your work, you will make friends, and that will be nice, and they will make your life easier and sometimes be of business use. You will also require allies, and that will be necessary, and they will make your life easier, and be of great use to you, and sometimes even be friends. Know the difference. If you like to sit around your offices with a colleague, trash-talk about the boss, have a few drinks after work, she's a friend. If you find yourselves spending your time together plotting out the destruction of your common enemies, she's an ally. If you plot the destruction of your enemies while getting plastered over dinner, she may be both. In the construction of your business persona, remember: A man or woman is known by the friends they keep. Choose them well. And use them well.

7. Substance Abuse

Imagine, if you will, a group of Yaqui shamans sitting around in the sweat lodge. Together, they are attempting to summon the spirit that will bring them victory against their enemies. They chant. They share legends. And then, amid the smoke and sweat, the Chief Executive Shaman produces a flagon of steaming brew that contains a heady narcotic that will give them all a common vision. Slowly, with pomp and a sense of shared camaraderie and danger, the bubbling potion is passed around the circle until it comes to Pat, the senior vice president of Tribal Relations. "No thanks, I don't touch the stuff," says Pat, who passes the ceremonial container to the next celebrant.

How far do you think Pat is going in the tribal ladder?

Every culture has its steaming brew, generally a legal one. And the big bones go to those who can take their share and handle it without losing their shorts. Some rules apply:

- Always remain one drink behind the most senior executive in the room.
- Do not hug or kiss a senior officer under any circumstance.
- Do not hug or kiss a drunken member of the opposite sex, even if they want you to, if they are junior to you in corporate standing.
- Try not to hug or kiss anybody at all unless you both have a lot to lose in the exchange.
- Do not throw up on anyone, junior or senior to yourself.
- Always be a happy inebriant, unless those around you grow truly lachrymose, at which point you may fall silent and appear to listen. If they begin to indulge in the kind of ultraconservative ranting to which rich people are prone, refrain from engagement; you will only hurt yourself.
- Do not get drunk and trash the boss, even if those around you are doing so.
- Never remind a senior officer what he or she did last night.
- Eat moderately when you drink a lot.
- On the other hand, never beg off from a bout of festivities because you "have a cold," "are tired after a long trip," or because of any other excuse that makes you look like a short hitter.
- *Never* have one or two "for the road." More damage has been done by those last quick pops than by a whole night of steady and responsible drinking.

Debilitating Effects of Alcohol

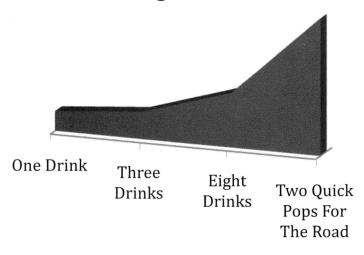

One Drink   Three Drinks   Eight Drinks   Two Quick Pops For The Road

- If you intend to drink a lot, it is the advice of this professor to stick to moderate amounts of spirits taken over the course of the evening. Those with low sugar content, like vodka, are best. In fact, let's keep it simple. Stick to vodka. If you are a man, try to avoid brandishing white wine as if it were a real drink.

- And please. Don't do cocaine or any other illegal drug in a business context, even if others are doing so. It gives more sober enemies a legitimate lever against you. You could also get arrested.

8. *Craziness*

Just a touch. Nothing more. You are simply too small, Grasshopper.

But keep this in mind: Our culture has decided, for its own reasons, that genius is always attended by madness. Some people have gotten confused and concluded that the reverse is also true—that madness is a sign of genius. Hence, they believe, no madness, no genius. It may be true in some cases. In many others, it's bogus. In your case, it means having the courage—and creating a tolerance in the organization—to give a tiny peek now and then at just how crazy you can be, and how that might be good for the business.

When we reach the tutorial section of *The Curriculum*, you will learn how the implementation of measured, strategic madness can confer enormous power and influence, and also how it can make people hate you and ruin your life, making all the wealth and power you have accrued meaningless and empty. But that is for another day. For this moment it will suffice to enumerate the most effective forms of madness within a business environment:

- **Paranoia:** Fear and suspicion are powerful allies, and the attendant delusions of grandeur are a prerequisite for executive life.

- **Obsessive-Compulsive Disorder**: Super-organization can be a tremendous asset, particularly in finance.

- **Bipolar Disorder 1:** The less virulent form of this mental illness confers focus, energy, and a form of brilliance, at least in the manic phase. The other side of the affliction—depression—is nothing but a pain in the neck to colleagues, friends, and family, not to mention yourself, but it certainly does make them more careful around you, and that's not always a bad thing.

- **Anxiety:** Trouble sleeping creates more hours in which to work and send e-mail.

- **Attention Deficit/Hyperactivity Disorder:** Present in virtually all senior officers, characterized by a short attention span, bursts of frenetic activity, and other business-friendly symptoms.

- **Asperger's Syndrome:** A low-level form of autism that generally operates on a spectrum, with severely affected individuals more incapacitated than those you will meet in a business environment, unless you work at Facebook. Look for individuals who are intelligent, sometimes quite witty, fail to make eye contact, and are loath to be touched. They seem to cluster in the parts of the operation that rely on strategy and spreadsheets.

- **Dementia:** Only available to the very highest levels of corporate life, but perhaps the most compelling and powerful mental disorder of all. From Alexander of Macedonia to Kim Jong Un, history is chock-a-block with the deluded and demented who were incapable of moderation and foisted their craziness not only on others, but on the world. In the later stages of your career, you could ascend to be one of those.

These are just a few of the conditions that are a liability in everyday life but can be viewed as an indispensable asset to a business career. As you assemble your sustainable fabricated personality, it will do you well to begin laying the seeds of the big dark tree that may grow within you as you go along.

Cultural Considerations That Will Affect Your Business Persona

All effective and sustainable business personalities are made up of two parts: the individual and the cultural. As difficult as it may be to accept in a capitalist world based upon the hegemony of individualism, the cultural by far dominates the mix.

Sustainable Personality

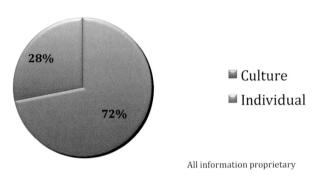

All information proprietary

In addition, the concept of "culture," although it may be represented by one bold color on our pie chart, is itself a complex entity, and a thoughtful consideration of each portion should be made in each student's personal case. Consideration must be given to environmental issues external to the company as well as internal cultural ones.

Components of Culture
That Bear Upon Business Persona

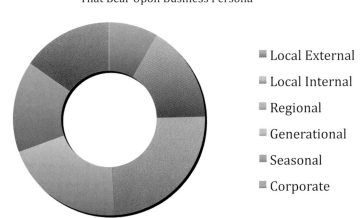

■ Local External

■ Local Internal

■ Regional

■ Generational

■ Seasonal

■ Corporate

To proceed, pose yourself the following questions in each segment of this circle.

- **Local External:** How do people approach personal style in the town or city in which you do business? What is a mature adult on the job expected to look like in your town? When you go to get a sandwich at noontime, do you look like an appropriate member of the business community? If conforming to such expectations meant wearing a small brass name tag that said "Phil," would you be willing? You probably should be.

- **Local Internal:** At your company, is everybody around you a slightly smelly male in a T-shirt? Then you're probably in a Silicon Valley start-up. What are the implications of this style when you are required to make a business call at Martha Stewart Omnimedia? Likewise, what happens when you're supposed to do business with the dudes at Apple and your gray suit, gray tie, and button-down oxford shirt make you look like you came from the old Soviet Union? One must at the same time conform to local internal standards but not be willing to accost the world as an outsider, like the Amish or Hare Krishnas, neither of whom play well before a live audience.

- **Regional:** Where are you? The Southwest, where a string tie may be worn without irony, or the Northwest, where one is deemed deficient if one doesn't carry a coffee cup on their twenty-four-speed bike with them at all times? The Northeast, where a man must wear a tie if he is to be considered a serious person? Los Angeles, where the wearing of that same tie may be viewed as a badge of servitude?

- **Generational:** Young people have a different compass in matters of personality construction than do older ones. How old are you? Do you want to look your age? Younger? Older? What portion of your generation do you want to embrace? Are there benefits to looking like a hopeless slacker? There are in IT. Think about it.

- **Seasonal:** Is it fall? Why are you still wearing that white suit? Is it summer? Why are you in wool? It is possible that women need not spend much time dwelling on this seemingly rudimentary issue, but it seems to be a necessary way station for their male counterparts. I know a guy who listens to Christmas country music in his office in July. He is considered strange.

- **Corporate:** Finally, beyond the local environment of ten or twelve local colleagues, how does everybody in the corporate ecosystem look? Do the senior vice presidents have a soul patch like yours? Are they wearing black? What do their shoes look like? Are the low-level droids expected to mirror the appearance of their superiors, or is there a standard for them that differs? Do people come in at 8 a.m. and leave at 6 p.m.? Or do they arrive at 6 a.m. and leave at 8 p.m.? If it's the latter, can you abide by those hours or should you consider carving out something different for yourself?

These larger cultural issues must inform the decisions each student must make for him or herself as the components of sustainable personality are developed and adopted.

Final Thoughts:
On Conforming to Expectations

The core concept the student must master, as he or she goes about the gradual and serious business of fabricating a sustainable business personality, is the necessity to *conform to cultural and preestablished personal expectations.* This may sound like sheer conformity, but it's not, not really. It is recognition that one's appearance and behavior—in any organization, from the Boy Scouts to the Supreme Court to a hip-hop posse on tour—must be in accordance, within a certain zone, with what people expect. Falling outside that zone will make people uncomfortable with you. But more important, it will make them begin to see you as *not part of the program.* This will, after a time, delegitimize you in the eyes of the group and, perhaps more important, its management.

The benefits of living up to the group's expectation of consistency and predictability fall within a traditional bell curve:

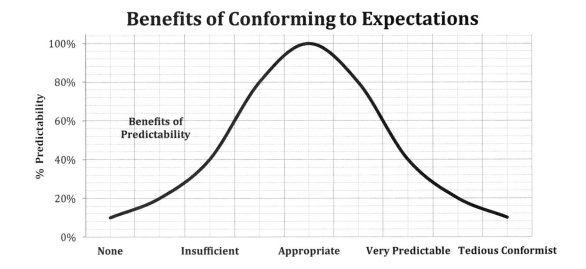

Benefits of Conforming to Expectations

As you can see from this vector, the highest benefit is attained by those who are appropriately predictable and conform to most reasonable expectations. Before and beyond that point, the benefit curve falls off quickly. Some latitude, in other words, is not only expected but permissible as long as it falls within, that's right, expectations.

To do this, personal latitude must itself be preestablished and authenticated by management and the group, but once laid in may be fully enjoyed by each. The quality and quantity of this latitude are determined by several factors:

- Audacity rewarded by longevity and affection
- Rank, which as we know has its privileges
- Propriety. A neck tie or panty hose, for example, may be worn as a headband at a raucous boondoggle but not, if one wishes to survive, at a board dinner.

The key factor in this matter, it should come as no surprise, is the place you occupy in your career arc:

Personal Latitude as a Function of Career Arc

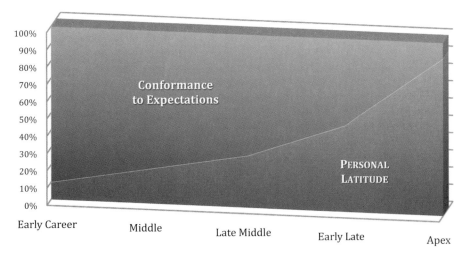

Establishing consistent expectations and then meeting them is at the heart of corporate life. It is as true for entire corporations as it is for the individuals who reside within them. Consider, if you doubt this, the kind of punishment that is reserved for companies that do not hit Wall Street's expectations on their quarterly reports. The reaction is immediate and severe. If that same company is expected to disappoint, however, the Street gives barely a grumble. That's why one firm can produce growth of 1 percent and see their stock go up, while at the same time Google can post 120 percent growth and watch its stock tumble. It's all about expectations.

As you fabricate your personality, make sure to keep that fact firmly in mind, because the creature you create will have to be sustainable, admirable, and capable of growth. It also helps not to hate yourself when you're done.

Exercises

1. Purchase a very serious business suit and wear it around your house for a week, including the weekend. How does it make you feel? If you begin to have the urge to order other people around, do so.

2. Purchase a bottle of vodka. Mix it with your favorite juice, if you wish. Drink it, preferably after dark. Then go about in polite company for a while and see if you can function without attracting notice. Practice this exercise until you can do so successfully. All points are deducted if you fail to make it to work on time the next morning.

3. Men: Grow a soul patch or tiny mustache. Women: Insert a purple, green, or bright red stripe into the front of your hair. Note: Those who work in environments where such accouterments are already present may remove them for the same effect. Now go to work on a Monday morning with this addition to your personal presentation. Note how management relates to you. Is this eccentricity an asset at this stage of your development?

4. Make a list that enumerates what people expect of you. Do not consider your list complete until it has at least twenty entries. Now consider in what regard you consistently meet or exceed these expectations. How did you do? And how are things going for you?

5. Put on a Bluetooth earpiece and go to a Starbucks. Conduct a business conversation in an audible tone until people look annoyed with you. When you are able to do so without flinching, throw the Bluetooth away and never use it again.

COURSE 103:
Selling, Marketing, and Negotiating

Today we will tackle the rudiments of getting people to buy the thing you're selling. This is the heart of all activity of any kind in the human sphere. Along with the opposable thumb, this capacity—to sell others something they perhaps did not even know they wanted—is what separates *Homo sapiens* from its ancestors. Cows do not sell each other hay when they are hungry. Monkeys do not sell each other bananas. Only human beings can create the perception in other human beings that, even though they have showered, they still smell bad and need an underarm deodorant to set things right.

Unlike in *Death of a Salesman* or *Glengarry Glen Ross*, salespeople are not simply gray men dragging their sample cases behind them or vulgar, desperate Ricky Romas cursing and honking their way to their next handshake. Everybody sells. Every human being with a shred of ambition sells in one way or another—and in the process engages in the ancillary necessities of marketing and negotiating. Consider this lineup of salespeople and the products, services, and ideas they have sold:

SALESPERSON	BUYER	PRODUCT, SERVICE, OR IDEA SOLD
Christopher Columbus	King Ferdinand and Queen Isabella	Wacky idea of new world
Cleopatra	Julius Caesar/Mark Antony	Egypt as the new Rome for cool people
Marc Antony	Friends, Romans, and Countrymen	Their ears (on loan)
Saints and martyrs	Bored heathens	A whole new religion with a much better afterlife
Joan of Arc	France	God
Giuseppe Garibaldi	Friends, Romans, countrymen	A united Italia
Otto von Bismarck	Germans	One big Germany

SALESPERSON	BUYER	PRODUCT, SERVICE, OR IDEA SOLD
Sigmund Freud	The Western world	Id, ego, superego, childhood sexuality, psychotherapy
Henry Ford	America	Model T, and later, Nazis
Josephine Baker Bananas	Jazz Age hipsters	Banana dance

Adolf Hitler	Germans	Deutschland Uber Alles
Abraham Levitt	Postwar petit bourgeoisie	Levittown and twentieth-century suburbia
Edward Teller	United States military	Hydrogen bomb, for when the atom bomb just wasn't enough.
Hugh Hefner	Men	Airbrushed sex with decent articles around it, making customers feel good about themselves in two different ways
Grover Norquist	Republican Party	The vast, right-wing conspiracy, as long as it lasted
Angela Merkel	World economy	Germany as the most trustworthy and appropriate steward of Europe
Martha Stewart	Confused and insecure Americans	Taste
Madison Avenue	Hungry Americans	Velveeta
Sheryl Sandberg	Women in business	Leaning in or whatever

Throughout the ages, success and fame have come to individuals who were capable of thinking up an idea, a service, or an object and who then, through the force of their personality, their knowledge of their audience and their product, and their unabashed need to close the deal, sold that thing through. Ludwig van Beethoven, for example, is often thought of as a consummate artist, and of course he was. But in between compositions, he spent all the time he wasn't writing or shaking his fist at the heavens selling his music to any nobleman or bourgeois with eardrums in working condition. Any biography you read about the guy is roughly 70 percent taken up with his various mercantile activities. Aside from selling, he was also a very good composer. But he was very, very interested in money.

For a more recent example, ask any journalist what he does all day. He or she writes or "reports" for perhaps 20 percent of the day. The rest of the time is spent selling editors on story ideas, selling potential sources on the benefits (often illusory) of talking to them, selling the finished and unedited story to their editors again, fighting for space and attention in the paper or online version, which is a form of selling, then going out at night, drinking and selling projects of one sort or another to book editors. All day long, selling, selling, selling. And occasionally they do a little writing. Artists, too, spend a huge amount of their time branding, positioning, and marketing their stuff to critics and gallery owners. Who would want anything by Jackson Pollock or Andy Warhol on their walls if it hadn't already been branded, explained, super-marketed, and presold as a valuable object by the establishment that packages these things? The only person who was an absolute loser at the sales part of his game was Vincent van Gogh, who produced several paintings a day for his entire working career and sold not one of them. He finally shot himself in a field not far from his home. That's what happens when you suck at selling.

The ability to get into people's faces when they have no interest in you, to engage them and eventually make them want to buy what you're selling—that is a real, God-given gift. Here are some further examples:*

---

* "Innate Talent Calibrated by Profession," © 2013, National Association for Serious Studies.

Innate Talent Required

Amount of Innate Talent

You will perhaps have noted the relatively small amount of innate talent required in the field of politics. A short note on the subject may be instructive before we move on, because it is a case in point. It is very, very difficult and expensive to run for major office like president of the United States or, to a much lesser degree, Congress, so politicians of that caliber must have very great sales talent indeed, creating belief in other people about their viability and succeeding, as all great sales professionals do, in getting them to part with their money. On the other hand, it is very easy indeed to run for local office if you want to. Some city councilors in New York, for instance, run unopposed. Others serve year after year after being accused of various noxious things. Still more return in triumph after having served time in jail, like former Washington mayor Marion Barry, for smoking crack with a bunch of prostitutes. Local and state governments, in many locations, simply reek of mediocrity. It doesn't take talent to get there, just as it does require talent to win certain beauty pageants. It takes desire and energy and a big enough ego to push people into an agreement.*

That's good news for the rest of us who don't really have a talent to sell. Because business, in many ways, is like politics or beauty pageants. The talented do, at times, rise to the top. But those with guts, gumption, unbounded energy, hot desire, and the ability to push people around do very well, too, even the ugly ones. So if you're timid, inarticulate, or even a bit slow at times, rest assured that you can rise to an acceptable level of proficiency in selling if you understand the craft of it, and learn the drill.

---

* Students of this issue continue to study Toronto mayor (and possible future Prime Minister of Canada) Rob Ford for additional insights.

The Basics

There are three legs to the salesman's stool, without which the salesman would be sitting on the floor, a position less congenial to negotiating a deal than some others. The three legs:

Marketing

Negotiating

Selling

- **Marketing:** It is sometimes challenging to ascertain the difference between sales and marketing. Think of it this way: Marketing was invented to help sell things people don't need. It's the fluffer. Products and services that people actually need do not require marketing's song and dance. That list, however, is limited: food, functional clothing, running water, some form of heat in the winter. When you depart from those essentials, marketing is needed. The more silly and useless the object or activity to be sold, the more intense the marketing needs to be.

   Root concepts of marketing include branding, positioning, and, when necessary, repositioning. We will explore each in brief as we move through this portion of your Core Curriculum.

- **Selling:** After the product is manufactured and made available to the market, and after sufficient marketing has been applied to the product and has raised the appropriate level of awareness, the time comes to sell the thing. The art of selling transcends the product that is itself the subject of the enterprise. Selling is persuasion, an exercise of self. Product knowledge is important, of course, but even the most knowledgeable salesperson is lost without the capacity to pitch, convince, and close. Selling involves getting another human being to part with something, usually money, in exchange for whatever it is you are telling them they need.

- **Negotiating:** One of the most important skills of all, negotiation is the seductive dance of all business relationships, successful or not. It involves, at one time or another: bargaining, wheedling, cajoling, bullying, reasoning, and, when necessary, threats and promises in equal measure. Obviously, the finer points take a lifetime to learn, but the fundamental basis of success here must be grasped early: Both sides must believe they have, in some sense, won. This is not to say that *you* shouldn't be the one who actually won. But unless you've got some mighty leverage, or never expect to do business with the other person again, you should let them walk away with at least one lung left in working order.

Going forward now, the assumption will be made that you have very little talent for this stuff, in other words, that you are normal and uninitiated. That's okay. You will learn a certain approach, practice that approach, and then hack away at it the way most people you see doing things for a living do them. This will prepare you up to a certain point. But hopefully, somewhere along the line, you will discover the part of your personality that can be good at this stuff. This Curriculum can teach you the steps. But you have to want to dance.

We're going to look at marketing before we move on to sales, because marketing precedes the actual intent to buy. Once that decision is made by the buyer, a certain amount of negotiation takes place, in some cases more than others.

Marketing

Those who are contemplating a career in marketing have much to look forward to. Marketers move the world! The job itself, however, is a little hard to grasp. Let's try to understand it before we send out our resumes.

The function of marketing is to implement a cycle of need:

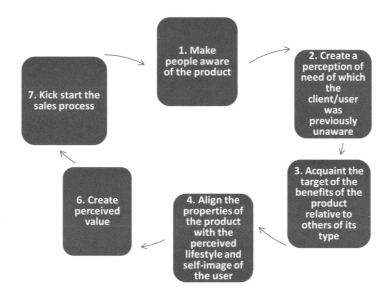

Constituent parts of this process have been mastered by a variety of hucksters and social philosophers in the field since the advent of the marketing culture in the mid-nineteenth century. As laid out in the prior illustration, they include a number of steps, which themselves generate a number of substeps. Let's look at each step in that marketing process now.

Step #1: Make people aware of the product: For a long time, this involved advertising, billboards, and other forms of crude, analog announcements. These days that effort has extended to "following" brands on Twitter, "friending" them on Facebook, and subscribing to video messages on YouTube and other pipelines of that genre, among many other platforms that seek to invade personal space with public messaging.

The goal here is to go *viral* via combination of social and traditional communications:

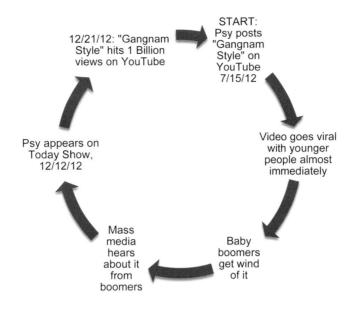

Going Viral: One Famous Example

Marketing also is useful in defining products that either have many uses or no discernible use. An example: Silly Putty, a popular toy since the mid-twentieth century, originally invented as a replacement for rubber during World War II. It proved unsuitable for that purpose. In 1949, a toy store owner became aware of the useless substance and contacted a marketing consultant. Together, they marketed a small amount as a toy. It did well, but the toy store owner bailed on the project. The marketing guy, however, saw the potential, gave it the catchy name, packaged it cleverly in a plastic egg, and the rest is silly history. By 1961 it went national, then international. By 1987, the new owner of the product, Crayola LLC, was selling about two million eggs annually.

Step #2: Create a perception of need of which the client/user was previously unaware. Classic examples of this marketing phenomenon are all around us, and include:

- **Deodorant:** The concept of body odor was invented by Madison Avenue sometime in the 1920s or 1930s, when new products to cure new ailments needed a market. This phenomenon hit its absolute apex (or nadir, depending on your position) with the development of vaginal spray in the 1960s, and has since somewhat abated. But the multitudes of vitamins, minerals, placebos, nostrums, supplements, additives, wheat germs, liquids, solids, powders, tablets, pills, and sprays that we consume for mysterious reasons are a wonder of modern marketing, while we smugly laugh at the ancients who applied leeches to cure headaches. True, leeches weren't branded, but they were so primitive back then.

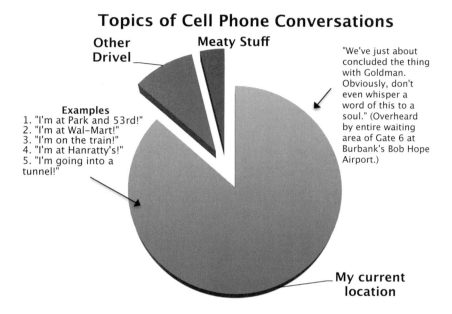

Topics of Cell Phone Conversations

Other Drivel

Meaty Stuff

"We've just about concluded the thing with Goldman. Obviously, don't even whisper a word of this to a soul." (Overheard by entire waiting area of Gate 6 at Burbank's Bob Hope Airport.)

Examples
1. "I'm at Park and 53rd!"
2. "I'm at Wal–Mart!"
3. "I'm on the train!"
4. "I'm at Hanratty's!"
5. "I'm going into a tunnel!"

My current location

- **TV dinners:** The idea that it was easy, convenient, and fun to eat lousy food in small portions on little trays in front of the television set was invented by the advertising industry, which delivered its messages over that implement.

- **A superfluity of hair products:** Did you know that you can wash your hair with just about any soap? Now go to a supermarket, superstore, or super drugstore and regard the vast army of shampoos and conditioners that march down the shelf as far as the eye can see. Each has been defined, researched, tested, branded, targeted, and set loose on some portion of a marketplace full of people who believe that they have bad hair, and have been convinced by marketing that they can do something about it;

- **Bottled water:** If in the year 1970 you had transported a confused hippy to the year 2014 and shown him a football-field-long cooler full of beverages, many of them various waters in a variety of clever bottles, he would have thought he was tripping. Further, the whole idea that people need to be hydrated every two or three minutes from water bottles that are choking the environment in plastic would have seemed insane to that visitor.

- **Mobile communications:** Yes, it's a real improvement in our collective lives to be available 24/7!

The ship has also sailed on delayed correspondence. We have all been marketed into a new zone where mobile communications has replaced the kind of thought that people were once capable of in silence.

Step #3. Acquaint the target with the benefits of the product relative to others of its type. This means branding and positioning the product or service by creating either real or fictional benefits to the product. Crest toothpaste, for instance, has Fluoristat. It used to have Fluoristan, which was the original name of the toothpaste until they changed it to Crest. Presumably, people would rather brush their teeth with Crest than with Fluoristan. For its part, to compete with the power of Fluoristat, Colgate put sodium lauryl sarcosinate in their toothpaste to create the "Gardol" shield for your teeth. The point is, products must carve out a reason to buy *them*, not the other guy. That's what marketing brings to the table, turning a commodity to a unique product, with Fluoristat or Gardol; whatever they are!

The benefits of a product or service are conveyed to potential consumers via its **brand**. Every serious entity that is offered for consumption has a brand. To put it another way, the moment a thing is branded, it begins to exist as something that can be sold at a premium. This concept includes:

- **Soap:** There are innumerable brands, each with its own ostensible benefits, most made of pig fat and other repulsive stuff with a handful of additives thrown in, each brand conferring different supposed benefits than the next.

- **Foodstuffs,** as opposed to food itself. For instance, Frito-Lay legitimized the concept of binge eating in a campaign essentially daring the consumer to try to eat "just one" Lays potato chip. Of course, once that gauntlet was tossed down, no American could do so. And so Lay's became the chip you had to stuff your face with *because you can't eat just one*. Ruffles responded with aggression, asserting the fact that, unlike its competitors, it in fact possessed *ridges* that made it a priori superior, since objects with ridges are more effective when employed with a dip. And so each carved out its brand benefit—one for greedy, hungry folks who eat their chips by the handful, the other for those who like to dip their chips in a variety of substances and not subject themselves to associated break-age as they convey the loaded platform to their mouths.

◦ **Religions:** A profusion of brands and sub-brands floods the marketplace for this product. In the nineteenth century, there were not one but two major brands of Presbyterians, neither of which could stand each other. There are, of course, dozens of other kinds of Christians, several kinds of Buddhists, a host of Jews, with several different kinds of Orthodox brands alone, with differing practices, attitudes, and hats.

◦ **Political parties:** Republicans are red. Democrats are blue. Republicans are wary of any limitations on semiautomatic weapons. That's part of their brand. Republicans are also more tenacious and less prone to compromise, at least at this writing. They are truculent and inflexible in the face of opposition and sometimes even common sense. Democrats, at this juncture, appear to be excessively conciliatory. Some rebranding in that area may be called for.

◦ **Clothing:** Take a plain black T-shirt that may be found at Kohl's or Costco, and you can take home a pack of three for $14.99. Take that same shirt, put a small embroidered pig or lemon tree on it, give it a foreign name, and you can charge $29.95 for one of them. Location also has an impact on branding. I was once in Paris in the arrondissement near the Ritz Hotel. In the window of a shop was a black T-shirt that had no visible branding on it and, further inspection revealed, absolutely nothing remarkable about it whatsoever in terms of its material or design. It was selling for 249 euros. Most often, however, the simple naming of the thing is enough. People believe, for some reason, that Dutch ice cream is better than plain old American ice cream, for instance. So Reuben and Rose Mattus got the idea of making ice cream in, of all places, the Bronx, New York, and calling it Häagen-Dazs. Voilà. Premium ice cream that costs three times the norm was born.*

◦ **Entertainers, artists, politicians, and celebrities:** Increasingly, people are themselves walking brands. Here are a few individuals who have augmented their worth in the marketplace by successfully branding themselves:

---

* I always believed that it would be interesting to take a quantity of Sealtest ice cream, rebrand it Saelden Teszte, and make it available only through specialty stores and upscale food courts. I believe the price point of the product would be vastly expanded immediately and permanently.

PERSON	BRAND
Lindsay Lohan	A hot mess who had better clean up her act or she's going to end up either dead or boring.
Sean Combs	Former musician who is now a walking brand for virtually any product he'd like to put his name on, immediately conferring his own coolness on you when you buy it.
Warren Buffett	Your rich uncle whose advice should always be heeded.
Oprah Winfrey	You get a dream! And *you* get a dream! And *you* get a dream!
John Boehner	He's a tough bastard—and he cries real tears!
Arnold Schwarzenegger	Fuck you, asshole. He'll be back.
Mark Zuckerberg	Brilliant but obnoxious billionaire in a hoodie.
Rush Limbaugh	Big, fat asshole loved by millions.
Lady Gaga	Who knows what she'll do next? And you know what? We care!

One last point about branding: It is essential. There is life without it—basic, simple, everyday life as it has existed for 100,000 years. But there is no Big Business as we know it. Branded things confer status upon those who purchase them. Nonbranded things do not.

Step #4. Align the properties of the product with the perceived lifestyle and self-image of the user. Once a thing is branded, it is the job of the marketer to make consumers see that product and its brand as potentially part of their selves, their lives, their concept of who they are and how others see them. It is the job of marketing, in other words, to make the consumer feel the need to acquire that which is marketed in order to complete him or herself. "I've got to have that watch, dress, hat, shoe, skin cream, or car—or something inside me will forever be incomplete," the consumer's little interior voice says to itself. "Worse, something inside me that is very important is diminished when my urge to purchase, to augment my life, is denied. And I've got to have whatever it is that is being marketed to me right now. Now, I tell you! Waaaaa!"

A number of products and services have been brilliant at sucking people's self-images into their vortex, including:

⋄ **Image-based vices:** Before they were banned from the airwaves, the tobacco industry crafted out self-defining images for a variety of smokers—appealing to people who wanted some form of self-definition lacking in their daily lives. Tareyton smokers preferred to see themselves as so belligerent they would rather fight than switch brands, even going so far as to sport faux black eyes earned in fistfights to protect their chosen smoke; liberated women who had "come a long way" in the 1960s had their own image booster, too: Virginia Slims, a cigarette as long and skinny as the models who appeared in the marketing effort. Men in search of enhanced macho had an icon to worship as well—the Marlboro Man, with a face as leathery as his saddle.

Now that smoking is deglamorized and ostracized in most social venues, it has fallen to liquor to help define the image of those who feel something vague about themselves. A bunch of hipsters arrive in a private plane. They sweep down the stairs of the G5, laughing, clearly preparing for a night in Gomorrah. Look! Who's that? It's Diddy! Who's that with him? Jesse from *Breaking Bad*! And just look at the ladies with them! God, don't you wish *you* were there? Well, you can't be. But you can drink the vodka they're drinking. It's Cîroc. There isn't a word said about the taste or quality of the vodka in the spot, by the way. Its association with these playas is enough. A little bit of that life can be yours if you buy into it. That's marketing, and it works. The vodka isn't bad, either, even if it is made from grapes.

On the other hand, you may want to be the one Beck's drinker among a bunch of yutzes drinking domestic beer. That will get you a really good-looking girl, too, because girls like upscale guys like you. Or you may want to be a friend of "the most interesting man in the world," who drinks Dos Equis (right). This is a marketing effort that actually makes fun of marketing. He is not interesting, in fact. He is rather pompous and slightly ruffled. Of course, he appears to have just had sex with three or four women, so there's that.

Marketing has also wrestled with the problem of image associated with the consumption of Viagra, Cialis, Levitra, and other drugs that enhance sexual performance in men. First, a major effort was undertaken with the medical community, which as always performed as an efficient and engaged member of the pharmaceutical marketing industry, to rebrand the problem, giving it a new name that bore with it no hint of shame or ignominy. The condition formerly known as impotence would henceforth be known as erectile dysfunction, a properly scientific term that was then conveniently shortened to ED. Who among us doesn't have a friend named Ed? Then the marketing guys got busy trying to address the social stigma men might feel about needing such help. First, they got a former United States senator to be a spokesman on the subject, get it out of the closet, as it were. This was not 100 percent effective, possibly because Bob Dole was not anybody's idea of a sexually attractive individual at that stage of his life and also because he was, at the time, quite old. And while old men might form a good potential market for the new drugs, its marketers certainly didn't want to limit its sales to geezers. There were so many young, occasionally virile men around who, if properly marketed to, would line up to get in on the action. What to do?

The most interesting man in the world.

It wasn't long before a solution to this issue was found, and now all ads for ED drugs feature the men formerly found smoking Marlboros, manly, manly men in their forties or early fifties engaged in manly pursuits, some of them with big trucks, most with wives at least ten years their junior who are clearly in an amorous frame of mind, a fact that disturbs them not because they . . . are . . . ready. In fact, it is often difficult to know, when these well-crafted messages come on the air, whether you are watching an ad for Viagra or for a Ram pickup truck. That, students, is effective marketing. The tagline warning users that if they experience an erection lasting more than four hours they are to call a doctor added an exciting tang to the proceedings, particularly for the target audience.

- **Cars:** For many, the purchase of a vehicle is the largest single expenditure, other than the house they buy with their partner (I mean their bank, of course), that they will ever make in their lives. In the 1950s, Detroit marketing was extremely successful in convincing the American family that, in order to retain its dignity and standing in their community, they would need to purchase a new car every year. When that ploy faded as a tactic due to its extreme ridiculousness, carmakers were forced to get more subtle. It was no longer enough simply to sell size and newness as inherently great attributes. They had to do what all marketers in the late twentieth and early twenty-first centuries have had to learn how to do: target the product, service, or idea to a narrow portion of The audience, and charge more for whatever it is. Yes, there are still little anonymous cars that look like all others, targeted to people who value function and gas mileage, and their marketing and sales positioning is as boring as that audience. But most vehicles are now designed and marketed to confer personality upon their owners. Those who are targeted by makers of the Nissan Cube (below) are meant to be young urban professionals who don't mind a quirky little car whose rear window wraps around the body an odd way. It is possible that the target is intended to be white, square, young urban and suburban types who want to distinguish themselves from owners of the Kia Soul, a similarly bizarre little box favored by the rapping residents of Hamsterdam Avenue (below).

Cube.

Hamsters.

Conversely, pompous, affluent individuals who want people to celebrate their pomposity and affluence are clearly the intended audience of the Jaguar. The marketing for the Jaguar is all leather and chrome and sexy sleekness, with a murmuring, cultivated voice that sounds like it intends to put you to sleep and then have its way with you. For a while, the campaign went so far as to pronounce the name of the brand as "Jag-You-R" but this proved so amazingly pretentious that it went over the line into humor. Today, the name of the car and the name of the animal are one, and haute bourgeoisie in great numbers can feel distinguished. Likewise, if you are a mogul in Los Angeles at this writing and do not have a Bentley, you're a loser. So get one.

Step #5: Price the product correctly. It is a mistake for marketers, and for self-marketers like you, to price the product being sold either too high or too low. For some products, particularly commodities of one kind or another, a low price is all-important. Gasoline, for instance. While Chevron and others may try to sell you on the idea that their gas cleans your engine and other nonsense like that, there isn't a person driving on the road who isn't looking for gas at the lowest possible price. If, however, the gas price falls *too* low, a driver begins to suspect that there may be something wrong with it.

The same thing can be said of many products. While shopping for fruit, for example, one will often choose not the cheapest peach, nor the crazily expensive, ugly one that claims to have been fertilized with real animal shit instead of bad chemical shit, but the middle-level peach, which looks fine and isn't the, you know, cheap one. The middle peach is priced correctly and is therefore the most attractive.

Other items benefit from being expensive. While many people want a cheap hotel on vacation, a fair number of people on their time off are looking for a little luxury. If a Four Seasons or a Ritz-Carlton sells that image—along with eight-dollar Cokes and twenty-five-dollar martinis—it can't price itself at a reasonable level. Vacationers will say to themselves, "That can't be where the rich stay. It's too cheap." The same can be said of certain items like watches. These days any cheap watch can tell time within nuclear levels of accuracy for the next ten thousand years. Yet rich people scour the globe for the most expensive and ostentatious of chronometers. And, true to branding form, they even give them a different name than the rest of us. They don't wear watches. They own timepieces.

Pricing can also be variable for virtually the same item sold to different people.* Some

---

* Some years ago in New York City, there was a hangout for the rich and famous called Elaine's, presided over by a wonderfully cranky, enormous, charming woman in a muumuu named Elaine. The important people had tables along the wall. To sit at one of those ten or so tables was to immediately enter the zone where people felt they should know who you are. It imparted incredible and lasting sociological glow, and in some cases extended the shelf life of shoppers who go on cruise lines are looking for good value and enough repulsively grandiose food displays to make them fat in ten days—for a reasonable price. Others shopping for the same venue on water want to feel like they are the Astor family setting off on a glorious, luxurious adventure on a great ocean liner, (hopefully not *Titanic*). They don't want to spend too little. So the big boat has to have many levels of pricing to fit the self-image of the many kinds of people who may want to avail themselves of the facilities. The rich people get a slightly larger small space to cram their stuff in. All share the same seasickness if the weather turns bad. But the rich do it in more congenial surroundings, as always. It doesn't hurt if the name "Royal" is attached to their branding, either, or, if the intended audience leans more toward young people who still want to get laid every night, "Carnival."

If the product one is marketing is oneself, the issue of pricing is equally important. At the beginnings of their careers, young people are very often selling value and will work for virtually any salary. Later on we will discuss the wisdom of saying, "I'll do anything and I don't care what you pay me," which very often yields limited returns. Suffice it to say, in this regard—and I believe I am speaking for parents everywhere—one should try not to accept a pay package that requires living at home after college. Those who do miss out on one of the great incentives to advance that exist in the workplace. Nothing can drive a young person to ask for a raise faster than the experience of living with nine other kids in an apartment with a 1,000x ratio of tenants to insects.

Step #6. Kick-start the sales process. All of this intense effort means little if the marketing of a product doesn't drive its targeted customer to the store, the online destination, the church, synagogue, mosque, or pagoda. There has to be a little nugget in the cake that, once eaten, moves the target to take action. Marketing cannot do it.

That's where sales comes in.

---

midlevel writers who hadn't produced a successful book in many years. People who sat at those tables routinely paid significantly more for their herring appetizer, Caesar salad, or sirloin steak than those seated in the Mesopotamia, back in the restaurant. To complain about this pricing discrepancy when one became aware of it was considered the height of bad manners, and risked permanent expulsion from the hot zone. The food was pretty terrible, too. Those who loved Elaine's miss the place, though. Status is hard to come by these days, and worth far more than an overpriced plate of pasta.

Steak?

Toy?

Cool Leather Jacket?

Marketing Thought Experiment

Above you see a cow. At right, you see three possible products that could be derived from that cow. What are the various challenges that are posed by the task of marketing each product? How would each be positioned? How important is branding to meat? To the toy? To the leather jacket? Conversely, how would an animal rights activist, who sees the cow not as a product but as a viable living creature with rights of its own, view this entire exercise? To what extent is every product's essential nature violated by the process of being marketed?

Sales

In a world full of things that nobody inherently needs, including you, marketing is essential, but it still doesn't move product. Fortunately for our economic system, it doesn't exist on its own. It fits within a large cycle that makes up the entire sales process. This is one such cycle, and will give you a fair idea of what might take place on any given day, in any given industry, with any given product, service, or idea:

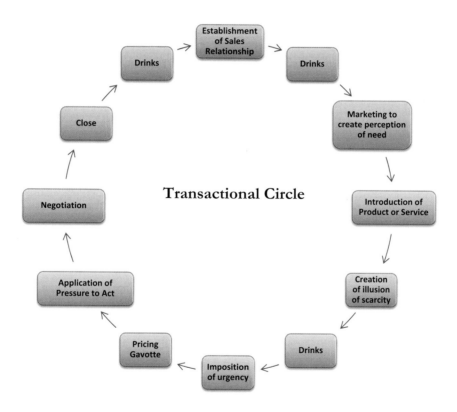

This circle does not encompass all transactions. The things that people genuinely need—basic food and water, heat in the winter, air-conditioning in the summer, serviceable footwear, health care and life-sustaining pharmaceuticals—need not be heavily marketed or sold through a cycle like this. If one wanted an apple in Neolithic times, you went out and got an apple. You didn't go to a section of a gigantic food emporium and attempt to select just the right apple from a selection of perhaps a dozen of internationally sourced varieties. And even then, with all that choice, there still is no need to advertise. The store itself, perhaps, will do some marketing, positioning itself as higher in quality or lower in price. But branding, positioning, repositioning, aggressive pricing strategies, etc., are not necessary for commodities and staples, unless the marketer is attempting—as in the case of water and certain forms of sticky rice—to redefine the product as one that is necessary for the maintenance or growth of the user's self-worth.

In these cases, the salesperson has yet to enter the picture, except perhaps as a dray horse toting product from one place to another.

On the other hand, in an economy that drives people to an increasingly byzantine crossroads of ever more choices, and a deepening sense that enough is never enough, the resulting confusion and insatiability can only be satisfied by the hard sell.

The more complicated needs, like those filled by religion, automobiles, and fine whiskey, require pomp, circumstance, fancy costumes, the smell of fine Corinthian leather, peat, or incense. Or perhaps the desire is time-sensitive, and must be met before it grows stale, rotten, or disappears altogether, as is the case with hotel rooms, airplane seats, and the time that is sold for the occupation of radio and television commercials. Or sometimes people need to be scared into purchasing what is being sold, like medicines and poultices, or convinced to purchase the thing in spite of the fact that there are ample reasons not to do so, as anyone who has considered the side effects of Lyrica, which include death, will agree.

In these cases and many others, selling is tough. It takes talent, and in some cases, genius. It takes the kind of person who can simulate or (in certain rare cases) forge actual relationships that are not sullied by the fact that they are essentially mercantile.

What kind of person are we talking about?

The rare and gifted sales professional will evince qualities found in one form or another and, to some extent, in all of them, mingled together in one throbbing energy source at the heart of their being. Let's look at some of these types for a moment (see graphic next page).

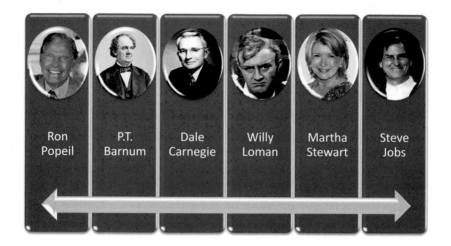

Ron Popeil | P.T. Barnum | Dale Carnegie | Willy Loman | Martha Stewart | Steve Jobs

○ **Ron Popeil** invented silly kitchen appliances that nobody needed and sold them by the millions by shamelessly and joyfully hawking them on his own paid-placement television segments. When you saw a Popeil infomercial, you wanted to buy whatever it was he was selling, no matter how unnecessary it might be to you. There are many explanations for this phenomenon, but none of them is wholly satisfactory. The first of these inventions was the incredibly influential Veg-O-Matic, which sliced, diced, and did other interesting things to vegetables. It was invented by his father, Samuel Popeil,[*] but brought to fame by Ron and his company, which was, of course, named Ronco. Other inventions of Ron Popeil include[†] the Chop-O-Matic hand food processor, which was self-described as "the greatest kitchen appliance ever made"; the Popeil Pocket Fisherman, which requires no explanation; the Inside-The-Shell Egg Scrambler, which solved the problem of incompletely scrambled eggs; and the Solid Flavor Injector, which injected solid ingredients into meat or other foods and went hand-in-hand with the Liquid Flavor Injector.

There are other inventor types who were their own best salespeople, including such luminaries as Thomas Edison and George Westinghouse, each of whom owned thou-

---

[*] In an interesting sidelight, in 1974 Samuel Popeil's former wife, Eloise Popeil, was convicted, along with her boyfriend, of trying to have her former husband rubbed out by two hit men, presumably for the money she could get in his will from the proceeds of the Veg-O-Matic.

[†] List courtesy of Wikipedia.

sands of patents, but neither of whom embodied the raw primacy of the man who invented and sold the Cap Snaffler, Ron Popeil.

○ **P. T. Barnum** said "there's a sucker born every minute," and made a lot of suckers happy finding interesting things for them to look at and basically inventing marketing and advertising as the world had never known it before. The disabled people he displayed in his wandering sideshows became some of America's first celebrities in the contemporary sense, people like the original Siamese twins Chang and Eng, both of whom were married, raised families, and were every bit as sought after, and famous, as any celebutante of the current moment.

○ **Dale Carnegie** invented the self-help book with his iconic *How to Win Friends and Influence People*, published in 1936 and updated in the 1980s, with 15 million copies now sold. There have been many how-to books since then, but all were modeled on this one. The essence of the book was simple: Business and interpersonal relationships were problems to be viewed strategically, not emotionally, and could be solved by determining a course of action and embarking on that willful path toward certain success and personal well-being. The advice was rudimentary but achievable, and dealt with such things as getting out of a mental rut, increasing your popularity, and making more money. Carnegie also hit on the great gimmick of all self-help books—numbering things. "Twelve things this book will do for you," and "Six ways to make people like you," were among

the headings on his table of contents. People in need of help have a weakness for numbers. Just look at all women's magazines, which are read not only for entertainment but for guidance. Every magazine targeted to women is festooned with so many numbers that one might be excused for believing that the editorial staff is into numerology. Research is now under way as to why this should be. But the numbered list has been a staple of all self-help since Carnegie.*

○ **Willy Loman** is the fictional salesman created in Arthur Miller's play *Death of a Salesman*.

---

* One could also consider that most influential of all books—the Bible—with its ten plagues, Ten Comandments, etc.

He spends his entire life lugging around a suitcase full of samples and getting no respect from anybody, including, he thinks, his own family, but he keeps on selling and selling even when nobody is buying, because that is his fucking job and he's going to do it until he dies, which he does at the end of the play. You don't want to be him, but there are days when you have to be. If you haven't read or seen *Death of a Salesman* by now in your puny young life, drop everything and do so immediately. This goes as well for *Glengarry Glenn Ross* by David Mamet, which is about how horrendous salespeople are and what it takes to live the life. With just these two depressing-as-hell works of the business arts, you will be able to deploy intelligent jokes for the rest of your career at an endless number of sales cocktail gatherings.

○ **Martha Stewart** is a never-say-die self-marketer who has, throughout her life, been able to parlay her image of herself, her taste, her interests, and her self-created image of personal development and perfection to other women and, to some extent, to metrosexual men. She has faced many reverses, most of them self-created, but since she is a pillar of self-creation anyway, she has been for the most part forgiven. She is living proof that sales requires a religious belief in the marketability of your own self. When people buy your product, they are buying *you*, because no matter what, you are worth that investment.

○ **Steve Jobs** was a visionary, a bit of a lunatic, a rather unpleasant fellow at times, and a complete and total genius at seeing the potential in stuff other people invented and had not yet exploited because they themselves didn't understand what normal people actually wanted. For instance: the computer mouse and the small hard drive that became the iPod. When you bought something Steve Jobs had marketed and sold to you,[*] you were happy, and remained happy with your decision.

For the purposes of our Curriculum, the student might consider achieving the following mix.

---

[*] Steve Jobs did not negotiate.

The Effective Sales Persona

That is:

a. A strategic approach driven by positive thinking (Carnegie, 31%)
b. A relentless pitch regardless of the stupidity of the product (Popeil, 23%)
c. A healthy dose of showmanship and commitment to bullshit (Barnum, 15%)
d. Courage in the face of rejection (Loman, 8%)
e. A dash of religious self-belief (Stewart, 4%)
f. And a clear eye and creative brain to bring your own personality and vision to terrain where others may have gone before and not seen the potential (Jobs, 19%)

The great salespeople, then, are those who perform all of these functions and then bring a healthy tranche of their own particular talent and genius to the mix. That last element is very important. The field is full of terrific professionals of all different personalities and stripes—quiet guys who get the job done with a minimum of fuss, noisy boosters with natty pocket handkerchiefs, scientific technicians with reams of documentation under their arms. It doesn't really matter, as long as you, the sales professional, have your act together. And there are no right answers.

Let's look at an example. As you can see from the following graphic, Edie and Bob are equally effective salespeople. Edie's style is relaxed and based on deep knowledge of the product. Bob, for his part, seeks out the kind of people who can be shoved from a cliff if they think it will please another person. Both do very well and their assets are almost completely balanced.

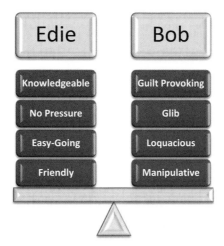

In the end, Edie may end up with more friends and long-term clients than Bob, but Bob may get more action in the short term, since the world is full of people who can be manipulated by a crafty and obnoxious operator.* You can choose, as you get to know your fabricated self better, which of these types of salesperson, if any, you may want to be. Perhaps you may even have a choice. Or not. Character is destiny.

The corporate life of a salesperson, even a natural one, is anything but easy on a day-to-day basis. The salesperson is pressured not only to maintain, but to grow the bushel of dollars that come in every year. And this is the worst kind of pressure, the kind that comes not from one's own boss, the sales vice president, or executive vice president, or even the president of sales. It doesn't matter what the sales title is to whom the sales weasel must answer. For above that operations person is the vast force of the corporation's finance organization, which runs on the fuel provided by sales revenue.

---

* See *A Disposition to Be Rich*, by Geoffrey C. Ward (Knopf, 2012).

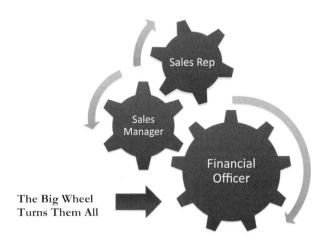

It should come as no surprise, then, that there are times—many, many times—when the well runs dry, the downward slope is devoid of snow, the pond has run out of fish, and even the greatest of sales professionals needs some assistance.

Which brings us to the subject of liquor.

Liquor is the spark that lights the campfire, the Sterno that keeps the chafing dish warm between courses. It is the final key element of virtually all sales environments worthy of the name. Here's how it works:

You may be censorious about this fact of business life, but think about this: In the 1950s and the 1980s, everybody was pretty much drunk all the time. Serious drinkers began at breakfast with an eye-opener. Lunch was two or three martinis,* often followed by a glass of wine. Dinner was a river of cocktails, followed by wine, followed by after-dinner drinks, capped off by Sambuca Romano with a coffee bean floating in it. If you didn't drink the Sambuca, you got a wedgie from the executives at the table. Then everybody drove home. Both decades were marked by precipitous, almost vertiginous growth in revenue and profit. You had to back a truck up to the back doors of most sales-based corporations to offload the money.

From the 1990s onward, behavior changed. No one drinks at breakfast anymore. The big decision at lunch is whether to have bubbles in your water. There is still some drinking at dinner, but people are generally careful, even in sales, not to get too sloshed. And business has sucked from that time forth. There are good years, of course, but the atmosphere of What the Fuck is gone and people make far more rational decisions. Those who remember the old days miss them greatly, particularly the sales guys who often wrote up millions of dollars of business on the back of their cocktail napkin.†

Negotiation

We will conclude this chapter with a brief discussion on the art of negotiation.

There are many styles of negotiation. There are the heavy-duty types who stand outside the situation with a bullhorn and make sure nobody gets killed when hostages are taken. There are those who simply sit in the middle of the road cross-legged when the convoy rumbles up with business to do and doesn't move until their demands are met. There are others that actually hug and kiss and slobber over everybody involved so that after a while there isn't a person in the room who doesn't want to give him what he wants just to get him the fuck out of there. And then there are the tough mothers who don't want to negotiate at all. They just want what they want, and they want it now.

---

* The martinis in those days were not the enormous vats of booze now served in most restaurants. They were relatively small, containing perhaps half the volume of the current beverage as served today. Anybody attempting to have more than one of these monsters either is a very capable alcoholic, has no important meetings with senior management that day, or is with someone in senior management who has no important meetings with his or her senior manager that day.

† In 2012, the steak house Ben Benson's, on Fifty-Second Street in Manhattan, closed. This was the equivalent, in the world of media sales, to the Vatican closing its doors to the faithful. It marked the end of an era, one that will be mourned by all who ever sold an entire season of inventory at one drunken lunch.

The process of negotiating with other people is not altogether dissimilar to the circle of events that attends a sale—the sale of a house, for instance, or a car. Everybody has a number in mind. Both sides know that in the end that's exactly the number that they'll end up at. Then, for some reason, everybody has to fight. The reasons for this are unclear, but it seems virtually unavoidable. In 90 percent of all negotiations, whether the issue at stake is turf, money, rights, etc., here is what happens:

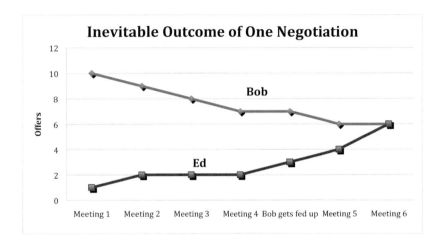

The truth is, in virtually every negotiation, no matter how fierce or supposedly intractable both parties are, the ultimate solution ends up being some number in the middle of the two parties' opening position. In the above case (see chart), Bob got completely fed up after Meeting #4 and put his foot down. Ed needed a deal in order to use the inventory Bob was offering, and always assumed he would pay a bit more than half of what Bob was asking. So everybody ended up pretty happy, although Bob fully intends to crush Ed between a rock and a hard place during their next negotiation as payback for the bullshit Ed put him through during this process.

As in all transactions of any sort, it is helpful to think about the cycle of events that attends a negotiation. This will save you from many sleepless nights during the process. If one knows that there is an inevitable circular dance about these things, one may be less likely to throw the cat against the wall during the midpoints of the process. Here is one such typical cycle, followed by a brief explanation of the events:

Ten Negotiating Strategies for Beginners

1. Start from a neutral position. That way you can move in any direction without losing your balance.

2. Know your adversary. Study the deals made by this company and this individual in the recent past. If the guy is a dick, don't get mad. He's just playing the game that got him here.

3. Feel the room. Who's going to make the first move? Does he or she seem anxious to do so? Let them. If not, move into the void.

4. Don't start with bullshit and you won't have to contend with too much bullshit later. Make your overall position pretty clear from the get-go. This will encourage all but the most dedicated bullshitters on the other side of the salad bar to do the same.

5. Give yourself room to move. Ask for what you want plus, perhaps, 20 percent.

6. Lock the door and establish a clock. It is generally disadvantageous to let negotiations drag on for too long. If you want to get it done, get it done. Nothing is going to happen if everybody is sitting around with their thumbs up their sphincters.

7. Be prepared to walk. You will never get a good deal if you're not prepared to leave it on the table if the offer stinks.

8. Get emotional if you have to. People are afraid of the dark side. In the old days, the great negotiators were willing to kill the other guy to get the deal. "I'll make him an offer he can't refuse," wasn't just a figure of speech to the Romans, the Mongols, or the Huns. Of course, these days, you can't kill people. But you can scare the shit out of them.

9. Don't sweat the small stuff if you've got what you want on the big stuff.

10. Kiss and make nice afterward. Extol their negotiating skills. Contend that you've been taken to the cleaners when everybody knows you kicked butt, took names, and went home with the bacon.

✔ *Greetings:* The process begins with a variety of hellos and how-ya-doin's, with varying degrees of bonhomie, depending on the situation. It is helpful to keep in mind that even at events like Appomattox and Yalta such formalities were exchanged. They mean little to the eventual outcome, although if the other guy won't shake your hand you're off to a pretty bad start.

✔ *Narrowing of issues:* There ensues a bunch of palaver about what the supposed issues are. The real issues rarely surface at this time, but what is often revealed are ...

✔ *Areas of agreement:* As the parties surface the superficial stuff, vast areas on which they agree often pop up. These should be captured immediately and formalized, since they will now make room for the real, difficult issues that have yet to be wrestled with.

✔ *Song and dance:* The parties now put on their bonnets and feathers and parade about the campfire, chanting and stomping their feet in preparation for the real engagement.

✔ *Staring contest*: The two sides now sit across the table from each other, shuffling papers and expressing doubts. The issue at this point is which side will surface the big, lumpy material that needs to be processed if there is to be a deal.

✔ *Further narrowing:* Here it comes, whatever it is. The size of the guarantee? Who gets control of the kazoo? Hopefully by now there are fewer than five such hairy, intractable monsters in the room. Too many of them means you may as well go home now and wait to see whether anybody is really serious around here.

✔ *Final issues:* Ah, good. Now we have them. The only problem is . . . we're miles apart, particularly on the Watanabe aspect of the transaction. That's a bear. How will it ever be resolved?

✔ *Who wants it most?:* The thing is, the party of the first part has to make this deal or a bunch of horrible things will happen to it, and the party of the second part knows it, although it doesn't know that the party of the first part knows they know it although it doesn't know that the party of the second part will have to merge with a party of the third part if it doesn't grow scale immediately, which is why both parties want it, but in the short term the party of the first part wants it 15 percent more and the party of the second part doesn't know it yet.

✔ *Ascertainment of leverage:* After a while, however, it becomes pretty clear from body language, as well as the pressure they are putting on to keep up the pace of the negotiation, that the party of the first part is hotter to trot, which gives the party of the second part some leverage. Imagine the fulcrum moving a bit to the left and the party of the second part on the right of the seesaw now has the weight. That's what's going on here.

✔ *Wind and rain:* Now comes a tsunami of hot air, meeting a cold front from the other side of the table, which produces more mini-storms and perhaps some big ones.

✔ *Deadline:* Everybody is now pretty much fed up. Both sides are camped in their positions. Now either one of the two parties walks, or the other starts mewling like a little kitten and moves off its supposedly intransigent stance. Everybody shouts Huzzah!, declares victory (even though one has received the short end of the straw), and goes out for drinks.

✔ *Deal:* Now comes the papering of the transactions, when both sides try to capture what they think they agreed to. It's astounding how, at this juncture, one side or another or both will try to cheat. The party of the first part said 3 percent, but all of a sudden their lawyers put in a 2 where the 3 used to be. Whoops! Good thing the party of the second part has a sharp attorney! Papers fly back and forth and eventually everything is signed and voilà, we have a deal.

In the end, the only questions that truly matter are: 1) Do both parties truly want enough to justify this tortuous experience? and 2) Is there somebody in the room who knows how to close a deal? There are many, many lawyers, finance types, and big swinging dicks who know how to dominate a discussion and move the ball into the red zone. It's the guys who can actually punch the pigskin over the goal line who earn and deserve the blue ribbon and all the trimmings that come with it.

Finally, here is a tiny road map for you, Grasshopper, whose sole negotiation, at this stage of the game, may concern your own terms of employment as you enter the game. Using the insight and skills you have acquired during this chapter, proceed as follows:

1. Be respectful but not servile. This conversation collapses the entire process of marketing, sales, and negotiation into what may be a twenty-minute window. Make those twenty minutes count;

2. Have a bottom line in both the job description and the compensation, even if that line is very, very low. For instance, if you want to be a sales assistant, you may not want to take that job as a janitorial engineer, even if it meets your salary requirements. Being a file clerk, however, may lead directly to the post you want, so perhaps it should be considered. Do not undervalue yourself and start off on the wrong career path. It's not as easy as you think to hop onto the right one, since that track may be occupied by the guy who got there first.

3. Be honest about yourself—both to the potential employer and to yourself. Do not sell yourself short. But do not claim expertise in editorial services if you have a bad case of dyslexia.

4. If you walk away, do so without prejudice and thank them for their consideration. They may want you back for subsequent conversations if you didn't come across as a dick.

5. If you accept, do so with graciousness and gratitude, and a firm determination—which is communicated—to do a fabulous job for the nice people who just hired you.

Concluding Thoughts

In this chapter, we have looked at the role of marketing and how it relates to sales, and dipped our toes in the water where, if we're not careful, the negotiating sharks can bite them off. You can't have marketing without sales, or in most cases sales without marketing, and you can't close a deal you can't negotiate. Give deep thought to the relationship between the three, and then execute the following exercise before we move on to the rudiments of management.

Exercise

The product you are going to prepare in this exercise is yourself:

◦ Make a list of positive attributes for this product. What is it good at? What are its most attractive features? What sets it off from the rest of the pack? Don't stop until you have at least eight to ten items.

◦ Now make a list a things your product does *not* do. No product can be all things to all people. A liquid can't be both a breakfast drink and a floor wax.

◦ Work up a slogan for this new product. You know slogans. You've heard a dozen of them today if you're a television viewer, and have seen even more if you read magazines or newspapers. What's a short, pithy statement that synopsizes the product's appeal?

◦ Is the product named properly? Think about this—would you have the same feeling for the following products if they were named . . .

   ◦ Mike Buonarotti
   ◦ Ed Poe
   ◦ Larry Beethoven
   ◦ Ted Dostoyevsky
   ◦ Gabby Chanel
   ◦ Stefani Joanne Angelina Germanotta
   ◦ Barry Obama
   ◦ Curtis Jackson III

◦ If not, consider a rebranding effort, recognizing that any such change may risk losing whatever existing brand equity you have in the original name.

◦ What does your product actually do? What are you selling?

◦ What is your pricing strategy? Are there tiers of service with different price points, like cable TV?

When you are finished with this exercise, ask yourself whether the position you now occupy and the price you command are commensurate with the potential of the product you have created. Of course it isn't! Now . . . what are you going to do about it?

Before you mount the campaign to rebrand, repackage, and reprice the great product that is You, make sure to master the unit on branding yourself in the advanced phase of this Curriculum.

COURSE 104: Managing

No matter how small a fish one might be in the great pond of enterprise, one must know how to manage. Those who do not manage will, in short order, find things unmanageable. There are four directions in which an effective manager must manage. They are:

- *Managing up:* No individuals are more in need of guidance and assistance than those whose job it is to provide leadership. No mastery of business arts is complete without full understanding and the beginnings of competence in this arena. So in this portion of our Core, we will do that.

- *Managing down:* Infinite drivel has been offered to putative leaders on their way into the workplace, and it is a subject more vulnerable to fads, enthusiasms, and cheese* than any other. But the secret of managing other people is complex. Intimately involved are several arts: listening, thinking, questioning, validating, encouraging, and appropriating other people's ideas as one's own.

- *Managing sideways:* A most neglected skill rarely identified or studied, the ability to manage peers and colleagues is also crucial. Included in this unit will be exercises in basic colleague development, delegation without the actual right to do so, manipulation, coercion, exploitation of friendship and exploration of mutual self-interest.

- *Managing the center:* Finally we delve into what may perhaps be the most important management challenge of all, one that is often the province not of business texts but of philosophy and religion: management of yourself. Manage the woman or the man inside

---

* *Who Moved My Cheese* by Spencer Johnson is the mega-bestselling book, supposedly on how employees can deal with change. It is, in fact, an odious primer on submission to authority that instructs little mice on how to accept that which their bosses have decreed for them. It is no wonder that it has been championed by senior management the world over, and handed out to grumpy employees tired of having their cheese moved.

you, and it shall follow, as the night follows day, that thou will then be good at managing other people. Shakespeare said that.

The Management Quadrants:
Up, Down, Sideways, and Center

L et's take a systematic and hopefully somewhat streamlined look at these four quadrants of management.

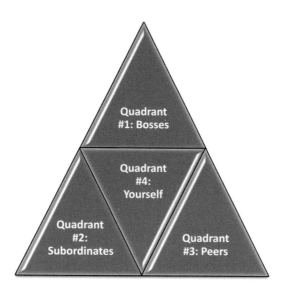

Each of the smaller triangles of the larger one has its own special challenges and component parts. Management of each takes it own very special consideration, strategic approach, and tactical focus. Upward management, for instance, involves a great amount of cold calculation and hard, daring manipulation of an entity that could injure you at any time. Sideways management may require use and abuse of friendships, not something everyone will be keen on doing. And downward management may be the most difficult of all, because then *you* are the authority figure, and that takes some getting used to.

You will note, however, which quadrant has been placed in the center: management of yourself. Discussion of that aspect of management really should come first in our overall consideration of the subject, but since the issue is somewhat more philosophical than purely strategic in its content and approach,* we will consider it after we have looked at the three other directions you will be managing—upward to your bosses, downward to subordinates, and sideways to peers.

Philosophers of
Self Who May Be Helpful in
a Business Environment

Buddha • Plato • Descartes • Adam Smith • Kierkegaard • Nietzsche • Sartre • Steinem • Oprah • Chopra

---

* The graphic above offers just some of those who have wrestled with the issue of the self and its relationship to the cosmos. The Buddha was helpful in his exploration of how mastery of self can carry with it incredible liberation and power. Plato taught, among other things, that the physical world is just a pale figment of the true ideal that drives truth. This seems useful, particularly when you're aggravated. Descartes defined Being as Thinking, which is often true except in certain top-down management structures. Adam Smith was one of the original Greed Is Good guys, although his fans will tell you otherwise. He looked deeply into the close bond between capitalism and selfishness, and found nothing wrong with it. Soren Kierkegaard saw the essential problem of self as one of loneliness in an uncaring universe, a problem that could only be solved with what he called a "leap of Faith." Anyone who has worked in a post-merger environment will find this especially poignant. Nietzsche posited the existence of an "ubermensch," a super-human being who could conquer anything. Students of the mogul—or aspirants to that status—need not be exhorted to take a look into that philosophy. Jean-Paul Sartre defined meaning as action, which was very businesslike of him. Gloria Steinem has yet to be improved upon as a motivator for both women and men who believe that gender should not impede anyone's prospects. Oprah is not only a great proponent of positive personal empowerment—believe it and you can do it!—she is its prime example. And Deepak Chopra makes a ton of money lecturing to people who need a life coach, which is encouraging to those who want to make a living advising confused people.

QUADRANT #1:
MANAGING THE BOSS

Managing the Boss: Explanation of Components

Errands: At the top of the stack of imperatives you will have in your upward-management initiatives, none is more important than the fulfillment of errands.* While errands look minor, they are in fact crucial to the psychic heart of the manager.† When one attains a certain status, even if that status is very low indeed, one assumes that there are certain menial activities that one should have left behind. While working like a slave may still hold a certain plausibility for the status-conscious manager, their self-image no longer includes the necessity of doing little piddly-diddly stuff. So in a sense, it is the moments when you are doing the small and insignificant things for the boss that he feels most like a significant person who no longer has to do such things. This is why, while errands are not a huge portion of the effort you are making to manage your manager, they are at the top of the stack.

Disaster control: Those close to a crisis can either solve it or, if it doesn't get solved, come perilously into the circle of blame (see

---

* This may be why, while employees of all types come and go during a manager's reign, his or her assistant is very often the longest-lived in the hierarchy—and the one who has the tightest stranglehold on the boss's time, schedule, priorities, and attention. In any organization, if you want to find the person who probably is the best at managing up, you need look no further than the assistant who serves the CEO.

† Such errands may include the arrangement of dinner engagements or sports tickets, the fetching of information, as in newspaper or online articles of one sort or another, getting him a cookie when he wants one, buying him a tie or her a scarf, or even just going out with her at lunchtime to get a manicure or find a Christmas gift for his wife.

graphic below). But the individual who can make a nice serving of chicken salad out of chicken-shit is nonfungible to the manager who finds him or herself in some kind of trouble. If you are the kind of employee who can solve problems over and over again, a hard crust of expectation and need will be constructed around your tenure and function, and you will achieve and maintain a precious power over the person who is supposed to be the one in control.

Problem.

Solved!

Wait a minute.

Bob failed to solve it.

Bob's a loser.

Kill Bob.

Having Fun: A Career Story
Four Snapshots

1990   2000   2010   2020

● Everyday Things ● Family Life ● Horsing Around with the Gang ● Counting Money

Fun: The closer you get to ultra-senior management, the less fun you have.

Explanation of Bubble Chart: This amusing bubble chart tells us an interesting story about our prototypical executive at four points in his or her career.

- In the beginning of this story (bubble stack #1), the future big cheese's four major ways of having fun are in relative balance, with the critical metric "counting money" (in purple) all the way at the bottom, below even "having fun with the gang" (in light green), and the juicy bubble measuring "family life" (in red) residing where it should be, right above "everyday things" (in blue) at the top;

◦　As the boss matures (stack #2), his or her pleasure in everyday things diminishes, but the commitment to family life increases, probably as the children grow to be more interesting and sleep through the night. The growing boss also enjoys "horsing around with the gang" a bit more, since the drinks continue to be on the house and he or she now has the right to order from the top shelf. The urge to count accrued money has also bumped up a notch, a trend that will continue until it is the most dynamic urge felt in any given workday.

◦　In the third stack, the executive is now a member of high middle management. Family no longer occupies much of attention. Possibly the children are in college, away from home, and he/she is fooling around with the new CFO since she/he is really very sexy and not against having some fun on a business trip as long as there are no residual strings attached. Counting money is now at the top of the bubble stack.

◦　In the fourth stack, our executive now has only two things that she or he enjoys. The first, by far, is keeping track of investments and petting that pile of money. The second way, although it pales beside the counting of money, is still "horsing around with the gang." The "gang," which is made up of senior managers of both sexes, is a last link with humanity. The rest of the successful executive's life, stripped of pleasure in family and everyday activities, is really not too much fun at all.

This is why, if you are our bubble executive, you require all the trappings of title and status—to fool yourself into the feeling that you're having a lot of fun in spite of all the pressure, the constant demands on your time and your sanity, the feeling that it could all go away if some stupid security analyst fucks with your rating. How could you not be having fun?! You have a jet! You're making millions! Your suit costs as much as your first car! You have new teeth! You have a goddamn Maybach! Fuckin'-A you're havin' fun!

Except, as we have seen from our chart above, you're not. You can't sleep. You drink more than you did when you thought you had a problem with it. Except now it's not a problem. It's a solution. The only narcotic that really works for you is to be in the company of other big, flaming giants of industry who remind you how big you are and that's a little bit of fun. And it's fun to look at the stock price every couple of minutes, except when it's down.

Oh, and yeah. It's fun to hang with Bob. Bob is the major player in that green bubble, because

Bob is fun. Bob sort of doesn't give a shit about a lot of the stuff he really should. And he likes you. You can tell. And it's not just because you're the boss, either. Bob reminds you of the guys you went to school with, and hung around the Chicago Merc with before everything got so fucking big. Yeah. Where is Bob, anyhow? Carole! Call Bob! Ask him if he'd like to get some burritos for lunch!

What amazing power Bob has, right, students?

Cleanup: I have observed elsewhere that bosses in general and executives in particular show many of the characteristics of babies,* including:

- the need to be conveyed everywhere in their own vehicles,
- reliance on others for the preparation of their food,
- the expectation that they will be serviced immediately if they start screaming, and
- bad hair.

One of the other major things that babies do is make a mess when they play with things, go to the bathroom, eat, drink, and engage in all the activities of a typical working day. What they do *not* do, what babies and executives never do if they can at all help it, no matter how many people might ask them to do so, order them to do so, plead and beg for them to do so, is clean up after themselves. The mess around the baby isn't malevolent. It's just offensive to adults. The baby knows that, and doesn't care. Any parent (or manager) knows that you can scream "Clean up your room!" a million times, but the only time the room actually gets straightened is when the parental units can no longer stand it and do it themselves. The initial reaction of the baby, by the way, is almost inevitably one of resentment at stuff being moved.

Fantasies: A small wafer (approximately 5 percent) of your management of your manager will involve tapping into his or her fantasy life. Over time, the engagement with the world populated by dragons and demons or the spirits of good fortune or the evil droids that threaten the well-being of honest men and women everywhere, or the fabulous nine-thousand-square-foot palace by the seashore or the trip to Zimbabwe to chase the rare white rhino or whatever the hell is on the boss's mind, will be offered to you. This will once again build the bond of dependency and need that will give you admirable control over your controller.

Duties: The largest thing you can do for the boss is their work. To make bosses feel better about

---

* *Board Room Babies*, Amazon Kindle Single, © 2001, Stanley Bing and the National Association for Serious Studies.

this, they created a word for it.* It's called delegation. The more of his or her work that you can do, the more nonfungible you will be. You will also get a good sense of what you will need to delegate later on, when you're the boss.

Desires: Desires, like fantasies, give you a hook into the soul of the executive. They are, however, fantasies made flesh. You have to be somewhat careful here. A friendly visit to the strip joint on a boondoggle to New Orleans is one thing. Getting blind drunk with the guy and ending up seeing things you shouldn't is another. There always comes a time when you should peel off and leave the boss to his or her own demons. Some healthy abetting of the natural desires of your charge, however, is a good thing and definitely part of our portfolio of ploys and strategies.

Fears: Perhaps the most potent tool of all. In the effort to hold sway over the seething psychic cauldron of your executive, there is nothing more crucial than keeping paranoia, suspicion of others, and rank terror of failure bubbling. You are the solution to all of that. And you can't be a solution if you don't maintain and cultivate the problem.

Keeping the boss a bit nervous may be an important part of maintaining your nonfungibility.

---

* Fobbing your work off on other people is rebranded not as an abnegation of any sort but actually the proof that the delegator is a superb example of management at its finest.

QUADRANT #2:
MANAGING SUBORDINATES

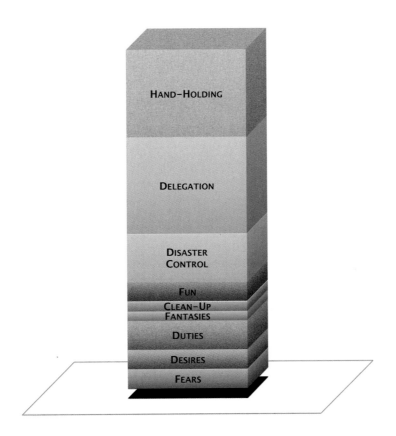

HAND–HOLDING

DELEGATION

DISASTER
CONTROL

FUN

CLEAN–UP
FANTASIES

DUTIES

DESIRES

FEARS

Managing Subordinates: Explanation of Components

Hand-holding: The emotional importance of the senior manager to his subordinates is incompletely understood and often undervalued. As nervous and tormented by fears as is the average ultra-senior officer, employees are just as crazy and paranoid, and probably for equally good reasons. In the current workplace they have ample reason to freak out more than at any time in human history since the Spanish Inquisition:

Employee Bummers

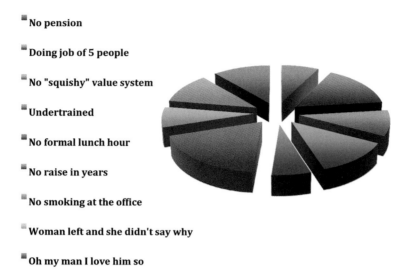

- No pension
- Doing job of 5 people
- No "squishy" value system
- Undertrained
- No formal lunch hour
- No raise in years
- No smoking at the office
- Woman left and she didn't say why
- Oh my man I love him so

Of special note is the complaint about the lack of "squishiness" in the current corporate value system. In every decade since World War II, there was a push toward some kind of humanizing concept to offset the general dehumanization of organizational life.

- In the 1950s, there was the myth of infinite progress, strong unions protected the defenseless fungible masses much better than they do today, and in corporations there was a fair amount of drinking and screwing around at the office.

- In the 1960s, there was a certain seepage of countercultural values into the rabbit warren of the workplace. Today, if one looks at the head shots of lower, middle, and even senior management in a corporation like Westinghouse, which was truly as close to the Kremlin as an American entity could get, you will see a surprising number of Fu Manchu mustaches, mutton chop sideburns, and even the occasional crooked tie. There were also a host of organizational theories then in development that were supposed to humanize the workplace.

- The 1970s were a time of loopy human potential movements, and self-help books like *I'm OK, You're OK* (1972) found their way not only into the living rooms of narcissistic, solipsistic former hippies, but into their new offices as well. The entire decade may have been dumb as a post, but it gave people a feeling of something soft and accommodating around them, even while they worked.

- ○ The 1980s saw the flowering of a fad that had been around in different forms since books like Frank B. Gilbreth's *Cheaper by the Dozen*, in which a demented father suffering from obsessive-compulsive disorder visits a plague of hyperorganizational time and productivity mania on his surprisingly jolly family. This kind of crazy nonsense morphed into an actual corporate phenomenon known by various names but most commonly as the Quality Process. Participants went to meetings, were rewarded with lapel pins and office toys, and everybody generally had a dopey, unifying experience that was very, very loosely tied to improved productivity and customer service. It was a leveler of hierarchies. In a Quality circle, an executive vice president and a junior submanager in the print shop could rub shoulders, get drunk at a Quality boondoggle, and end up singing the corporate song together.

Then came the greedy 1990s and the incessant cutback culture fostered by neofascist consultancies and, as they say, there you go. Since then there is no such softening agent in the mix. This puts increased pressure on the manager to be father, mother, brother, sister, or just a friendly hand ready, when need be, to rest on the shoulder of the human being who spends most of his life laboring for his living under the authoritarian footwear of that boss.

The demand for emotional sustenance is omnipresent and crucial to successful performance of the function. Consequently, as a downward manager, it will be necessary for you to deliver certain minimum levels of empathy and cordiality:

- ○ Say "good morning," "good night," and "hello" to people in the morning, the evening, and when you see them in the elevator, respectively. If you do not, the sensitive among them will grieve and the truculent will give you a bump on their personal asshole curve. The fact that you are hungry and are thinking about your morning muffin, or tired and dreaming of a short nap behind your door, does not occur to them. This is about Them, and whether you love them or not.

- ○ Keep your door open a fair amount of the time, so that if they wish to pop by for a little personal interaction, you are emotionally available to them.

- Anticipate the moments when they may have something personal to share with you, an anxiety, a fear, a little newspaper or magazine clipping, a new raisin bran cookie from the local bakery. Like housecats, they want to bring you a little gift and lay it at your feet, and then receive appropriate petting. If you do so, they will purr; if you do not, they will pout and, at critical moments, show a claw or two.

- Understand when they act distant and weird because they get mad at authority sometimes, and that's you.

- Outlandishly note the excellence of their work with regularity, sometimes in public at staff meetings so they can achieve standing with their peers.

- Forgive them their trespasses and never hold a grudge.

And so forth. This pressure to be essentially familial within the context of the workplace is one of the key components that remains untaught and basically unnoticed by traditional business training. But it's crucial in the construction of the kind of love that you want from your people and, more important still, the type of loyalty that you will need from them if you're going to demand the extra 10 percent that comes after the first 100.

Delegation: In the previous section, we saw how the good upward manager sucks up functionality from his boss. In this section, we validate that from the boss's point of view. You, as the senior officer, have better things to do than grind away at the butter churn. You have thinking to get done! You have to . . . set stuff up! Politics! Rub shoulders with Big Bob when the time is right. That's why the less you do, the more you are really doing.

Disaster control: Not the disaster control you perform when you are managing your boss. This is the kind of annoying shrapnel that you have to contend with when others lower than you on the totem pole screw up. There is also the highly aggravating work that requires your attention when subordinates need constant coaching, validation, and supervision after a task has been delegated.

Boss Satisfaction During One Employee Transaction

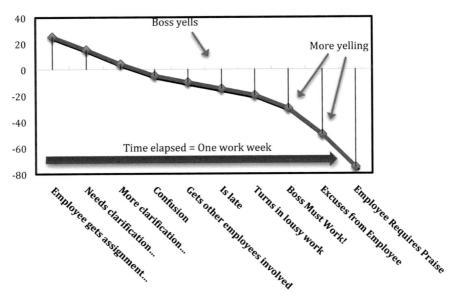

Notes on the Chart: This graphic tells a simple story. It chronicles the level of satisfaction that the boss feels in regards to one employee throughout the process of a single assignment, beginning with a moderate positive and concluding deep in the pit of a murderous negativity. Some points of yelling are also indicated. The X axis is our timeline.

➤ At the extreme left, the employee receives the assignment from his manager.

➤ He immediately needs clarification.

➤ Next, this initial clarification appears not to be sufficient.

➤ After the second clarification, there is some confusion about timing, formatting, delivery specs, whatever.

➤ Immediately after that, several other employees are suddenly involved, having gotten related duties from the employee who was supposed to be handling the work in the first place.

➤ On the date of delivery, the work product is not in evidence. It is late.

➤ The manager, now very aggravated, demands to see something. She is then presented with a document that is not only late, but also bad.

➤ She then has to rework the thing itself, requiring several hours of her time and attention, and calling her away from a lunch she was planning to have with a bunch of congenial suppliers. Instead, she has a sandwich at her desk.

➤ The next day (in our final entry) the boss looks up to find the employee standing in her doorway with his metaphorical hat in hand, all affable smiles and trembling, needy aspect. It is clear that he is seeking praise for the excellent (in his own mind) job he has done on the assignment.

A sorry situation, and all too common. How is it possible for the manager to a) not kill the employee and b) make it a learning experience for them both? In general, she has two choices, both of them popular with management professionals:

a) Take the employee aside, sit him down, and describe the concept of true delegation, and the kind of trust in the employee's judgment and capabilities that it demonstrates; that a task, once delegated, should be accomplished *by the employee himself* (unless additional personnel are cleared after discussion with the manager), and all this is to be done with minimal disturbance of the executive and presented, on time and under budget, with excellence.

b) Take the employee into her office, close the door, and tell him, "You really disappointed me on this one, Larry. I guess I overestimated you. Now get out of here before I say or do something we will both regret." Then shun the employee for several weeks, denying him his morning hang time and otherwise making him feel like crap until one day she's no longer angry with him or needs him for something, whichever comes first.

Both are effective and provide residual psychological benefits to one or both parties. I leave it to the student to decide which kind of manager he or she would like to be.

Fun: The good downward manager provides not only inspiration and guidance, but also a modicum of fun for his employees. But just as it is wise to be careful when one is having fun with one's own manager, the senior officer in a hierarchical relationship must never fall to a level of abasement that would negate her authority. Levels of substance abuse (particularly illegal substances), sexual indiscretion (including inappropriate comments to subordinates), and obvious misuse of company funds and expense accounts in pursuit of hedonistic pleasures are to be avoided by both master and servant alike.

Think of it like a marriage. You can do a lot of things in an affectionate relationship, but some things can never be forgotten or taken back, even with all the goodwill in the world. And in business, goodwill sometimes lapses. And then people talk. Don't be paranoid; just keep it in mind. And in your pants/skirt.

Things you can do to have fun with your employees that will build community, loyalty, and love for you:

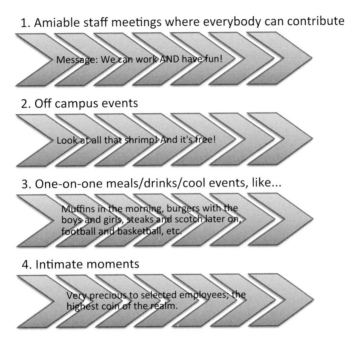

1. Amiable staff meetings where everybody can contribute

Message: We can work AND have fun!

2. Off campus events

Look at all that shrimp! And it's free!

3. One-on-one meals/drinks/cool events, like...

Muffins in the morning, burgers with the boys and girls, steaks and scotch later on, football and basketball, etc.

4. Intimate moments

Very precious to selected employees; the highest coin of the realm.

Cleanup: Employees can clean up their spaces and places for themselves. Your job here is to surround yourself with a work environment that pleases you. You're the boss. Standards that are too lax in this area can lead to crazy cubicles filled with Star Wars toys and, in certain extreme cases, porn. There are also many complaints registered by employees in an "open" work location that features a minimum of privacy, of fellow colleagues who have bad body odor or dental hygiene, and not just men, either. Believe it or not, there are many cases in which part of your duty as a manager is to improve the sanitary or grooming standards of one or more of your subordinates. I suggest delegating the job to the senior assistant in the department or, lacking that, the most sensitive junior officer.

On the other end of the scale, there are many tales of anal-retentive, overly controlling officers who do not let employees put knickknacks on their credenzas. At CBS, for instance, it was illegal until the 1980s to have anything at all on your desk, including pictures of the kids. That seems excessive.

You want people invested in their space, particularly these days when every effort is made to knock down walls, force people to sit cheek by jowl, and otherwise homogenize them into a big blob of flesh, bone, and hypersupervised anxiety.*

Fantasies: You can listen to your subordinates' dreams of future greatness, if you want. Be aware that these fantastic flights very often drool and drip into a discussion of their compensation.

Duties: Sometimes employees get to take vacations. While they are on these little jaunts, they get a chance to recharge and express their personalities and engage in pursuits that don't have anything directly to do with you as their manager. If you do not let them do this, they will hate you, and for good reason. Be advised, however, that when they are away, you may be called upon to do some of the duties that they normally perform for you. Your powers of delegation will be degraded, since there is one less person around, but you will also remember what it's like to actually run a program, talk to a vendor, write the first draft of something, or take a meeting with a nugatory person. All of these things draw you back to your roots as a working person, as opposed to an executive, and are good for you.

It may be humiliating to admit this, but the need to occasionally perform the duties of your subordinates—whether they are on vacation, maternity leave, out sick, or just taking a day off—may reveal that you don't know what you're doing when the time comes to actually do something, rather than just sit around on your ass issuing orders. As an employee yourself, you know the effect that interrupting your overworked subordinate during their time off has on their state of mind. Calculations done by real scientists in white coats reveal the following . . .

---

* This widespread fad, instituted by organizations as disparate as Bloomberg and Facebook, wants to give the appearance of democratization but is actually a totalitarian attempt to control every waking moment of the employee's life while he or she is on the job. At Bloomberg, for instance, the boss's "generosity" provides free food, all day. Employees are therefore discouraged from leaving the gulag for lunch, to the point where, when their computers are inactive, warning lights that are visible to everyone in the organization who cares to look are displayed.

$$D = 60x/20$$

. . . where D is the disturbance created in the target individual—in minutes it takes to restore peace of mind—and x represents the number of minutes the subordinate is forced to attend to business matters while out of the office. Thus a one-minute phone call (x=1) from the boss while you're on vacation creates a disturbance factor of 5, meaning that the one-minute call requires a five-minute period of agitation before peace of mind is reestablished. This seems somewhat tolerable. But regard what a thirty-minute conference call does to the day of the poor employee on a much-needed vacation:

$$D = 60 \text{ x } 30 = 1800 = 150 \; minutes = 2.5 \; hours$$

More than two and a half hours out of the middle of the day before the poor bastard is able to sink back into a relaxed state of mind! Seriously. Leave the guy alone, for chrissake. Do what you have to do yourself for a couple of days. Your employee will thank you.

Desires: There may come a time when you have to deal with extreme employee behavior due to deep human needs and desires. It's odious. People's business is their own, right? Sometimes, however, the activities of one or two employees have an effect on the morale of the group as a whole. In the opinion of this Curriculum, there are only two things that a manager truly needs to establish in this arena:

1. **Discretion:** Nobody needs to know about things that nobody needs to know about. The moment a grotesquerie of humanity is on excessive display, however, or is flaunted in any way or made an issue between people in the workplace, it presents a problem, and will need to be managed.
2. **Business standards:** A lot of the time, employees whose desires are out of control demonstrate lack of judgment in other areas as well. They disappear for long hours doing who knows what. They suddenly take business trips for wafer-thin reasons. In certain outlandish instances, the occasional charge slip from Tiffany's has been known to show

up on an expense report.* People are human. They occasionally go off the rails. But for both operating and legal reasons, bad social, sexual, and financial behavior cannot be tolerated in any but the most senior officers.†

   If the employee is valued, he or she should be taken aside and led back to earth after their visit to the Planet Mambo. View the employee involved as an individual who is in the grip of a form of mental illness, which is a disability. We don't punish people for their disabilities, do we? No. We help them manage them. Of course, if they went to Mexico with most of the third-quarter cash flow, well . . . that's what corporate security is for. Try to manage things before it gets to that point. It could reflect poorly on you as a manager, you know, if your employees are allowed to go completely out of whack.

   Fears: Honestly? How boring. Everybody has them. Tell your fearful employee to suck it up and get back to work.

---

* I once knew a guy who put a BMW 300 series convertible on his expense account. Seriously.

† At boondoggles in the 1980s, the author of this Curriculum routinely saw the president of his company and the executive vice president of something important arrive in matching Baby Benzes wearing identical green terry-cloth leisure suits. Such behavior in anybody but the very top officers of the corporation would never have been tolerated, even though their bosses were doing it. Subordinates did have a good laugh about the situation, though. Particularly about those jumpsuits, which were a nasty shade of Day-Glo green with jaunty black racing stripes down the leg.

QUADRANT #3:
MANAGING PEERS

Managing Peers: Explanation of Components

"SHARING"
WORKLOAD

FOOD, FOLKS &
FUN

GOT YOUR BACK,
MAN

"Sharing" Workload: The budding future manager will have a lot of work and nobody else to do it for them. This means that while you are a work in progress, you will need to build solid operating relationships built on mutual self-interest and some genuine dollop of affection. You have no inherent authority to wield over your colleagues—just the sense in them that it would probably be good for them, as well as easier (because you're not that pleasant when denied), to shoulder your burdens when you ask them to do so.

In essence, what you are practicing here is the art of *exerting influence without power.* This is a somewhat complicated concept. For while it is easy to understand why one person will do what another person tells them to do when they have a gun to their head, it is less clear why some people are able to get over on others with no other weapon in hand other than the strength of their personality. Yet it is those very people—those who can act like a boss when they are not the boss—who go on to be the boss. And that, students, is precisely what you are being trained to do.

There are many reasons why a person will agree to grant another person's wishes even though they are not forced to do so:

**Reasons for Successful Imposition of
Influence Without Power**

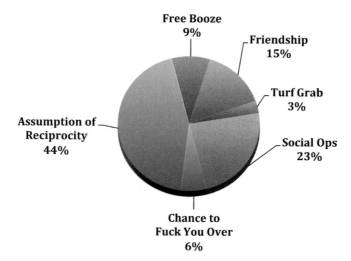

Notes on Chart: There are both positive and negative reasons why another person would accept your influence. Some are obvious, some less so.

➤ **Assumption of reciprocity:** Barb scratches your back. When the time comes, she will expect a back-scratch in return.

➤ **Free booze:** If Luis is doing the work for you, he may end up getting the free drinks that come along with the assignment. That's a sales point.

➤ **Friendship:** Chuck may actually like you. You can use that.

➤ **Turf grab:** Perhaps Elaine is looking to snatch up all the work that you do for the Large Rotating Object Division,* which has been on your turf for years. You've got to be careful you don't throw out the operating turf baby for the comfy bathwater of leisure that her involvement may grant you.

_____

* See *The Big Bang Theory*, Chuck Lorre/Bill Prady, CBS Television Network, 2007–.

➤ **Social opportunity:** Suppose the assignment involves a chance to mingle with the chairman's assistant, who is a belly-dancing snake charmer in her spare time. You're not interested. But Barry down the hall? He's interested!

➤ **Chance to fuck you over:** You have to be sensitive to the possibility that Melinda is out to get over on you. It's not a big slice of the pie, your little empire in the bullpen. But it's there. Thank goodness Melinda is your friend, right? Right?

Of course, you're not going to work this magic if these various peers don't feel much like your pals, or if they don't see how it's going to benefit them to take some of the weight off your back. That's where peer management differs from authority-based transactions, and takes more subtlety and, whenever possible, sincerity. Most of all, nobody is going to bend their will to yours if you don't exert it. This may sound tautological, but it really isn't. The desire and ability to exert one's Jedi-like will is a learned talent achieved by those who are dedicated to its study, practice throughout their lives, and are to some extent born with the gift. We'll get into this in our upcoming unit on power.

Food, folks, and fun: Finally, an uncomplicated metric. You're going to manage your colleagues not only through mystical exercises of your will, but also with beer. If beer doesn't work, try steaks.

Got your back, man: The occasional demonstration of selfless courage on behalf of your colleague is also a good idea. The conviction that the guy next to you has got your back goes a long way in achieving your goal, which is the creation of a posse that works to each member's personal advantage when the need arises. And if you expect to get something from that, you've got to give something to it, too. Modulating that balance of get/give is the management challenge. Give them a nugget of information or gossip to which they might not otherwise have access. Sharing is a beautiful thing.

QUADRANT #4:
MANAGING YOURSELF

Managing Yourself: Explanation of Components

If you are pleasant to yourself, and honest, and don't go around screaming like a little piglet every time something ugly rears its head, you will have begun the first and most important step to self-management. Beyond that, there are these components:

Getting it done: Until you reach a certain level of executive importance, you will be judged solely by the quality of the work you do (Figure 1). The 10 percent of Other is important, don't get me wrong; if you're nothing but a drudge, people will be bored by you and think you're a weenie. And nobody views their self-interest as being inextricably linked with a weenie. Given the fact, however, that you are *not* a weenie, we will leave that consideration for the moment.

Fig. 1

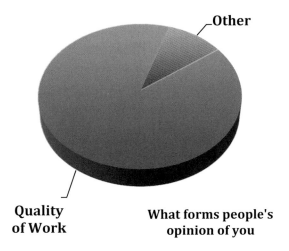

Other

**Quality
of Work**

**What forms people's
opinion of you**

Your work is defined as excellent if it:

1. Does not need to be reworked by others to the extent that they feel like they wished they had given the assignment to somebody else;
2. Is on time, under budget and realistic, based on obvious parameters and conditions;
3. Has an element of surprise—good surprise not bad surprise—that puts a very light fingerprint of yours on it.

"Wow," your boss should think. "Fred really went all out on that out-year projection table." That's all it takes. In that tiny acorn of originality or extra effort comes the eventual oak of your nonfungibility.

Thinking hard: Set aside time to think. Time when you do nothing but thinking. The kind of thinking you don't even know you're doing, because you're thinking. This is harder than it looks. Where do you go? In Internet circles on the West Coast, people can't even call a conference room their own. You have to sign up for it and then vacate it when your meeting is done, leaving it to be occupied by guys from, like a completely different floor. Who are they? You don't know. You just know there is no space you can call your own. In these same locations, people don't even have desktop computers or their own laptops. They borrow a common laptop to make periodic visits to the cloud. Where to go?

Take a walk. Sit in a quiet office that was recently vacated during the third cutback of the Bain year. And then just . . . be quiet. Keep yourself company for a while. It's amazing what bubbles up.

And don't forget to have that drink after work (Figure 2). They say drinking alone is bad for you, but corporate studies show that most people actually get into a lot more trouble drinking with others.

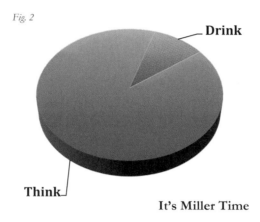

Fig. 2

Drink

Think

It's Miller Time

Fighting fear: Businesspeople are frightened all the time. Frightened of the economy. Frightened of Wall Street. Frightened of the new senior management structure, the new boss, the new consultant, anything new, in fact. Frightened that in the coming reorganization they will lose their office space. Frightened that they are not core or in the loop. Frightened that the finance department will take a more aggressive look at their expense account. Frightened that there will be some event that could spoil their vacation plans. Frightened that their industry is in a cycle of inexorable decline. Frightened that there will be layoffs. Every day has its specific fear, with an undertow of other, more general apprehensions. To be in business is to be afraid at least some of the time, and sometimes all the time. During a merger or acquisition scenario, everybody walks around with a knot in their guts for months, sometimes years.

This fear expresses itself differently in the various strata of the company infrastructure. Lower-level people feel it as simple fear melding into terror, it shows up as pervasive anxiety in middle managers, and is magically transformed into ferocious anger in senior executives. This is because people without power don't have the right, organizationally speaking, to be angry yet. You need power in order to turn your fear outward and use it to assault other people. Middle management has a modified right to inflict their fear onto subordinates, but often isn't narcissistic or self-justifying enough to do so without an overlay of guilt, which is an anger inhibitor.

In terms of our goal—self-management—our objective is not to eradicate fear. Fear is a wonderful motivator and clarifier of confusion. A middle manager who is not afraid when McKinsey Consulting shows up is a moron. As we incorporate this issue into our overall search for mastery, our task is to segregate the fear so that it does not seep into everything we do, to limit its impact and expression in our daily routine and psychology. Some find it effective to focus the fear into a session of squash or tennis, channeling fear into aggression and competitive spirit. Others let it cloud their drinking time, which is a mistake. Drinking should be exclusively for pleasure and not tainted by other considerations. Serious executives often find that the best time to wrestle with and master their fears is the critical hour between 3 and 4 a.m. (Figure 3).

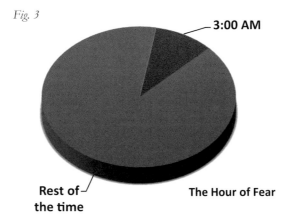

Fig. 3

3:00 AM

Rest of the time

The Hour of Fear

This is, for many, the hour when a variety of unpleasant doubts, terrors, dreads, uncertainties, suspicions, and lesser qualms rear their heads from the blackest hour of the night and assail the soul in their purest form. The fearful businessperson can then, with some practice and determination, fall back into a fitful sleep, waking at dawn, all of his or her worries evaporated like dew in the sizzling dawn.

Not fucking up: Everybody does. The size of permissible fuckups depends on the size of your compensation package (Figure 4). Small people can sustain small fuckups. Big ones will sink them.

More substantial fuckups can be tolerated in those of larger size, with an almost unlimited carte blanche for smaller snafus and screw-ups. Titans can make enormous, bone-headed fuckups and be celebrated for a time in the business media for them. Jamie Dimon, the head of JPMorgan Chase, presided over one of the really big banking screw-ups of 2012, when his company lost billions on bad investments under his watch. He was rewarded with a headline in *USA Today* that said, "Jamie Dimon Screws Up the Right Way," and applauded by his fans in Congress when he went to Washington to tell them why additional regulation was unnecessary to prevent screw-ups like the one he just oversaw.

Fig. 4

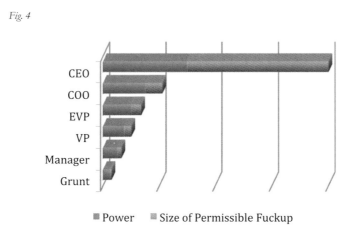

■ Power　　■ Size of Permissible Fuckup

Men and women of normal size can take a tip from Jamie Dimon. He accepted responsibility for the problem immediately, without really appearing too contrite. There is a good lesson in that for us all. People who apologize too much after they fuck up compound their problems. Manly admission of responsibility is good; begging forgiveness is not. In our culture, for some reason, a full apology always seems to be the preamble for additional punishment and recrimination. So blame yourself all you want but don't fall on your sword in public. Use your fuckup as a chance to request some humble schooling from your boss. Bosses love to give instruction to guys who are courageous enough to ask for it. But don't wallow in the sea of contriteness. You have better things to do—like move on to your next engagement, which hopefully will not be a fuckup, right? It better not be, Sparky. You've only got so many bites at the poison apple, you know.

Stayin' frosty: Frostiness may be understood as the state of readiness that precedes battle. Great warriors stay frosty even in their sleep. The cowboy sleeping in the middle of the prairie is approached by a gang of desperadoes who are going to steal his horse. Just as the lead outlaw is about to knock him over the head with the butt of his pistol, up pops the cowboy and shoots the bad guy between the eyes. Hopping on his trusty steed, he chases the gang into a gully, where they are killed by falling rocks. That's frosty. A team of marines sometime in the future is in the bowels of an alien spaceship. Around the next corner is the alien mother with a large cadre of acid-spitting creatures waiting to cocoon them and impregnate them with their alien spawn. The marines do not run. They turn on their flamethrowers and head deeper into the ship. That's frosty.

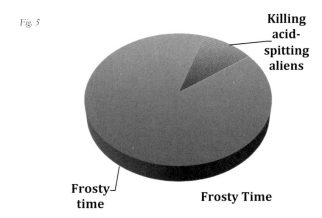

Fig. 5

Killing acid-spitting aliens

Frosty time

Frosty Time

Business is all about frosty. There's work that needs doing during frosty time. But clean your weapon. Grapple with the monster when the alarm goes off.

Chasing the dream: Never lose sight of it. Maybe yours is grinding out the yardage every day so that in about fifteen years the little kid at home can go to any damn school she wants to. Maybe it's making a million dollars before you're thirty and moving to Fiji. If you don't have one, find a new job. If you can see the road in front of you, then you're managing. That's basically all you can ask of this line of work. Keep it up.

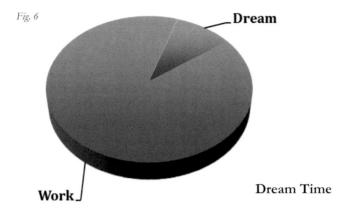

Fig. 6

Dream

Work

Dream Time

Concluding Thought

We haven't said too much about what just might be the most important quality of great management and those who have the gift for it. It's listening. The capacity to listen. Not just to hear and react. Not talking, although God knows your average manager does more of that than anything else. It's listening.

Listen to your boss. Yeah, he's making all kinds of familiar noises, but what's he really saying? What is he not saying? Can you listen to that? What would he like, actually? What is that thing behind what he believes he's telling you? Listen for it.

Listen to your employees. They're telling you things, too. They don't think you're right on that thing you've been working on. They're telling you that by their silence when you express your naïve enthusiasm in it. If you were listening, you might be on the way to preventing a disaster. Listen to what they're saying and what they're not saying. Listen.

Listen to your colleagues. They're probably as smart as you are. Some may be even smarter, if that idea seems at all possible to you. Listen to the finance people when they express an opinion on financial matters. Listen to the lawyers on all legal matters and even some ethical ones.* And listen to your friends when they are annoyed with you.

Listen to your clients, your customers, your family, your research people, your vendors, your critics, and even, at times, to the media, when the spotlight beckons. Listen to it all.

And finally: Listen to yourself. The great ones do that better than normal people. And who knows? You may be one of them. But you won't know if you don't listen.

Exercises

1. Have a conversation with your boss. Ascertain some area where he is nervous about something. Very carefully and subtly, see if you can make him even more nervous than he was before. If there is no such problem or issue, see if you can create one. Then see if you can get the assignment of solving that particular problem that didn't exist before you generated it.

2. There is certainly a very rude person that you encounter in your daily transit, acquisition of food or coffee, or some other daily exchange. You have always been very polite to that person, in an attempt to manage them and their nastiness. Tomorrow, go to that person, and at the first indication of rudeness on their part, be even more rude back. See what happens. Report the results to www.serious-studies.com.

3. Organize a drinking event for you and the five people you like best in the company. Pick up the check. Observe what that does to your subsequent relationships.

4. Wake at 3 a.m. Sit in a chair in the dark. Go back to bed at 4 a.m. Repeat the exercise until you are able to fall asleep after sitting in the chair.

---

* You probably don't have to listen to them on matters pertaining to public relations and marketing, even though for some reason they seem only too eager to offer the help.

Group Dynamics

Some years ago, the author of this Curriculum was a midlevel functionary in a large multinational corporation whose name is still on appliances but whose ownership is now in a former Axis nation. Back then, it was highly hierarchical, led by a rather cold-blooded MBA CEO who didn't like me. He determined at that time that, in a battle for the head of our small department, the title would be given to another who was less qualified, for reasons I won't go into. Budgets were tight, however, and this decision meant, in the eyes of the CEO, that I was fungible and had to go. I was at the time a member of a small group of friendly diners and drinkers, all of whom enjoyed each other's company on a regular basis, perhaps too regular, but that's another story. One of this group was the head of HR and the other was the COO. Without telling the CEO, these two colluded to hide the costs associated with my employment in a secret budget line managed by them both. Thus I was saved. The CEO's selection for our department leadership lasted for eighteen months, at which point I took over my current chair, which has survived three mergers, a gigantic acquisition, and a host of other corporate traumas. And when I say "my current chair," I mean that literally. It's the same chair.

Business is often seen as a personal occupation; it is not. It is the functioning of the individual within the context of groups, not just one group, but a series of groups that form, dissolve, and reform hourly, daily, over months and years. Understanding group dynamics and what an important role they play in any business career is critical. Up until now we have looked at the core issues from an individual point of view, and this is as it should be. In this life, as well as in our careers, we begin and end alone. In between, however, we do encounter other people, sometimes in more than just a superficial fashion. In this unit we will investigate the following preliminary subjects.

➤   *What is a group?* A group is not simply more than one or two people sitting in a room. It is a living organism, as long as it lasts, whose workings have an impact on each of its members. We will look at that, and then move on to how this variety of assemblages functions in a business context. Before we truly wrestle with the complex issues that surround group behavior, we must first engage on the question of . . .

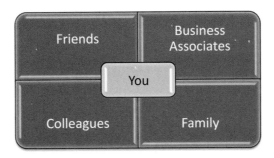

➤ *Understanding other people:* What are they? Gifted businesspeople tend to be self-obsessed, driven narcissists who often have an incomplete grasp of the nature, and indeed the existence of, "other people" as entities distinct from themselves. Yet this task must be learned as well. We will take two turns around this track. The first will be for beginners who have never recognized that other people really exist. Some never learn this and fail in the workplace, or go on to be preening egomaniacs who run everything. The second lap will offer thoughts for those who enjoy the existence of groups and draw power from them. This easily transitions into our subunit on . . .

➤ *Social relationships as a function of group dynamics:* To succeed in a group, the business-person must build and sustain what are apparently not purely business relations with a variety of people in whom he or she would have no interest in any other context. How? When? Human (and semihuman) interactions also improve quality of work life. No one but a true ultra-senior executive can do without them. Beyond the questions of how the individual interacts with the group, there is the massive subject of how groups interact with themselves. The most obvious and inescapable way they do so is through the most ubiquitous phenomenon in business life, that is:

➤ *Meetings and other formal gatherings as a form of work as well as an alternative to it:* We'll look at the how-to, the what-not-to, the setting up, the criteria for inclusion, and so many other factors that make a decent meeting. The meeting is the spine of much of the "work" that people do at any office; it is also at times the antithesis of work. In this layer of the Core, the green and unpracticed students will be schooled on the difference between good and bad meetings and tutored on the basic techniques so they don't spit up on themselves in public.

Let's get started.

What Is a Group?

A group is an entity that is created when a collection of individuals are brought together, often but not always voluntarily, sometimes to achieve a purpose, but not invariably so. There are as many kinds of groups as there are groups themselves, but in the workplace, these are the most likely to be found in one form or another:

Short-term Task-Oriented	Amorphous	Long-term Status-Related	Intense Deal Mode	Cadre
•Fixed purpose •Fixed membership •Disbands when tasks are completed •Loose emotional bonds	•Called together by manager •Specific purpose unclear •No escape possible •Usually a regularly-scheduled event at the convenience of the manager •No fixed beginning or end date •No emotional bonds	•Attendance is considered a perk •Regularly scheduled •Extremely formulaic content •Some faux camaraderie •Exit only on career death	•Laser focus •Time-sensitive •Stakes very high •No love lost among members •Success in the group may determine role in future enterprise •Failure is not an option •Money on the table	•Membership based on loyalty •High degree of emotional bonding •No specific tasks—other than to build the power base of the group itself •Very long-term duration •No exit sought or granted

Each of these groups comes bearing different expectations, shapes, risks, heat, depth, and emotional demands on its members. The Amorphous group, for instance, is usually some kind of staff meeting that the senior manager has decided is a good thing for one reason or another—and he or she may be right. Staff meetings of this kind interrupt the flow of work for members of the group, but they also serve several very real functions in certain cases. They improve communication within the work unit, as people report on their activities and compare notes. They reveal flaws in the operation, as these reports lay bare duplicative efforts or stupid things that are about to happen or have happened already. On the downside, within the context of an Amorphous group people tend to say things that, due to the lack of genuine loyalty, often travel beyond the confines of a gathering.

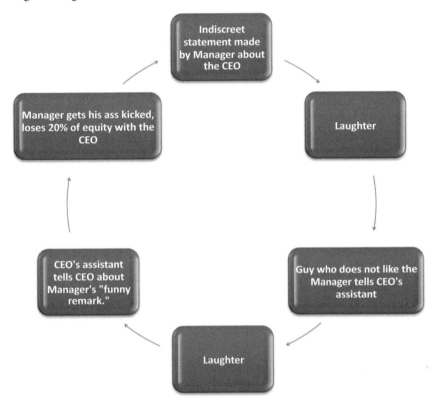

Very unfortunate. All the kinds of groups noted above come with similar risks, as the needs of each individual interface with those of the collective. In the deal-making group, the purpose of the collective may be to create an entity that will destroy everything that each member has known and loved for years, including, sometimes, their careers. This lends a certain crazy desperation and, in some cases, hostility to the proceedings. The Long-Term Status-Related group can carry with it the extreme danger of falling asleep during its gatherings, because the sole function of the event is simply to have it. The content is insignificant. And yet such groups provide important glue to a large organization that requires it. The cadre is the only form of group in which the individuals and their group are truly one, with each member identifying entirely with the needs of the whole.

It takes talent for a person to be a good member of a group. A transformation takes place in a person called upon to join one, a shifting of the perception of self, from this:

To this:

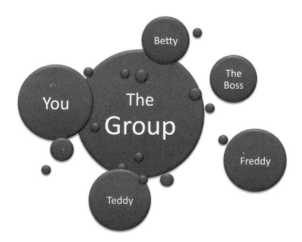

Not everyone can make this transition. It requires nothing less than revolution in a collective perception on a Copernican scale.*

One last point to keep in mind: Groups do not only exist when its members are assembled. A real group exists even when each member is nowhere near the center. Families, for instance, exist even when members have not seen each other for years except at weddings and funerals. Likewise, management teams can break up, travel to the far ends of the earth, never laying eyes on each other for months at a time, except in tele-presence rooms, and still be tightly bonded together as a unit by common economic interests and loyalty to the company leadership. In very rare cases, groups of former employees of the same company outlive their tenure with the organization, with elderly members of yesterday's executive team meeting on golf courses or in bars and restaurants, long into their dotage.

A group is the antidote to loneliness and isolation in business life. A good one is a precious resource. Bad ones are a real pain the ass, taking up time, attention, and effort and exposing members to the bleak prospect of hanging with the wrong table in the student lunchroom of hell.

Understanding Other People for Beginners

Only those who care about this subject need take part in this level of the course. If you don't, you may be one of those great, bloated Godzillas who are destined to take down a major city, and more power to you. The rest of us will continue on from here. On the other hand, maybe you've come quite far without being interested in other people beyond what they can do for you in the next five minutes, but feel that something is missing from your business life. In that case, hang in here.

Here is the core concept that you are going to have to accept if you are to engage in groups, enjoy them, and get them to assist you in your quest for Mastery of Business Arts.

> *Other people are real, living, breathing, thinking entities. They believe*
> *their lives are as central to the cosmos as you do of yours. They are the*
> *hero or heroine of their movie, not supporting players in yours.*

---

* That is, in a typical American workplace, where everybody is taught to "look out for number one," the act of putting the group in the center of one's universe is not unlike the major change imposed upon European orthodoxy in the early sixteenth century, moving the earth from the center of the cosmos into its proper position in orbit around the sun. Scientists who tried to do so were often excommunicated.

Some of you may need to copy this down and post it somewhere on your desk or wall. You may have been raised differently, or come to another conclusion early in life, and developed a conviction that everybody is there to accommodate you, follow your orders, and make your life conform to your personal mythology. If this is so, you have an executive point of view built into your DNA. It is, in the end, a weakness, although the religion of self as practiced by powerful executives does yield short-term benefits.

Long term, however, it is a crippling liability, one you should recognize and seek to understand and, eventually, seek professional help for. It is based on a lie, and lies eventually collide with the truth and create tremendous discomfort for everybody, including the individual you care most about: you.

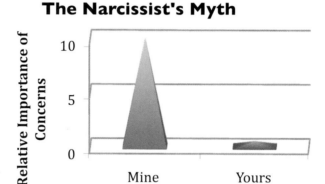

The lie in question is that, due to their immense importance, they have control over the universe. This, of course, is patently false, and eventually, in one way or another, will be proven so. When that happens, as it will over and over again, a profound cognitive dissonance erupts. There are two ways to deal with this:

- Change your worldview to a more rational one where control is limited to a human scale and one's fate is inextricably bound to that of others.
- Get very, very angry and make everybody around you miserable, thus proving that you can control at least some portion of the universe by torturing it at will.

This is why senior executives are angry so much of the time. They choose the second option when the world does not conform to their solipsistic view of it. This enrages them down to their narcissistic nub and they dig in, refusing to compromise, which only makes life worse for them, because 1) people hate them even more now and 2) they continue to be tormented by a cosmos that constantly contradicts their view of themselves and their place in it.

For instance, if you are Napoleon and convinced that you are destined to rule the world, the idea that you should not invade Russia during the winter never occurs to you. The lives of the men lost in the stupidity of your campaign are of no concern to you. And yet look at what happens! How can it be? Your men stop just short of Moscow and . . . die! This wasn't in the script! In business, fewer people die but the decision-making process is equally driven by individual frailty.

- April 23, 1985: The executives at Coca-Cola, using copious market research, decide that they are going to improve Coke. They don't. The new product is a huge flop and almost sinks the company. In short order the original Coke is reinstated and a second product, New Coke, makes an appearance. It also flops.

- December 2008: Jeff Zucker of NBC decides that drama at 10 p.m. is dead because NBC can't develop a hit drama. He puts *The Tonight Show with Jay Leno* at 10 p.m., completing the destruction of the network and nearly ruining all two-hundred-plus NBC-affiliated stations in the Armageddon that follows. He is rewarded with the top job at CNN a scant two years later. In the media business, you have to fail big enough if you want to stay relevant.

- June 2012: Apple, in its executive arrogance, eliminates the superb and deeply researched Google Maps app from its mobile devices and offers its own proprietary, hastily assembled map program instead. It is the worst launch in the company's history. In a truly unfortunate development for Apple, one of the most influential industry writers, David Pogue of *Scientific American* and the *New York Times*, uses the Apple Maps app to find his way to a speaking engagement and ends up hopelessly lost. He writes a damning column. The executive who developed the app is fired.*

In all cases, somewhere in the lead on these things was an executive who didn't listen to people.

---

* This guy was also responsible for development of the artificial intelligence program offered with the iPhone and iPad—Siri. Not only is Siri unhelpful and anything but intelligent; she also has a very irritating artificial personality. Surely somebody at Apple could have taken her out back and asked her to shoot herself.

This is understandable, because it is the very egotistical, bullying qualities that made the individuals executive material in the first place. This is a shame for the organization, and completely avoidable, if the leaders in question had simply listened to the collective wisdom of the group.

Understanding Other People (Advanced)

At this point you have wrestled with the notion that there are other people in the world who are not simply projections of your needs or agents placed on earth to accomplish the inconvenient things you don't feel like doing. Right now, I know, that is a vague, unsubstantiated concept to you. You have been running in forward momentum mode since you were conscious of yourself as a human being. This has warped your perceptions and only after encountering some of the ideas in the first section of this Curriculum subject have you begun even to consider moderating them.

There are two things standing in your way: this need for speed and forward motion that has defined your character and, second, the fact that a key, fundamental part of your personality has never developed beyond infancy, because along the way you discovered there were ways you could get those infantile needs satisfied by asserting a privileged status. Both disincentives to group life are difficult to overcome, but through a concerted effort, and the help of other people, it can be done.

If you are an afflicted narcissist, you must try to rip your head out of its comfy socket and look at the way you do things if you are ever to hope to belong to a functioning group. The behavior is ingrained and leads to all the associated difficulties:

Narcissistic Management Style Conflicts with Group Formation

Moving very fast	Insulated from others	Lousy group skills
• Not listening • issuing orders	• Alienated from group • Lonely and isolated	• Recognition of problem necessary • Rigidity of character is core problem • Possible solution lies in group love bombing

Only after these management failings become insurmountable, and impede performance (when things fall apart), is there some incentive for change. Sadly, one of the characteristics of senior officers is rigidity of character. It's hard for them to accept new solutions, new ways of seeing things. This explains why so many group experiences in hierarchical systems are tedious, top-down affairs that exist simply to bolster the self-importance of the executive sitting at the head of the table. Solutions lie in the power of a group to pour so much positive or negative reinforcement on the benighted executive that he or she begins to prefer the group to loneliness, egotism, and alienation.

Great groups do exist. This is because the pull of a group, if exercised continually and with determination and delicacy, can eventually produce change even in the most encrusted superego. The group has tremendous power. In this case that power can be used to humanize the relationships within its circle, to slow down the decision-making process, and, at least temporarily, flatten the structure of the organization.

In this regard, the group must assist the suffering individual by making the demand that this be done—in sales terms, by *asking for the order.*

Asking for the Order: The Sales Paradigm

Looking at it this way, the task becomes one of upward management, as discussed in our previous unit on the subject. We are, of course, assuming that the person having difficulty recognizing the existence of other people is the senior officer, because if he weren't, the other group members would simply tell him where to get off. This can't easily be done with the boss. A more strategic, sustainable approach is necessary. For this purpose, the group must develop a shadow leader who actually conducts the true business of the group—which is to bring the outlier into the fold. Tools are many:

- ◦ Humor: the great democratizer.
- ◦ Process: The group engages in sustained discussion of the issue, which reveals that the solutions are not amenable to simple bullying or order-giving.

- Silence: The group simply refuses to function when the boss is up to his old tricks. No fun is had. The boss doesn't enjoy the passive-aggressive group. It meets less often and this way of executive validation becomes eventually closed to him.
- Catering: It's tough to resist a less hierarchical approach when everybody is munching on a sandwich.

Social Relationships as a Function of Group Dynamics

Now that you have begun the process of appreciating other people as discrete entities worthy of attention and respect, you may begin assembling others around you, or joining aggregations already in progress, in more than what might be considered a purely business manner. The workplace offers a wide range of coming-together opportunities that look primarily social but are actually an elaborate form of organizational melding, positioning, and structuring. Careers are made and broken in these less formalized environments, where people gather for situational, simulated, and, occasionally, genuine friendships while taking part in . . .

➤ Breakfast: Sometimes there is a cafeteria in one's corporate tower, where waiting in line forms a common bond of inconvenience in the morning; sometimes small groups gather around coffee areas or, if the manager is convenient and amenable, in the office of the senior director, enjoying some of the most precious quality time with the boss that may be had.

➤ Meetings, where groups of employees band together for a few moments, sometimes longer, to discuss business, talk idiotic drivel about golf, or simply to make fun of the more senior people who are either on the way into the room or just departed.

➤ Getaways, which actually offer some the most intense forms of situational friendship available in a corporate setting. These "boondoggles" are fewer and farther between in the recessionary era, but they still exist and present both the greatest potential bonding venues as well as the most acute opportunities to destroy one's reputation, fabricated business persona, and home life.

➤ Drinks after work, a prime means of building not only interpersonal relationships but lasting groups that will stand the test of sobriety. Within these groups, however, there are those serpentine individuals who will be a valued member of the drinking group while intoxicated and continue to be a dangerous dick when the only glasses on the table are bifocals.

➤ Golf outings. These appear to be friendly, but often are not.

➤ Trips to the restroom. When a group of hand-washers get together the chances for team-building are intense, brief, and almost subliminal in their power.

Do not make a mistake here and assume that such group associations that shade into friendship automatically are transformed into business alliances that have operational value. Sometimes they are, based on my own personal experience over many years in a variety of corporate cultures (see figure, below). They certainly prepare the seedbed for operating alliances. But sometimes a friend is just a friend, and a group of friends is just that as well. Not everything can be a tool, although there are times when a finance mouse with whom you share a cigarette every day at 3 p.m. outside the door of the building might take a thorn out of your paw in a budget meeting, or a group might assert your importance to the grim reaper from Bain when he shows up at your staff meeting to evaluate the productivity of your operation.

Can Pals Be Used for Reliable Business Purposes?

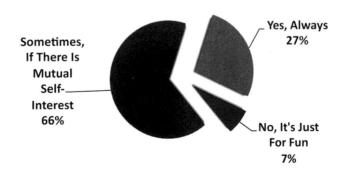

Sometimes, If There Is Mutual Self-Interest 66%

Yes, Always 27%

No, It's Just For Fun 7%

The hard fact, though, is that your best work friend will still heave you over the parapet if a situation arises where it comes down to him or you. It's not personal. The distinction between your private and your corporate lives is one that you will do well never to forget.

Meetings: Organizational Tool or Waste of Time?

Both.

Meetings are the way business organizes its collective brain. They are inescapable. When people don't know what else to do, they have a meeting. When they have ideas and want to move those ideas to decision points, they have a meeting. When they are lonely and have a headache, they have a meeting. When they want a free bagel and a little chat, they have a meeting. When they want to plan a meeting, they have a meeting. When they want to plan the meeting where they will be planning the meeting to plan the meeting, they have a meeting to set up the meeting to plan the upcoming planning meeting for the meeting. In Japan, when they want to put off making a decision, they have a meeting. In Stalinist Russia of the 1930s and General Electric in the 1980s, when they wanted to execute a person, they had a meeting to do it publicly.

During the length and breadth of your career, you will have to make a personal decision about what kind of meetings you want to take part in. At the start, you will have limited choice—but choice nonetheless. You will have to learn to exercise that choice, as practice for later on, when you will have much more sway in determining the meetings you attend, lead, or champion. To make informed choices, you should understand the nature of the meeting itself, how it can be used both badly and, occasionally, quite well. Let's look at that now.

Bad Meetings: The Revenge of the Nerds

At their best, meetings come together to form groups that will work, enjoy the process of doing so, and then disband when the work—both business and personal—is completed. Sadly, much of the time the great institution of the meeting is abused and tortured, rendering the vehicle a tawdry, tedious waste of time. There are several reasons for this:

- *Ego of the manager:* As we discussed previously, and probably will again, the large/small egotism of those in control of the group, an alternatively bloated and shrunken sense of self that blossoms under the pressure of leadership, can distort virtually every business and social transaction in the workplace. This is nowhere more evident than in the meeting context. The workflow of a normal meeting should look something like this:

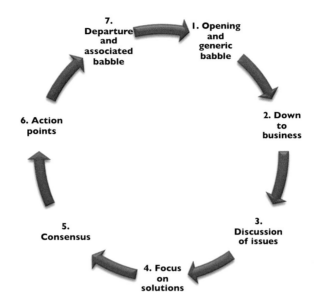

Instead, the intrusion of the self-centered executive or inappropriately egotistical peer transforms and ultimately damages the process all but irreparably. First, the possibility must be recognized that the meeting has been called for no other reason than to bolster the big ego's agenda, solidify his or her power, or pursue some other purpose of his or her devising. This is a total waste of time to start with, since nobody but this one individual has a reason to be in the room. Worse, the content of the meeting inevitably devolves into this:

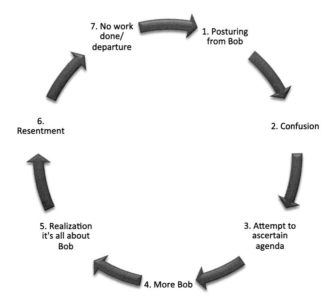

This kind of nonsense gives all meetings a bad name. Other causes of bad meetings include:

- *Lack of clarity:* Let's say there is a problem that needs some form of resolution. Perhaps it's as simple as it being summer and there not seeming to be as much to do as there was in February. Everybody is at sixes and sevens. Gotta have a meeting. Talk about the upcoming to-do list, even though there isn't any. Or there is a big presentation due in, perhaps, three months, and the boss hasn't been altogether clear on what comes next. Data is being collected. Assignments have been distributed. What comes now? Shouldn't something be happening?

- *Procrastination:* Everybody should really be working. But how much fun it is to have a whole bunch of meetings instead! Things that can be done in a good procrastination meeting include:

  ➤ Pre-crastination: All the good stuff you can do while leading up to the actual procrastinatory process;

  ➤ Crastination: More pre-crastination and additional crastination while work is being avoided;

  ➤ Actual Procrastination: The dark heart of the procrastination project, professional crastination is begun in grade school and involves a variety of activities—intense work on other projects, evolved excuse making, self-deception, symptoms of Epstein-Barr syndrome, and more;

  ➤ Work: to be done by others while procrastinatory meetings are still under way and completed in a swift and surprising move that makes everybody who didn't bake the cake hungry for a piece of the completed one;

  ➤ Post-crastination: Basking in the post-crastinatory glow is only part of the fun here, which beyond talking about how well the project went may involve a period of planning and other pre-crastination on upcoming ventures.

The only person not having fun here is the guy actually assigned to do the work that everybody else has avoided by having the meetings. He or she is dying inside while being trapped in this stuffy room while all his senior officers twiddle their thumbs. Then when his work is late, due to all the meeting and professional crastination that's been going on, he'll be blamed for it. Procrastinators are experts at blaming others for procrastination. Also:

- *Rotten decision-making capability:* Very often a surfeit of meetings is an indication that somebody who is supposed to be organizing, prioritizing, and ordering things, isn't. Other times nobody wants to make any decisions so they have meetings instead. The committee defers to another committee that doesn't have the power to make a decision on it, so it is passed along to a committee that makes a recommendation to an executive who doesn't have the decision-making power, either, so he makes a recommendation to an executive who does have the power but doesn't want to exercise it because it would be considered bad form for him to do so without consulting his superior, who doesn't give a shit and sends it back into committee.

- *Jerkoffs:* There are some people who just like to have meetings. There is no explanation for them; they just like to, you know, have meetings. "Let's have a meeting about that," they will say. And you ask, "Why?" And they don't really have an answer except that afternoon you get an e-mail saying there will be a meeting. Perhaps these people fail to see a reflection when they look in the mirror and, like other vampires, need an audience to verify their existence.

A Word About Committees

A solid committee dedicated to the unraveling of a specific issue, or the planning of a complex event that has many layers, is a necessary entity in an organization that has work to do. But the creation of a committee should be a somewhat rare event, since there are many other ways that things can be done before one becomes necessary, and there should be a limited number of committees in existence at any one time within a business organization. Operationally, the committee should be very focused, have a narrow turf, be essentially democratic, but also have a clear leader who has the power to make decisions and set agendas. The committee should have the ability to execute members who waste the committee's time. A surfeit of committees within a corporation or any serious enterprise is the sign of intense internal rot and incipient organizational collapse. Those who suggest the formation of committees must also be watched with care, and expunged if they continue to assert this view when difficult issues arise that could otherwise be resolved via decisive individual or small group action.

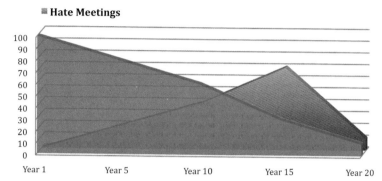

As you move forward, you will find it increasingly impossible to tolerate meetings that are superfluous, time-wasting ego-boosters for the wrong people. Your pleasure at being invited to meetings at first blush will be intense—to be included in anything will feel so rare that you just might burst into tears at the first indication that you are welcome, somewhere. Later, as hours and then days and then weeks and then years of your life have been wasted in fruitless meetings, the feeling will change.

You will note in the chart that at the end, many people hate meetings somewhat less. This is because they have once again reached the age of potential superfluity.

Now, having bathed in a fine mist of negativity about meetings as a group endeavor (as they well deserve!), we will now, in true business fashion, take the diametrically opposing point of view for the sole reason that doing so suits our purposes (itself a jerkoff move at a meeting).

There are many, many meetings that are important, at which critical, life-changing business is to be done, at which your attendance is a statement of your standing, and your absence a testimony to your unimportance. The next section is about those meetings—getting to them, managing them, and, when you grow to have the opportunity, running them.

The Eightfold Path of Good Meeting

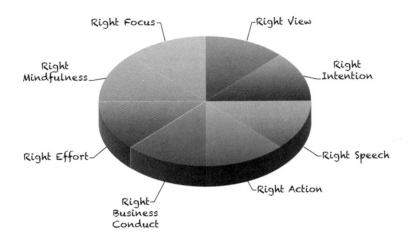

The Eightfold Path of Good Meeting is one of the principal teachings of the Buddha (originally Siddhartha Gautama, before he achieved fame and rebranded himself). The Buddha was in business more than 2,500 years ago but still found it possible to describe a variety of ways that people could cut through the miasma of daily living and achieve serenity, insight, and divine detachment, wiping out in the process the demons of greed, hatred, and attachment to false things. Key to his teaching is the fact that, if pursued with attention and patience, the practice of Buddhism works well to eradicate suffering, at least until you step on a nail or something like that. Among the suffering from which the Eightfold Path can lead you is the suffering that attends pointless and obnoxious meetings. Let's look at the path that leads to that goal.

1. Right View

Right View is the attempt we continue to make, throughout our time within the confines of our job descriptions, to figure out what is actually going on. The situation analysis. It is the effort we make to ascertain reality. It is the beginning.

Right View happens before the meeting. Just consider all the ways people generate suffering for themselves at meetings—a lack of clarity of purpose, bad feelings about the meeting and its participants, foolish hopes for the meeting itself, random hatred, envy, and free-floating anxiety. In this initial effort to position our perceptions correctly, we bring to the task all our knowledge of human behavior and how people impose suffering on each other. Our goal is, by this right view, to minimize the discomfort members of the meeting might visit on each other. That is the goal of Right View. In doing so, we recognize that:

1. Every member of the meeting has the power to affect the karma of others.* Good actions will produce good results; evil actions the opposite;
2. The meeting will end, and with it the specific suffering it appears to have created;
3. Suffering is inherent in the human condition as long as people are tied to the wheel of desire and disappointment. Those who accept the inevitability of meeting and the associated physical discomforts—claustrophobia, boredom, narcolepsy, hunger, over-heated or excessively air-conditioned surroundings—suffer first a failure of Right View. To abandon all hope and desire is the open door that is always open to us as an exit from the suffering associated with bad meetings.

Right View is a healthy outlook on things, strong but realistic, and very often involves healthy catering of the meeting with fruit, cheese, cookies, and, if it's a very serious meeting, smoked meat or fish. Badly or insufficiently catered events have a greater chance of morphing into less positive directions and straying from the Eightfold Path into peevishness, greed, misanthropy, destructive hierarchical lording, and hypercompetitiveness. Nobody can pull off that kind of stuff over a well-toasted bagel.

2. Right Intention

After one has taken a look at the overall reality of the situation from both ground level and forty thousand feet, one now has an opportunity to face the upcoming meeting with a firm desire to make it as good a meeting as possible. This would seem to be a given, but sadly, it is not. People come to the meeting not only with the Wrong View but also with Lousy Intention. These might include:

---

* For our purposes, karma may be defined as what is going to happen to everybody in the next five minutes, five days, five weeks, five months, and five years. Anything beyond that will cease being karma and begin to shade over into dharma, the fate of the cosmos, which is not really our concern in a world that operates pretty much quarter to quarter.

❖   Kneecapping Lazenby because I don't want her to get a promotion before I do.

❖   Not helping Brewster achieve his objectives because he hasn't ever been particularly congenial to my agendas; why should I be to his?

❖   Getting out the room as fast as possible even if there are some important things to discuss because I have a hot game of Words With Friends going on my iPad.

❖   Trying to impress the boss by acting like a sycophantic piece of shit.

❖   Trying to get Bridget Olivetti sexually aroused with salacious text messages.

❖   Killing every idea that is not my own.

These attitudes, among many others, demonstrate wrong intention arising from a failure to achieve Right View and the fact that, in each case, the speaker is being a douche. Douches do not achieve enlightenment, or have many good meetings.

In Right Intention, armed with a realistic Right View, those of us on the Path attempt to get rid of all this poisonous vapor and crappy baggage that attend the average bad meeting and enter the room with a firm intention to do good without being a chump. This Not-Being-a-Chump part is very important. A chump never prospers, no matter what discipline one is pursuing.

At its highest levels, Right Intention involves the renunciation of many of the nerdy, high-competition tenets taught to impressionable business students in the academy. Unlike those future Huns of corporate life, he or she with Right Intention is committed to doing no harm to others, to treading the path of cooperation and goodwill. What is interesting is how much power that stance actually bears with it in the face of jerks, assholes, and sleazy short-term tacticians. Going into the meeting with Right Intention arms us with purity of spirit, the desire to do good work, and a general disinclination to care about the nonsense other people are toting around with them. This is not only a good spiritual position but an excellent operational one as well.

3. Right Speech

Right Speech follows. In business, this involves thinking before one speaks and choosing words correctly, because words have meaning; they are not just the product of two gums flapping.

The penalty for talking trash is minimal in private life. In business, it can mean destruction, disrespect, or commitment to do something or pay for something you didn't really want to have to pay for. In groups, and in their meetings, the need for Right Speech is even more essential. The Path deals with several clear commandments in this regard:

❖   *Speak the truth or speak not at all:* Lying in an open meeting is never advisable unless you are a senior officer with only a glancing relationship with veracity because you are making your own reality or, in certain cases, have been ordered to lie for strategic purposes.

❖   *Avoid divisive speech:* Although you may disagree with others, never forget that you are reaching for consensus, not division.

❖   *Eschew punishing speech:* Business is full of people who like to kick ass and take names in public. This may be fun for the abusive manager or swaggering colleague, but it makes for dangerous and ultimately exhausting meetings. Cordiality and politeness count. Exaggerated respect for people you don't like is better than displays of contempt or snide aggression.

❖   *Abandon idle chatter.* Keep the shooting-the-shit phase to the little gaggle either before or after the meeting. Discursive, time-wasting cul-de-sacs about golf or fly-fishing may function to ingratiate blabbermouth subordinates with their bosses, but the rest of the guys in the room may have work to do. And Right Speech always keeps the fact that the meeting has a subject and an object in mind.

The Buddha generally advises that if something is unpleasant or unproductive, a meeting is not the right time and place for it. He was a very big guy for thoughts, speech, and action that produced a good result with a minimum of distracting, ego-driven emotion. Better a good meeting followed by a tough one-on-one with appropriate parties than a big, unpleasant gang bang.

If you have ever been in one of those, you will find it impossible to disagree with the Buddha. He wouldn't care if you did, anyhow. That's the kind of guy he was. Agreeable. Take a page from his book and you won't go wrong.

4. Right Action

In spite of what you may have been told, it really is often best to Do the Right Thing, at least at the meeting. Perhaps in other places you can swing a little looser, but at the meeting? It's down the middle the whole way (and as ethical as possible within the constraints of

> ### Phrases That Demonstrate the Peaceful Nature of Meetings
>
> ---
>
> Meeting of the minds
> Nice to meet you
> Nice meeting you
> Very nice to meet you
> Take a meeting
> Meet me in St. Louis

one's industry and corporate culture), and also, believe it or not, doing your best to do no harm to yourself or to others. Makes some of you want to gag, doesn't it? Maybe that's why you're having so many bad meetings. You might consider looking for an organization where the Right Action is doing Wrong Action. Try the mob. Or a big bank.*

Right Action is most counterintuitive to those who have been trained in gladiatorial schools where ferocious competition and cutthroat imperatives get the thumbs-up. And in a way, the old school has a point. You should most definitely be prepared to cut out another guy's guts and wear them for garters. Just not very often in meetings, that's all. Hamlet did not stab Polonius in front of the whole court. He waited until his future father-in-law was behind the arras to do it. We don't have arrases anymore, although we do have credenzas. But you get the point. Meetings are, simply, meetings. Places where people meet. Meet, as in . . . come together. Join together for a common purpose. When the gladiators faced each other in the Colosseum they didn't call that a meeting. Nor was the business meeting between Alexander Hamilton and Aaron Burr that ended with a bullet in the better man's liver.

Right Action, therefore, is the way of compassion, friendliness, open-handedness, and peace. One does not come to the meeting prepared to kill the other guy, mess with his agendas, or fuck him over. The Buddha is very clear about that. If you must gouge out his spleen, do so after the meeting.

5. Right Business Conduct

This is an easy one, unless Right Business Conduct for you is Wrong Business Conduct for most people. It remains Bad Meeting to be a human trafficker or arms merchant, for instance. The Buddha mentioned those in particular. Beyond that, it can get a little murky. Selling animal meat comes across to some people these days as Wrong Livelihood. Most businesspeople I know like a little bacon now and then, and we're not going to come down on the guy who brings it home.

Let's just say there are universal standards that apply to all businesses everywhere.

❖ No cheating, lying, or stealing, at least from your friends and colleagues.

❖ If your business has rough edges, try to smooth them out. For instance, if you raise

---

* An annual viewing of Francis Ford Coppola's Godfather saga (excluding of course the unfortunate *Godfather III*) is strongly suggested for those who are attempting to live by a strict moral code within a corrupt and immoral institution. Most of its lessons hold up fantastically well in a corporate environment.

chickens, you probably have better meetings if you raise them on tasty chicken feed and let them run around rather than rip off their beaks and stuff them into cages for their entire lives. If you make children's toothpaste, you probably have better meetings if you aren't the ones who put poisonous diethylene glycol in it.

❖   Does your business have humane policies toward employees? Good health plan, is it? How many times have you called a consultant in to fire people this year? Did you do a layoff on Christmas Eve? Do you have a lot of forced overtime that doesn't pay extra while the CEO makes millions and millions of big, greasy dollars? What kind of shop do you run?

6. Right Mindfulness

Mindfulness is a higher state of being. It's . . . transcendent. Suspend your conscious mind and get in touch with the . . . entire universe. What It is. You'll see and feel everything. Without getting in the way.

❖   You are eager and positive and aware of all around you.
❖   Nothing bothers you or upsets you because you don't actually care about anything.
❖   Your thinking has gone way down deep.
❖   Your perception is sharp, tight, well lit.

Open. Quiet. Alert. In the moment. Taking it in without comment or rising passion. Let it all go. You are *in* the meeting and the meeting is *in* you.

7. Right Effort

How many people who attend your average business meeting come in expecting to work hard? For the most part, nobody. This makes many meetings desultory, dragging, energy-free affairs . . . and longer, too. It's pretty simple. Come prepared to work hard and your meetings will be shorter.

8. Right Focus

Bliss is not a quality one would normally associate with the concept of the meeting, but even in the most inhospitable of environments bliss does exist.

❖ You desire nothing. All you want is here.
❖ There is tranquility here, the unity of mind and body and spirit.
❖ By detachment from joy you have achieved joy.
❖ And now there is real work to do.

Length of Meeting vs. Level of Effort

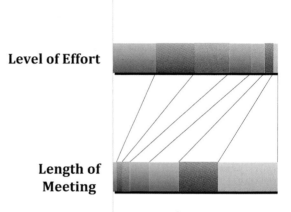

Level of Effort

Length of Meeting

Explanation: The greater the level of effort of those in the meeting (blue, red and green bars, top and bottom), the shorter the meeting will be in proportion to the weight of the work being done. A major meeting will still be long, but it will be shorter if those involved have come with Right Effort. Even minor meetings, however, are lengthened by those (in purple, aqua, burnt umber and light blue) who have arrived with Wrong Effort.

For those who have pursued the Eightfold Path with diligence and patience, you will suddenly and without warning be filled with a cosmic happiness, a sense that time does not exist, that no other group of individuals would be such good company, no other work would be conceivable.

That is Good Meeting.

Concluding Thought About Groups

Beware of people who tell you that there is no "I" in "Team" unless they are kidding about it. They are usually the people who put the "I" in "Team." If they're around, you probably should keep plenty of I in mind, too.

Exercise

Go to your local Starbucks, Waffle House, or local restaurant bar at the same time every day, find a seat, and occupy it for half an hour. Do this as often as you can over several weeks. By the end of the month you should have formed a group of regulars that see each other every day. Experience what it is like to be a member of a nonhierarchical group. After no more than thirty days, cease going to that establishment altogether. Note how that makes you feel on a scale of 1 to 10, with 10 being where you feel really terrible and miss the old gang a lot and 1 being you have no lingering feelings of kinship whatsoever and realize that in fact you never joined a group at all. The lower your score, the more you need to think about this. You're in for a cold and bumpy ride if you don't.

Fundaments of Power

Hard work and patient achievement is fine, but only a true master can transform labor into power. It is a talent that can be taught only to those possessing the four essential building blocks:

1. Desire: Powerful people *want it.* They are walking breathing gasbags of want.
2. Obsession: Watch a dog with a bone, or a cat disassembling a vole it has caught in the woods. Are they thinking about anything other than accomplishing the job that lies before them? Normal people think about a variety of things. The truly powerful have minds like laser beams. You may not. With thought and concentration, you may be able to develop a very serviceable flashlight, though.
3. Anger: There are many ways to acquire power over other people, and few are as effective as this one. Powerful people are always angry about something. You would think that their power would to some extent confer peace of mind, but you would be wrong. Anyone who has ever seen Barry Diller walking to lunch up Sixth Avenue, barking intensely into his Bluetooth, will understand what I mean.
4. Will: There are many names for it. Determination. Resolve. True grit. Power is self-generating. Title, rank, and position in the organization do not automatically confer it. Power begets power, and that is that.

There are, of course, the lucky few who do not need to learn any of these attributes or how to employ them, because they are innately powerful—and rare. We are going to assume, for purposes of this study, that you are not one of these people.

The First Element: Desire

Alexander the Great is said to have wept when he realized there were no more worlds to conquer. This is incorrect. There were obviously other such worlds. What he was crying about was that the rest of the globe, as far as he knew, had no armies, no huge, civilized cities full of merchants, soldiers, and kings. All there were, as far as he could tell, were modest people trying to make a living in ragged clothing. He wanted battle and was met by lots of trees and mountains and indifferent animals. He was crying over the fact that there were no more worlds full of people worth killing and stuff worth having.

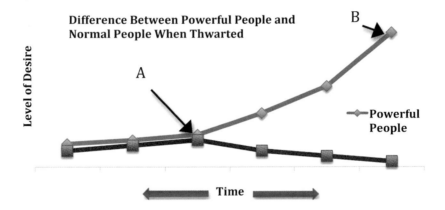

Above you see a chart that describes the difference between powerful people and normal people. At the beginning of a quest, there is little distinction as both types decide they want something. At the midpoint (A), it becomes clear that thing will either not be had or be difficult to get. The level of desire of the normal person then slacks off in an appropriate manner as the individual goes on to think about and want other things. In the powerful person, however, the lack of acquisition only amps up the level of desire until the wanting reaches epic heights and cannot be denied (B). This is usually where the infantile, radical behavior begins.

This undeniable urge to *get what they want* is what characterizes all people of power. And throughout history, those who were successful and became famous for their resolve in this area were those who were willing to kill people to get what they wanted.

Fortunately, in business it is unnecessary for many powerful people in powerful positions to resort to actual violence.* That doesn't mean they aren't willing to exaggerate, bully, and intimidate to achieve their goals. In your development, you will need to begin cultivating this irrational level of desire, the kind that justifies war, revolution, bloodshed, pain, and humiliation on the part of your adversaries.

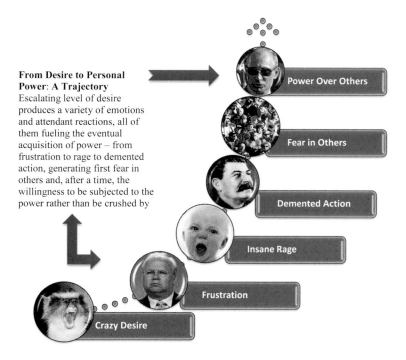

From Desire to Personal Power: A Trajectory
Escalating level of desire produces a variety of emotions and attendant reactions, all of them fueling the eventual acquisition of power – from frustration to rage to demented action, generating first fear in others and, after a time, the willingness to be subjected to the power rather than be crushed by

Power Over Others

Fear in Others

Demented Action

Insane Rage

Frustration

Crazy Desire

In this way, desire escalates through frustration and rage, resolves on a level of action that is frightening to other people, then uses that fear to achieve power. (See chart above.)

Naturally, you will need to modulate yourself to an extent determined by how powerful you already are, because this characteristic—intense desire that generates personal power—is *not* part of your fabricated persona. It is the real thing.

There will be many people who will, as a result of your lousy, grabby personality, come to hate you if you make things too obvious. Many people in business don't like to be hated. In some professions, in fact, it's a liability. I only know of two or three salespeople who get what they want

---

* Although I did see a fight between two agents at the Four Seasons bar on Doheny that ended with chairs flying through the air and both escorted out by the entire security contingent.

by being hated and shunned—and their tactics hew to the unpleasant and overpowering so that their clients will buy anything to get them out of the room. Even though this seems to work for them, this is not a reliable strategy. Fortunately, there is another, subtler way.

The Second Element, Part 1: Obsession

Beyond the extremity of wanting lies the unique ability of the powerful to obsess about the discrete object of their desire, to spend time cultivating that obsession, tending it, making sure it is fed and watered until it has grown into a solid, healthy trunk of obsession with deep psychic roots. Although all are forms of madness, some are power builders, and as such are useful. Others are power drainers and must be avoided.

Some powerful people have one obsession for their entire lives, and they make their apparent mono-focus into their brand. Hugh Hefner is obsessed with the fact that when you grow up and become an adult it is possible to have sex as much as you want. This would seem to be a rather pedestrian and boring idea. As nice as it is to get laid, some like to break for a sausage sub now and then, or take a nap, or listen to music. But then, they're not obsessed, and will probably not become king or queen of a highly effective business empire driven by that one powerful obsession the way Hugh is/was.

There are many kinds of obsessions that drive the will to power. Let's look at a few of them now.

➤ *Obsession with Money*

Here's a rule: Beyond a certain income that provides food, shelter, and a cable/Internet/cell phone package, money is nothing more than a way of keeping score to the powerful.* And as an obsession, money is perhaps the most frustrating of all, because the more you have, the more you want (see chart at right).

---

* The original quote on this subject was from a mogul now lost in the mists of time, Jack Kent Cooke. Cooke at one time owned the Washington Redskins and the Los Angeles Lakers, among many other properties. He is now all but forgotten, because his obsession was money, not fame.

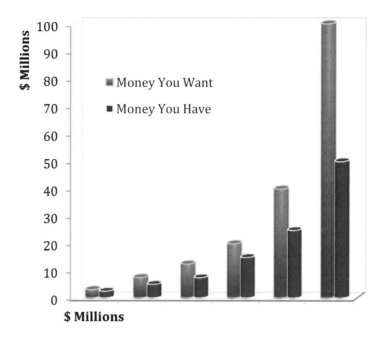

$ Millions

As we see, those who make in the mid-five figures might once have considered a salary of, perhaps $60,000 per year to be aspirational. Now their sixty grand looks paltry next to the magnificent compensation of Murphy down the hall, who makes the princely sum of $110,000. Murphy, for his part, sees his annual pay as something with which he might once have been satisfied, but certainly no longer. The number $250,000 seems far more appealing, particularly when he looks at McTavish, who is his age, actually, and pulls in even more than that if you count his annual bonus. McTavish, on the other hand, works cheek by jowl with Ted and Betty and Fred and all the senior guys in sales, who, if you count their salaries and bonuses and long-term equity compensation, pull down, like, a million dollars a year! Imagine that! Except Ted and Betty and Fred all feel like, hey, a million dollars a year is only about $500,000 after taxes and they all have kids in college, which costs nearly that amount for each one over four years. They look at Bob, the CEO, who is reported to make the unbelievable amount of *$15 million a year!* But Bob is aware that there are a lot of guys he has lunch with every day who are worth upwards of $100 million. He's not. He's still working for a living. That makes him dissatisfied with his $15 million, as he would be unhappy if it were $20 million, or even $50. How can he be happy with all those billionaires on *Forbes*'s list of the richest people in the world? Is he on it? No. Naturally he's upset about that. He's certainly as good an executive in his mind as they are! Why isn't he as rich? And those billionaires? Each of them looks at the other and wonders if he can grow even bigger! Why not?

No matter how much money Bob may be making, it only makes him more avaricious and frustrated, and these highly negative emotions are themselves a source of tremendous power for him. Greed may be an ugly emotion, but it's tremendous fuel, driving the greedy, obsessive individual to longer hours, heightened emotion, and a drive to get to the goal and go past it every single day. For this person, the measure of that success, if he or she achieves it, is money.

Not everybody hankers for the big bucks just so. If you, as a developing businessperson, lack this critical gene, more power to you. But you will have to replace it with some other dementia to drive your will to power. Fortunately, you have a lot to choose from.

➤ *Obsession with Things*

This may look like an obsession with money, but it isn't. Obsessives about money accrue money. Obsessives about things accrue things. They are collectors. Jay Leno and Jerry Seinfeld have buildings full of cars. Old cars, new cars, cool cars, square cars. Lots and lots of cars. More cars than they can ever drive. No one has video of either of them going down to their garages to pet their cars, but it's a safe bet they do so. Other objects that become totems of power include:

✔   Shoes for men and women
✔   Ties/scarves of great expense and flamboyance
✔   Timepieces
✔   Pens, which can cost tens of thousands of dollars for the serious collector
✔   Homes you seldom visit
✔   Planes, boats, islands for the ridiculous
✔   Fish/birds/llamas

These are just a few of the things that people of power can collect to make themselves more potent. In fact, there are as many things a person can draw to themselves as there are ways the human imagination can stoke itself. Gems. Hats. Wine, of course. Lots and lots of wine. Not to drink, mind you. Just to have, in cellars that could hold ten Fortunatos trapped for eternity.

Explore the depths of your mind. Think to yourself—what would you like to collect around yourself to give you power? Stamps? Guitars? Old turntables? Yo-yos? One famous star of television and motion pictures you certainly know has hundreds of hunting knives and a basement full of guns. It works for him. He's a winner. You might like tropical fish. I know a billionaire who has an entire house full of them. Some have gotten so large that they simply sit in their tanks all day, having outgrown their space, unable to swim, just floating, staring back at the mogul who stares at them.

When you are powerful, you will have some *thing* that obsesses you. What will it be? Why not start imagining your vast array right now? The size of your obsessions will be a further goad to prod to you forward.

➤ Obsession with Sex

Open up any history book or newspaper and it becomes evident that power does not only bring with it access to money and a host of people willing to perform any command you bark at them. It also hands those who are interested a lifetime pass to lots and lots of sex in a variety of flavors, because power apparently makes you attractive.*

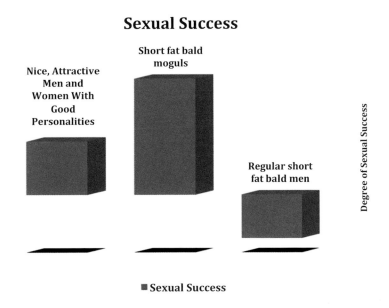

---

* Data accumulated after exhaustive review of all magazines, newspaper, online media, social media, and gossip pages, as well as personal observation at dozens of industry galas, awards ceremonies, etc.

For some reason, it is in the world of power politics where one sees the most evidence of this phenomenon. Perhaps it's the pressure of this kind of power at the highest levels, where one's decisions are matters of life and death in many cases, or involve the vast movings of money, men, and machines. This may explain a John F. Kennedy, who in spite of a bad back and a very sexy and marvelous wife, was pumping everything but the family retriever whenever he had the chance—movie stars, cleaning ladies, you name it. If he had a spare minute, he was employing Mr. Johnson, and we're not talking about his vice president, either. Likewise Bill Clinton, of course, who had state troopers scoop up groupies for his delectation when he was governor of Arkansas and, when he was president, initiated many of his male fellow citizens to the idea that oral sex was not "having sex," a notion still reportedly disputed by a majority of their spouses and significant others.

From Jefferson onward, American history is replete with men who extended their power in this way, from the Romans with their Sabine women to the former Anthony Weiner's display of equipment on Twitter. There would be more examples of women who did the same if there had been more women in positions of power throughout the march of recorded history. At this writing, the only individuals who are discussed in this light tend to be Catherine the Great of Russia, Elizabeth I of England, and a number of Kardashians.

These days, however, you may do many, many questionable things in pursuit of profit and power, but in many cases it is sex that will be unacceptable as an obsession. You can manufacture land mines or distribute semiautomatic weapons to schizophrenics, but you cannot hump your assistant. Perhaps this is as it should be. But it can lead to some distortions. Mark Hurd, for example, was the head of Hewlett-Packard until he took a consultant to dinner and put it on his expense account. Here's a bit of information: Everybody in American business takes a consultant to dinner and puts it on their expense account. No, he didn't sleep with the woman. His sin was that he didn't give her the business they were discussing, she got mad, made some allegations of flirtation and what is and has been perhaps the stupidest board of directors in the world kicked him out. He was immediately rehired by one of HP's biggest competitors, a freewheeling guy who basically doesn't give a damn about what anybody thinks, Larry Ellison of Oracle, the embodiment of wealth, excess, and power. Hi, Larry.

The top guys at Best Buy and Boeing were canned in recent years for having sex with an employee (not the same one). In perhaps the most scandalous episode of the 1980s, Bill Agee, the CEO of Bendix, then forty-three, fell in love with a bright, beautiful twenty-nine-year-old Harvard MBA named Mary Cunningham. They both left their respective spouses and eventually Cunningham resigned to go on to greater success. Agee left two years later. Throughout corporate America, journalists who were routinely banging each other after hours were thoroughly scandalized by this obvious example of inappropriate sex in the workplace.

Some do get away with it. Jack Welch was simply too cool to touch when he got involved with the editor of the *Harvard Business Review*. But for every one of him, and there is only one, there are too many of those who now perpetually walk the halls of shame, those who, like General David Petraeus[*] or golfer Tiger Woods[†] or almost-president John Edwards[‡] or sanctimonious prig and former New York governor Eliot Spitzer[§] or sportscaster Marv Albert[¶] or Congressmen Larry Craig[**] and Mark Foley[††] and so many others, lost their jobs and reputations when this particular form of personal power was exercised improperly.

The expression of power through sex, then, is not a particularly good idea. I'd tell you to knock it off, but those who are capable of listening and complying don't need to be told.

➤ *Obsession with Status*

These are the powerful who have to make you acquainted with every aspect of their supposed power, and constantly establish external proof of it through a variety of public displays. There are several pathetic subsets:

Repulsive repetitive name dropping: This sorry individual believes he draws power from the ritual, totemic repetition of names he believes lend luster to his. There is usually one in every organization, and they are to be pitied more than censured, although every bone in your body may cry out to censure them.

There are, in fact, two forms of name dropping. The first is more common. It is characterized by the name dropper dropping the name of one supposedly important person over and over again. Jane Austen captured this personality perfectly in *Pride and Prejudice*, when the fatuous cleric, Mr. Collins, constantly refers to his patroness, Lady Catherine de Bourgh, in tones of great

---

[*] Affair with attractive biographer, stupid misuse of e-mail.

[†] Multiple hookers.

[‡] Unstable groupie.

[§] More hookers.

[¶] Wearing ladies' underwear, biting sex partner.

[**] Propositioned wrong guy in men's room.

[††] Sent improper e-mail to congressional page.

reverence, to the point where it is clear that he has absolutely no value to himself beyond that which he ascribes to his association with the lady. In show business today, one may spot such people by their constant references to one famous person or another by their first names, primarily "Bobby," which always refers to Robert De Niro, or, on the West Coast, "Steven," which, of course, is Mr. Spielberg. Everybody in the business who has nothing going on is always just coming from a meeting/conversation/Skype with Bobby or Steven. In banking, of course, everyone is always dropping either Lloyd or Jamie at this moment. If those names mean nothing to you right now, it means they have been replaced by some other names that confer imaginary status on the user.

Lady Catherine

The second kind of name dropping is the more outlandish, with the afflicted person simply spurting one name after another out into the ether to see which one will stick with the listener and perhaps elicit a reaction. Within seconds of encountering them, they will tell you that they just saw six people whose names are supposed to impress you. He was, for instance, at a dinner with Brad Pitt and Jimmy and Bobby and Lenny and they all were hanging around with Warren and Jamie and blah blah blah and so on and it just never ends.

What's good about such people is how easy they are to please, and therefore to manage. You simply have to stand in their festering aura for a while and they will hold you to their hearts with enormous gratitude. Such bosses need subordinates who can minister to their disability, and are rewarded accordingly. You may have to wash out your brain every evening with some fluid or other. But it's a living.

Just don't be one of them. Name droppers are, at best, tolerated with grim good humor. At worst, they are despised and discussed behind their backs.

Tasteless bragging about personal wealth. Even more obnoxious than name dropping is the blabbing about how much money the power seeker has, how many houses, cars, airplanes, etc. I have sat at an executive dinner in total silence for more than an hour while some nabob goes on and on about how much return he's getting on his tax-free investments, and actually shares with me the amount of money in question, which is always in the millions. Other senior types will talk about their home in Gstaad or Vail, and how much it cost them, and how much it's worth now, and how much money they have made on it. One evening, an elderly gentleman of means discoursed for some time how much fun they had in their private apartment at the Ritz in Paris. "Why don't you pick one up?" he asked me, in all seriousness. At that same dinner, I had to spend a bit of time convincing another captain of industry that I fly commercial.

"Why?" he inquired politely.

"Because I don't have access to a personal jet?" I replied.

He has treated me with even more courtesy and sympathy since. Those individuals are at least kind, and as essentially naïve about real life as was George H. W. Bush when confronted with a supermarket checkout scanner. Far more egregious is the very senior executive who likes to stop by the desk of an assistant who makes $42,000 per year and share with her the size of his bonus, which is well into the seven figures. What are such people thinking? The answer is, they're not thinking. They're exercising a tiny twitching power muscle that is well outside their control.

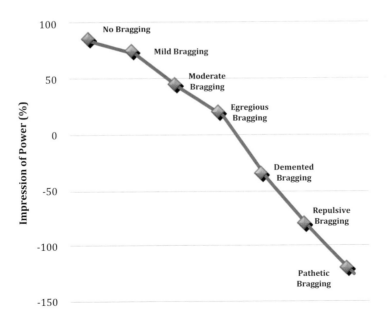

Bragging vs. Impression of Power

Excessive acceptance of honorifics: I know a senior manager who is generally seen by those who know him as a figure of fun. At this writing, to my knowledge, he has received no fewer than eleven major industry awards for excellence. Some were offered by organizations unknown to any but the most assiduous students of former executives in the industry. Others were events in which he was one of ten or twelve fellow luminaries honored for "lifetime achievements." Every couple of months, in some meeting or other, a participant pipes up, "Hey, I heard Squinty is being honored again." And everybody cracks up.

Several years ago, I worked for an industry nabob whose fame spread to the front pages of the business press with some regularity. He was a modest fellow, and sought no honors. One day I thought I had a piece of good news to tell him. A major industry group had announced they were giving him their Man of the Year Award. "Is there any way we can get out of it?" he said, looking somewhat crestfallen. "Why in the world would you want to get out of it?" I asked him. "You'll see," he replied. By the end of the process, I had.

The event cost the corporation upwards of $250,000 for tables and ads in the program; we had to torture every friend we knew to contribute to it in some way, either by attendance or by forking over a tidy sum. We also had to hire a speechwriter for his acceptance speech and an audiovisual company to help the sponsoring organization do a respectable video. On the night in question, he was incredibly miserable, nervous and angry at everybody who got him into it. The dinner was rubber chicken, and since the event was at the Waldorf-Astoria in New York, it was served by nasty, hasty waiters who had no sooner presented the food than they whisked it away. The whole experience was horrendous for all concerned but the honoring organization, which made a bunch of money for whatever it was they spent money doing. Imagine putting your company through all of that several times a year and you have some idea of the warped mentality that routinely accepts such things in order to plump up their power.

Serial club joining: If one wants to experience a level of boredom unknown outside of a high school physics class, one has merely to sit at a business dinner with a bunch of people talking about all the clubs they belong to. This one belongs to one in Long Island and one in Miami! And this one adds a very exclusive club in Jamaica—the island, not the section in Queens! Wow!

"Do You Know Who I AM!" syndrome: This is the last refuge of the status junkie when their public standing is questioned or found insufficient to resolve a situation, and they are made to feel not like a person of great power but like a normal individual trying to negotiate the sea of life. It's a sad moment. The supposedly powerful person is confronted with a situation in which their power is not recognized. They receive a bad table at a restaurant. Their reservation at a hotel is not

found, or the room is in the back facing the parking lot. They fail to get past a velvet rope at some exclusive club. They are bumped from their first-class seat when their airline changes equipment and the number of available premium slots is diminished. First, perhaps they are polite. Then they are stern. Then they get angry. And finally, in a supreme excess of pique, they raise themselves to their full height (which is sometimes not much) and, skewering the offending party with a razor-sharp and threatening glare, they bleat, "Do you know who I am?"*

The tragic truth here is pretty clear. If the person knew who they were, this wouldn't be happening. So in all cases, the answer is "No." This can only be described as a total and public Power Failure, only achieved by those sad fucks who are totally obsessed with status. Following is a synopsis of the power-destroying behaviors that arise from an overactive obsession with status.

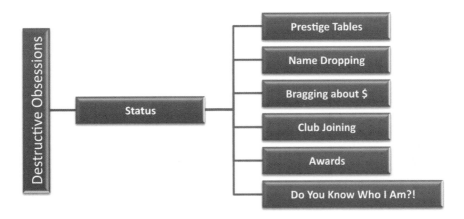

Other more useful obsessions include:

---

* Most recent reference in this regard may be made to actress Reese Witherspoon, who was stopped for driving drunk in Georgia and resorted to this tactic to dissuade the officer from pursuing the matter. She was arrested and her mug shot was made available to TMZ.

Obsession with not dying:

When a powerful force gets to the end of his or her career (or life) they become especially dangerous. Take the case of Marius, the Roman who was elected consul a record eight times. He lived a life of great achievement, conflict, and influence, and killed a lot of people in addition to doing many other important things that are of no interest to us here. As he got old and fat, he had his armor let out to accommodate his girth and then rode out on an extremely massive steed every morning on the fields of Mars to work out with the young studs. He was something of a laughingstock—the old dude who thought he could still keep up—but nobody ever laughed in his face. They even let him win a couple of contests, just to feed his ego. Along came one of those complicated political wars that characterized Rome before the Caesars came along to simplify everything, and Marius fell out with the other vicious bastard who was in power at that time. He could have lain down and died, as so many of his allies were forced to do, but instead he fled with his son to northern Africa, where he hid out in the marshes, at one point

actually stripping down and submerging himself completely in a dirty swamp, staying alive by breathing through a reed. Really tough guy. He was about seventy at the time, which is about 140 in current human years. He then went back to Rome, got back into power, and immediately killed twelve senators who had opposed him after he had been elected consul again. Then and only then did he consent to die in his own good time.

In current days, you see similar moguls who, while not being able to kill their adversaries, intend to stick around until the fat lady herself has not only sung but croaked. Colleagues, subordinates, and adversaries are forever counting the old fellow out, and continue to do so until he pops out of the swamp and cuts their throats.

In younger power seekers, the obsession to Not Die expresses itself in a mad pursuit of fame and notoriety. People who seek publicity and the glare of the red carpet seriously almost always have a shot at it. In a culture where Honey Boo Boo (next page) can be a well-known figure, just about anybody who seeks the limelight can clearly achieve immortality in their own minds, at least for a time.

Obsession with Winning:

Honey Boo Boo

The final obsession that drives people of power is a necessary one. No one achieves power without it. The degree to which an individual can moderate his or her obsession with winning is precisely the amount that their power will be diminished.

The Second Element, Part 2: Compulsion

There is a palliative for the pain and anxiety generated by the kind of obsessive thought/behavior that confers (or drains) power from your senior managers. It's called compulsion. Compulsion is the flip side of obsession. All these driving obsessive forces arise from and generate more anxiety, the feeling that something is very, very wrong and needs to be made right immediately if the world is not to fall apart. This horrible and pervasive feeling is at least temporarily assuaged by a variety of powerful, ritualistic behaviors that ease the anxiety and give the suffering obsessive an illusion of control, at least briefly. Here are just a few:

OBSESSION	COMPULSION
Money	*Money Management.* Sometimes the only thing that makes an anxious, competitive, money-obsessed person less crazy is to spend some time counting their money. These days they don't say "money," though. They say "investments." And the piles are not in a vault beneath their wine cellars (most of the time). They are in responsible "instruments." But it's touching the money that makes the obsessive happy. Short of touching, there is talking about it, which is also a compulsive form of counting it, an obnoxious behavior we have discussed above.

OBSESSION	COMPULSION
Things	*Conspicuous Consumption.* People who are obsessed with things never have enough material things. So they spend time collecting, which temporarily slakes the never-quenched thirst for the possession of objects. Computers, smartphones, pens, bottle caps, wine, little cards that used to come with cigarette packages, yo-yos, items with the company's logo on them that go back decades, shoes, handbags, women, men, subsidiary companies, the technology invented by a competitor. It comes down to arranging, counting, and touching, the three key palliatives of the compulsive personality.
Sex	*Golf.* Business players who have lost interest in sex often resort to excessive golfing. Talking about golf is their equivalent of telling dirty stories about their sexual escapades. They are tedious to any but their fellow sexual deviants.
Status	*Name Dropping, Club Joining, Party Hopping, Bragging, Boasting, Being a Jerk.* Status must be renewed constantly. While the effects of a round of golf may last for weeks, status cravers need almost constant massaging to maintain the feeling that they have status. Hence the high-energy nature of this particular set of obnoxious compulsions.
Not Dying	*Sex and Health:* It is interesting that those who seek immortality at both ends of the youth spectrum often turn to physical, rather than spiritual or emotional, solutions to the conundrum. People can live to a very old age, but death cannot be put off indefinitely. The trick is to live so long that one doesn't want to live at all anymore, either because one is too sick, too old, or too bored, or all three. This, sadly, rarely occurs. As powerful people get older, they don't want less power. They want more. So how do you get more power? You exercise!
Winning	*Kick Ass and Take Names.* The obsession with winning is not a liability, it's an asset.

But an obsessive is just a crazy person melting down if he or she can't transform that insanity into action. In that regard, there is no more muscular force for power than the lever that moves the world, that strikes fear in hearts weak and strong alike, and that converts suggestions into commands, turning every human interaction into a management issue.

The Third Element: Anger

Business is full of angry, angry people. Not all of them have power. But even the ones who don't have power to speak of have more power than they would have if they were not so angry.

Anger confers power because people who are not angry are afraid of people who are. Why? Why do large elephants cower before enraged mice? Because anger is a sword that, in the right hands, becomes the most effective tool in the arsenal of successful power players. There are other tools, but without anger they are simply less effective.

- ○ *Intelligence:* Smart people do better when they have anger to back it up. Smart people who aren't angry enough go into things like research, which has no direct access to ultra-senior management.
- ○ *Guile:* Manipulative people who aren't combustible enough are just sneaky.
- ○ *Planning:* Strategic thinking is toothless without a potential kick in the head to back it up.
- ○ *Loyalty:* The power to inspire great loyalty goes hand in hand with the ability to punish those who don't measure up in that regard.

Those are just a few of the attributes that are boosted into high gear with the addition of some level of potential emotional toxicity. However, as with most personal gifts, the aptitude for great anger comes at a cost. The greater the genius for anger, the greater that cost. People who are capable of flying into a rage at a moment's notice when thwarted generally have few friends and even fewer loved ones, and the ones they do manage to acquire are not, often, of sound mind. They also sacrifice tremendous operational agility. They are forever pounding around like the eight-hundred-pound gorillas they are, crushing the underbrush, baring their big, yellow teeth, and pounding their chests. Actually, the metaphor is unfair to gorillas, which are actually peaceable, kindly creatures. Think of an animal you don't like that victimizes its neighbors and associates. That's the animal we're talking about.

No, businesspeople interested in permanent, usable power learn to manage their anger and employ it for good purpose. In that vein, it is possible to ascertain no fewer than five separate levels of anger that, when wielded with thought, discretion, and cool blood, yield excellent working results. Working from the outside in, then ...

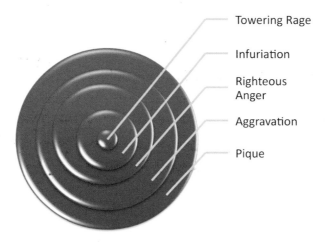

Towering Rage

Infuriation

Righteous Anger

Aggravation

Pique

1. *Pique:* The lowest level of annoyance, which may be demonstrated by a variety of means—the blowing of noses, slamming of the occasional door, look of crestfallen disappointment, short, frustrated outbursts, etc. The target of pique knows that there is much that he or she can do to right the wrong, set things straight, and make the piqued one happy again. Pique is an excellent motivator for the executive looking to wring better performance from a capable subordinate.

2. *Aggravation* is more personal. The aggravated person is genuinely bothered someplace deep within. There is something gnawing on her. It must be dealt with, and for the first time punishment is in the air. It should be. Managers who do *not* punish people who aggravate them end up plagued by a host of aggravating subordinates who feel they have the right to be as aggravating as they want to be. Far better to crush the source of the aggravation in a display of indignation, but not to squish them altogether, of course. This is just aggravation, after all. It's not serious. Yet.

3.   *Righteous anger:* Several years ago, an executive known to this professor was at a parking garage out of town and, exiting the structure in his rented Mercedes, offered his corporate AmEx, perhaps the most powerful object in the road warrior's satchel, to the attendant in the booth. The card was declined. This is a moment in organizational life unlike any other. In that instant, status, power, and credibility are revoked. One is as naked as a castaway on a desert island, left to rot in an inhospitable climate swarming with airborne insects, the woods around you throbbing with the sound of drums. The executive was forced to use his own credit card—his own MasterCard!!—and fork out ninety-five dollars of his *own money* for a charge that should have sailed through to Finance on wings of light. When he returned to the office, an investigation ensued as to why his corporate AmEx had been declined. The answer that emerged was truly shocking. His assistant, it turned out, had been undergoing a personal crisis of some sort for the past several months, unbeknownst to him.* During this emotional impasse, the assistant had simply thrust all of the executive's expenses into a drawer, and never submitted a report to American Express. The customary warning letters had been torn up before he had a chance to see them. And now, after this extensive period of neglect, a time in which the executive had traveled business class to a variety of locations around the nation and the world, his card had amassed a debt load of more than $22,500. Those familiar with corporate life will recognize the difficulty of clearing such a sum to be paid all in one chunk. Doing so involved the most horrendous thing that can happen to a manager: an internal audit.

We need not go into the pain this executive endured before he got back his status, his standing in the corporate tree, and his ability to function as a working member of that society. It took more than three months before sanity and economic integrity were restored. During that time, he was righteously angry at his assistant every single day and on weekends, too. And by the end of his term in that shallow level of organizational hell, she had been yelled at perhaps twenty times over minor matters and, finally, encouraged to find employment elsewhere, which she did.

Righteous anger demands sure retribution. Those who do not mete that out quickly lose their ability to do so and their sense of themselves as sources and repositories of power. Some things should not be allowed to stand. That knowledge alone confers power to the angry.

---

* This ignorance is by no means unusual. Colleagues in organizational life seldom know what is actually going on inside one another. This is why they wear uniform outfits and maintain high levels of decorum, and why people who work side by side are so often shocked when idiosyncratic human behavior emerges in plain sight.

4.　*Infuriation:* Ironically, it is at this point where the power associated with anger begins to diminish. One rarely sees a powerful person infuriated over something important. They are generally infuriated when their steak is overdone, their coffee is cold, they didn't get their way on a deal. Babies get infuriated when their bottle is late or their diaper is wet. So do executives, particularly the older ones. Several years ago, a friend of the National Association worked for a very angry executive who maintained only marginal control over his temper. One morning the angry executive called this manager in for a dressing down. That was intimidating, to be sure, and the manager was duly frightened for a time. It was when the angry executive began literally jumping up and down like Rumpelstiltskin that the recipient of this exhibition began to take an amused view of the situation. Shortly thereafter, the angry executive's gums began to bleed. By then it was impossible for our friend to take any of it very seriously. So he excused himself and left. Several days later, the two had another meeting and both acted as if the incident never occurred. Not an impressive display of power in any respect.

5.　*Towering rage:* This level of anger is reserved for psychos, murderers, dictators, and truly manipulative power players of the corporate world. In the first three cases, the rage is real. In the latter case, it is a show put on to scare the kids, and is highly effective for that purpose. In any event, it's an ugly thing to see. Displays of this nature may be seen in old footage of despots and fascists, and a number of college basketball coaches.

Each level of rage is meant to elicit fear, whether its object is an erring undergraduate linebacker who got called for a dumb penalty or a senior vice president whose presentation failed to meet the chairman's expectations. Interestingly, research among a very wide sample group over a period of many years shows some unexpected results.

Level of Anger vs. Amount of Fear Elicited

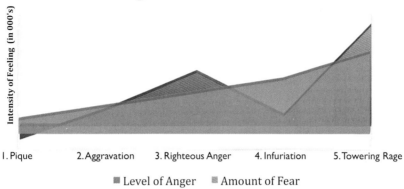
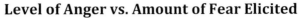

Note on Chart: While pique, expressed aggravation, and righteous anger elicit the expected intensity of fear, petulant infuriation just leaves the average recipient cold and resentful. As such, it is not a building but a destroyer of power. Inchoate, towering rage, on the other hand, remains a reliable cudgel.

The greatest impact in terms of the accumulation and maintenance of power, however, is not seen by those who are actually angry at any particular moment. It is experienced, in fact, by those who have *exercised frightening anger in the past and now wield the threat of doing so again at all times, as in:*

Fear in Others vs. Actual Level of Anger

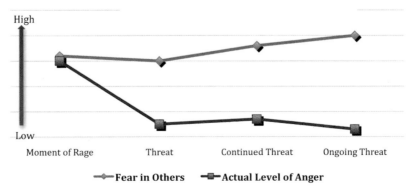

Note on Chart: The initial display of rage was enough to terrorize the employee for an extended period of time as long as a low-level threat was maintained. One show of credible rage (possibly followed by a scary public whipping or scourging of some kind) is enough to generate ongoing fear in others for quite some time. After that, restraint becomes a more effective cudgel. Even bacteria become immune to antibiotics when they are overused.

One final point in this regard does need to be stressed. While emotion certainly has its place in business, pointless emotion has its limits. That is to say, anger that is not followed by some form of action, penance, or retribution is a waste of time, space, and power. That does not mean, however, that the powerful person needs to go around kicking rears and collecting ears all the time. The action must be considered, thought through, and executed as an organic and integral part of the arc of anger that is embodied in the incident as a whole. Here is only one possible arc, and the points at which decisions and actions are taken:

Now that is well-managed anger, ending in appropriate punishment and subsequent amnesia. As I said, this is just one arc. But it should be instructive. Our study in this unit is not justice. It is power. The former is more useful in business than the latter.

The Fourth Element: Will

ome hypotheticals:

- When the boat is careening down the sluice and someone must step up and grab the wheel, will that be you?
- When the bomb is ticking down to 00:05, 00:004, 00:03 . . . and someone must rip off their safety helmet and decide whether it is the red wire or the blue wire that must be cut to save the day-care center and all the little babies . . . will that be you?
- When an entire room full of people is scared shitless of Bob and so nobody will tell him that he is wrong—and he is—will it be you who will tell Bob he's about to step in doodoo?

How much risk can you stand? How much guts do you have?

When a tough situation is staring everybody in the face that can only be resolved by an intricate, dangerous one-on-one engagement, will it be you who quietly says to the terrified group, "Okay, I'll do it"?

Power is seized, then used. If not fully utilized, it is lost. If not taken, it is passed to the next in line who wants it. The history of civilization, business and the arts is dominated by people and nations that see what must be done and step up to do it themselves, not always for the good, of course, but power is neither good nor bad. It's what you make of it.

So, do you want to make something of it?

Power: The Lion's Share of the Core

Every piece of the Core is useful to you, but the extent to which you can draw power to yourself and use it either wisely or, frankly, as stupidly as you want will determine the height and depth of your business career.

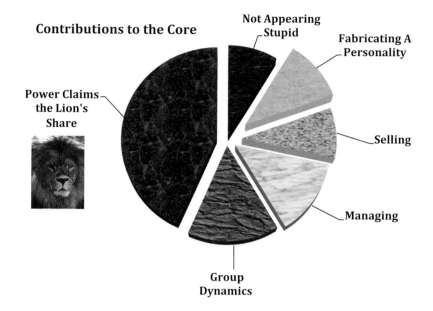

Exercises

1. Select a day when you have many things to do. Skip breakfast. Most important, deny yourself your morning coffee, tea, or other establishing beverage. Go all the way to lunch without sustenance. Note several things when you are operating at this level of frustrated desire, including:

    a. How much you want to kill other people
    b. How much you want the craving to stop
    c. How wrapped up in yourself you seem to be
    d. How everything looks different when you've slaked your desire

5. Select one of the little rituals you have for yourself, whether it is lining up your pens and pencils, playing with paper clips while you talk on the office phone, or obsessively checking your e-mail and text messages on your iPhone or BlackBerry. Count how many

times during the day you perform this compulsive ritual. Once you have established the nature and frequency of the behavior, force yourself to stop it for twenty-four hours. To the extent that you can do so without discomfort, you have either chosen an easy ritual to dispense with (in which case you have failed the exercise) or you have no such rituals (in which case you have also failed the exercise). If you are deeply uncomfortable or driven to distraction after the ritual is taken away, you have passed the exercise. You are an obsessive-compulsive person in at least this one regard, and therefore have access to the part of your psyche that establishes power.

6. Devote a week to figuring out a variety of ways to make other people do the things you don't want to do. This should include not just peers, subordinates, assistants, and significant others, but also bosses. If people notice what you are doing and challenge you on it, you have failed the exercise. If people seem to hate you more as the week goes on, you have failed the exercise. To the extent that you have more free time, enjoy your life more, and actually seem to have people requesting your guidance, you have passed the exercise.

7. Establish a meeting that has no other purpose than that you want to hold it. A passing grade is achieved if a) there are more than six people at the meeting, b) it lasts more than twenty-two minutes, and c) nobody says, "What was that all about?" after the meeting.

8. Take a group of peers out for drinks and pick up the check. Take careful note of how members of that group relate to you afterward.

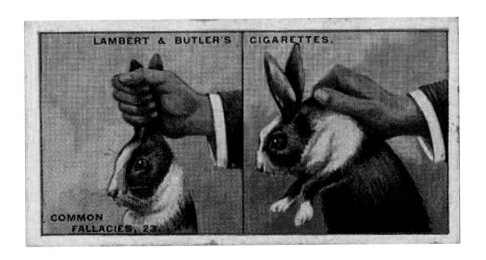

LAMBERT & BUTLER'S CIGARETTES.

COMMON FALLACIES, 23.

200.

The Advanced Curriculum

elcome to the Advanced Curriculum. Having established a strong Core, you are now ready for field-based and experiential studies to better prepare you for the vicissitudes of everyday work life. On the next page is a schematic of the various topics under study.

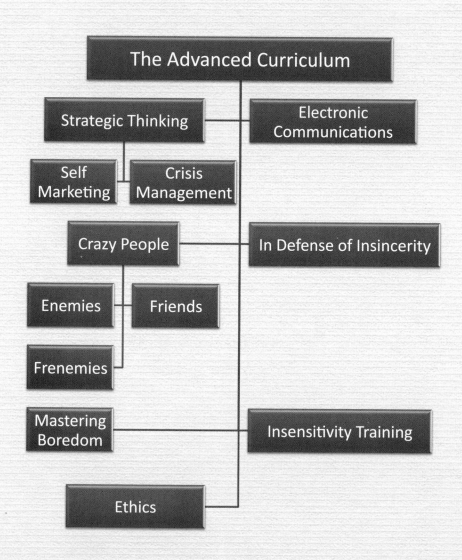

201.

Strategic Thinking

Successful people get to where they are because they think what is called strategically. Sometimes, it is true, they lash out and pulverize somebody, but most of the time they are thinking as much as possible in a way that you do not. Methodically. Incrementally. *Strategically*.

What, you may ask, is a strategy? A strategy is a plan that is designed specifically to achieve a certain well-defined goal. It is made up not of one but of several—sometimes more than several—actions. Put those actions together in a sequence and you have a strategy.

Strategic Thinking, then, is the kind of thinking that is utilized to produce a strategy. Thinking that produces something else may be very good thinking, but it is not Strategic Thinking. This may sound kind of simple, but you would be surprised how many management teams sit around thinking strategically without coming up with a strategy. That is not Strategic Thinking. It's huddling for warmth.

Is Strategic Thinking all about solving problems? No. Not always. The best kind of Strategic Thinking involves preventing crises. So I guess you could say that Strategic Thinking is prophylactic. Sometimes it's about as much fun as a prophylactic, too.

Strategic Thinking helps you come to the conclusion that all hairy situations are amenable to management, even when they're not. In the latter case, things stayed screwed up. Maybe even more screwed up. But at least you weren't bumbling around in the dark, blubbering like a little baby. Why? Because you had a strategy.

There are, of course, some professions where Strategic Thinking is not necessary. Being a forest ranger, maybe. But even they have fires, right?

Strategic vs. Nonstrategic Thinking

The great strategic thinkers take an empty landscape and lay out the shape of things to come. Because most other people can't. That's what separates the Strategic from the Nonstrategic Thinkers. Here are some of each who come to mind:

NONSTRATEGIC THINKING	STRATEGIC THINKING
Boeing deploys fleet of gigantic 787s called Dreamliners that unintentionally belch flame. Would it have killed them to test-drive the things for another couple of months?	Southwest conquers the boarding process. Three little letters. A, B or C. Line them up. Load them in, no assigned seating. Off we go.
AOL merges with Time Warner . . . reenacting the sack of Rome by one of the minor barbarian tribes, late in the history of the empire, when senior management had really gone off the deep end of the pool.	Google buys YouTube . . . making it possible to spend your entire day in the Googleverse quite happily while they harvest every single thing it is possible to know about you.
HP Fires Mark Hurd. CEO Mark Hurd of Hewlett-Packard wines, dines, and possibly flirts with, but does not have sex with, an attractive consultant of some sort. This doesn't stop her from complaining of sexual harassment when she fails to get the business she was pitching. They fire him, not for the harassment, but because he put the dinner in question on his expense report!	Larry Ellison hires Mark Hurd. In a huge fuck-you to Hewlett-Packard, Larry Ellison of Oracle immediately hires Hurd, who has just received a megamillion-dollar exit package from the dummies who fired him that does not include a noncompete. In doing so, Ellison conveys two messages: 1) Hurd is an okay guy worth having around and 2) it's a pleasure doing business when guys like HP are your competitors.

These are just a few examples of how Nonstrategic Thinking produces embarrassment, destruction, and loss of money. If such outcomes are to be avoided, the nonstrategic mind must be understood . . . and then retrained, molded into some useful shape. Otherwise, it should be sent out for pizza while the strategic thinkers get down to business.

The Non-Strategic Mind

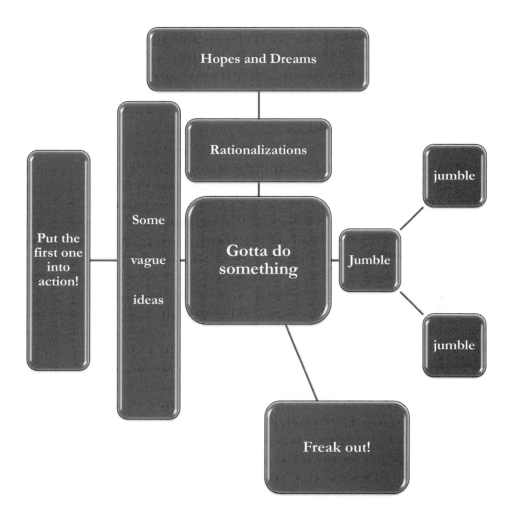

How different than that mental gumbo is the orderly march of the Strategic Mind, which furrows a row of thought with the powerful plow of its intellect, planting seeds of insight into neat, fertile tracks from whence will blossom clarity, wisdom, and a solid plan of action.

The Strategic Mind

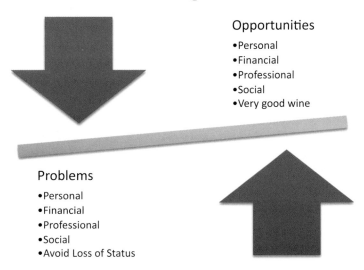

Opportunities
- Personal
- Financial
- Professional
- Social
- Very good wine

Problems
- Personal
- Financial
- Professional
- Social
- Avoid Loss of Status

So much clearer. Now all you have to do is to put these considerations in their proper balance and order—both in importance and in sequence. It isn't easy. But it can be done, if you have the right attitude. Which brings us to the whole question of opportunity. Opportunity is at the heart of good Strategic Thinking, because it produces a positive attitude.

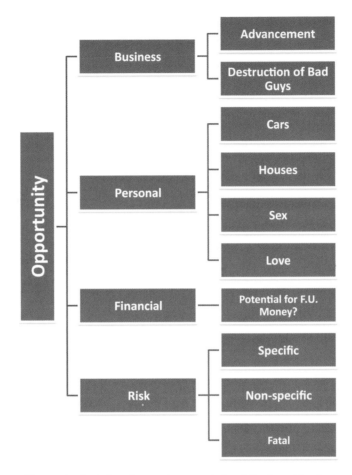

Note on the chart: A good strategy is opportunity-based. People are driven by many other forces: greed, hatred, fear, revenge; none is as likely to yield satisfactory results as just a simple look at opportunities that may arise.

We have now considered:

1.   The definition of Strategic Thinking
2.   The nature of the Strategic and Nonstrategic Mind
3.   The role of opportunity-based thinking in the creation of a positive and productive strategy.

We're on the right track. We're thinking in a clear, calm way and concentrating on the large number of considerations that pose challenges as well as opportunities. But all this means little if we don't harness all this good energy and channel it into ...

The Six Steps of Strategic Thinking

S trategic Thinking is not really like other kinds of thinking. It takes discipline and practice.

1. **Step One: Underestimating the Problem:** People who do not think strategically immediately go off on things, small and large, with a lot of emotion. They blow things up. They fester. The strategic thinker wants time to do some light cogitation in a good frame of mind, without freaking out. Consequently, the true strategic thinker is the first to say, "It's not going to be a big deal" when the company's $25 million celebrity spokesperson is found facedown in a bowl of oatmeal, dead. In my experience—in a business where there may be several crises before your mid-morning fruit—every one to which I have said, "No big deal" has mushroomed into a behemoth of world-shattering difficulty. Still, I believe that approach has helped me move on to the next step.

2. **Step Two: Fear:** The 3 a.m. kind. Something has happened. An episode has occurred that will require some Strategic Thinking! Shit. I hate Strategic Thinking. Yet danger lurks with failure and humiliation in the weeds. Fear is a terrific motivator. It does one of two things in people. Some run away. Some run forward braced and energized by how big and scary everything is all of a sudden.

3. **Step Three: Rage:** The mind turns black. *Why do these kinds of things always happen to me!* you scream, silently to yourself, unless you're the CEO, in which case you can scream audibly at virtually anybody you choose.

4. **Step Four: Intense, Microscopic Plotting:** Now it's time to focus. Focus. Can you focus? Maybe you can't. Maybe you're not good at focus. You could be good at other things. Charming people, for instance. Or selling them on something. Or just having fun with them. Those things are all important. But now, a certain kind of linear thinking is concerned, the kind that produces lists. Ones that start at 1 and go to 25. If you're not good at that, find somebody who is and have them start plotting while you perhaps take a little break to do some more Strategic Thinking.

   If, on the other hand, you're the list maker:

   • Get a big picture of where you want to go before you start listing stuff. Examples of a big picture include:

     ✔ Crush the mother!@#$rs
     ✔ Avoid a big fight at all costs

✔   Have as much fun every day as possible

✔   Convince the other party that a merger would be beneficial for everybody, even if it isn't, and it's just good for us

✔   Not really do much of anything, just watch it for a while and see what develops.

All of these big pictures demand different sorts of strategies, don't they? In the first case, in which we're looking to crush the mother!@#$rs, we might be working step by step to line up a team of assassins who can rip out their entrails a day at a time until they are no longer operational. If, on the other hand, we are seeking to avoid a big fight at all costs, we might be implementing a sequence of pointless, lengthy meetings with our adversary, as each of us lays out our positions while the other listens respectfully. At the end of each meeting, we all agree to meet again. As most Japanese corporations have demonstrated, that strategy can take years to get nothing done while everybody remains gainfully employed pursuing pleasant inaction.

The big picture is very important. Without it you're not building a strategy. You're just planning actions. Once established, the big picture should suggest a number of steps that need to be taken. Now it's time to . . .

- Make a List of Actions to Be Taken. Divide your list into three time periods:

  ✔   Immediate
  ✔   Intermediate
  ✔   Long term

Things to consider including in your list:

- If you are a manager, job one is selecting the team. Yes, the mission is impossible, Mr. Phelps. But perhaps if you select just the right people?

- If you are not a manager, what would you like your manager to do?

- What resources should be available to you? Xerox machine? Stapler? $150,000 for sales and marketing?

- Who would you like to eviscerate in the immediate, intermediate, or long term?

- What needs to be done throughout the strategy to make sure you personally come off looking as good as possible without compromising the effort?

5. **Step Five: Getting It Done:** Now, this is a huge, huge subject. The good news is that it isn't really a part of a unit on Strategic Thinking. So we'll wrestle with that part elsewhere, okay? Suffice it to say, however, that while the Getting It Done people are Getting It Done, really tough Strategic Thinking must be taking place by the Getting the Strategy people as well. With good communications between these two halves of the organizational brain, you cannot fail, unless you try very hard.

6. **Step Six: Mopping Up:** You may think for a moment that the beast is dead, because you chopped its head off yourself. But look. The body is twitching. Better get busy doing some more thinking!

Takeaway

It is always better to go into the engagement with a strategy than without one. Even if you don't know what to do, it is better to pretend that you do, and to do what you might do if you knew what to do. Most people in a conundrum of some sort have no idea what to do. They are not thinking strategically. Eventually, they will look to a person who appears to have some idea of what might be done if somebody knew what to do. That will be you. Pretty soon, they'll be calling you a leader.

202.

On Branding Yourself

Now we're going to take a look at how you might go about marketing the most important product you will ever sell: you.

In this unit, you will establish yourself as a brand just like Coke or Pepsi or Rolex or Tampax or Viagra or Skippy, one that speaks to who you are and is congenial not only to your business self, but to your authentic one as well.

When people buy your brand, they must know that they are getting something consistent, with known properties, that will live up to expectations again and again. That's what your brand must promise.

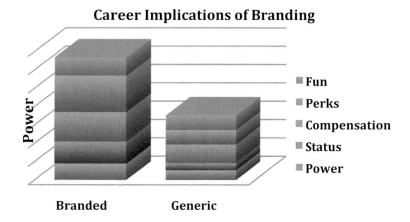

Career Implications of Branding

(Legend: Fun, Perks, Compensation, Status, Power; categories: Branded, Generic; vertical axis: Power)

Think about McDonald's. They don't make the best burgers in the world. Claims could be made for In-N-Out Burger, or possibly White Castle, or the little secret diner behind the makeshift curtain in the lobby of Le Parker Meridien hotel in New York City. French fries at McDonald's? Not the best. They're good . . . but Burger King's are better. McDonald's Coke is like everybody else's. But one thing you know about McDonald's is that every time you go there you will have the experience that you anticipated. You will have the same Quarter Pounder you first enjoyed five years ago, fifteen years ago, thirty years ago. The fries will be McDonald's fries. You will get what you anticipated when that McDonald's burger flashed in your brain pan at five minutes past noon. McDonald's lives up to its brand every day, millions of times a day, all over the world.

So does every great brand. It does a certain thing. It does it every time just the same way. You want a Bud? That's what you get when you open a can of Bud. You get Bud. If you wanted anything different, you wouldn't have gotten a Bud. But you wanted one, so that's exactly, precisely what you got. It's cold. Kind of nutty undertaste. And it's not French. It's not English. It's not some fancy-pants Belgian. It's 100 percent American. Drink a Bud, and you will be, too. It comes with the price of the bottle. The brand and the experience are one. God Bless America . . . and its brands.

Of course, you don't have to do it the hard way. Sometimes it's okay to take the store brand when you have a headache. A decent bar scotch can be almost as good as Macallan if you mix it with enough soda. So the question is, do you want to be generic ibuprofen or do you want to be Advil? It's easier to be the generic a lot of the time. But keep in mind—Advil can charge more, even though it provides nothing beyond the stuff in the plain-vanilla wrapping. That incremental cost is the value of its brand. I'm guessing you want that premium pricing, too.

So pay attention. There is minimal room for mistakes here. You've got to get it right the first time, because while a brand can be polished and tweaked and realigned now and then, you can't monkey around with it too much. Once established, you must live in your brand for a long, long time, and you mess with it at your peril.

What will *your* brand be?

Branding began very early, and has continued to the present day:

BRAND	BRAND QUALITIES	USP*
Noah	Serious. Solid. You can count on him. Generally seen with a long caftan, beard, flowing hair, and a staff— Moses with an ark, basically.	The only guy in the world decent enough to take care of all the innocent animals when God wants to wipe out every form of human life on earth.

* **The Unique Selling Proposition (USP)** is a marketing theory dating back to the 1940s. It suggests that people adopt brands that offer them something unique. All the great brands have one.

BRAND	BRAND QUALITIES	USP
Job	Really, really patient and understanding. Like to the point where you sort of wonder about him potentially being a schmuck.	If you have one person on earth to victimize, make Job the one.
Nero	A very talented and charismatic musician, the Mick Jagger of his day. Did not fiddle while Rome burned, but he did play the lute. And he did burn down a whole section of town to build more upscale housing there, like a lot of contemporary urban development projects. Widely viewed today as a lunatic.	Sure he's a flaky dude. But he rocks. Think of a Donald Trump who can actually kill people when he gets angry, and he gets angry a lot.
Socrates	Great philosopher. Liked little boys.	The one. The only. The original.
Huns	Covered with hair, unwashed, vicious, stink of animal fat and sputum.	They know how to party and they play to win.
Amazons	Legendary Brazilian female rulers of their powerful empire.	They know how to party and they play to win.
Investment bankers	You don't like them and they don't give a shit because they are so fucking wealthy.	They know how to party and they play to win.
Warren Buffett	Yoda with enormous resources.	Invests in what he understands and what he doesn't understand probably is not worth understanding.

BRAND	BRAND QUALITIES	USP
Politicians	Blue pinstripe suits a little down at the cuff, white thatch of frosty hair, some little gold pin that means something to somebody but not you, serious expression when called for, quick with a jolly laugh when necessary. Perhaps includes a peccadillo or idiosyncrasy, like crying (Boehner), taking a leak in the presence of his aides (Lyndon Johnson), or drinking and cursing like a sailor (Richard Nixon).	Lethal issues here. Totally discredited as a profession for the most part, although there are still individual politicians capable of generating respect. Task is to repair the entire brand so that new recruits to the profession may be found. First, a new Unique Selling Proposition must be developed. Possible elements might include honesty, compassion, and intelligence.
Angela Merkel	Leader of Germany—tough, resourceful, and scary.	The only Eurozone nabob worth listening to. But really? Germany again?
Vladimir Putin	Wacky he-man capable of any hijinks you can imagine. Swimming! Weight lifting! Hang-gliding! What a man!	The wrong look from those squinty little KGB peepers could send you to the gulag for twenty-five years.
Miley Cyrus	Has way too much fun for her own good. Really scandalous. Something should be done about her.	Sort of nice that there's still somebody capable of shocking people because they're so naughty.

Some Notes on the Table: As you see, brands are divided into two parts. Brand Qualities involve the physical presence and perceived image of the product. The second element is the Unique Selling Proposition—what makes the product different from others and crystallizes that inimitable ability or quality into something a customer might be interested in purchasing. Vladimir Putin, for instance, creates a complex, multicolored mix of various macho characteristics, a Wild and Crazy Guy who can also order somebody to put dioxin in your cream of mushroom soup.

At this writing, the world is filled with branded people. Some personal brands are strong, solid, well defined, and basically positive.

- **Bono:** ostentatious philanthropist and rock star.
- **Bill Clinton:** master marketer of the Bill Clinton brand, one of the most complex and well-cultivated public brands now operating on a global scale.

- **Hillary Clinton:** Very strong Unique Selling Proposition. Enormous development still possible.
- **Donald Trump:** Very strong brand with high negatives. Iconic hair solution to what could have been a problem.
- **Sheryl Sandberg:** The entire media universe united to publicize her book, *Lean In,* an exhortation to women to lean in. Immediate punditry ensued. Duration of punditry is still an open question, but in a crowded field she now occupies the corporate speaking engagement niche once owned by Tom Peters.
- **Marissa Mayer:** the president and CEO of Yahoo, smart, dynamic, perhaps a little too outspoken at times, has taken a fading and besieged brand and given it a legitimate shot at relevancy and even possible coolness.

On the other end of the spectrum are individuals with very strong, very bad brands. It's not pretty, but you can't say they have no profile:

- **Kim Jong Un:** This generation of North Korean psycho despots. Fed his uncle to the dogs, literally. Right now, he is probably in a workshop somewhere building the one nuclear warhead his nation can afford.
- **Arnold Schwarzenegger:** Once great action star and politician, currently being punished severely for having a child out of wedlock with a woman who was not attractive enough for people to imagine it was worth it. Then spoiled his brand further by mismanaging his comeback/apology tour. Subsequently gave himself the final coup de grace by starring in several unsuccessful movies. People can tolerate spectacular meltdowns—witness Charlie Sheen, whose brand is as strong as ever (assuming he is still alive at the time of your reading this). What people cannot accept is disgraceful behavior paired with bad box office numbers.
- **Greedy Wall Street Bankers:** Before 2008, this brand had a certain panache. After the meltdown they caused, nobody likes them very much. They tend to hang together, drinking and eating, like turkey vultures. No, that's not fair. Turkey vultures are very ugly birds, with black suits, red necks, and bald heads. That only describes some of this group. The rest are hawks with plenty of feathers.

Whatever brand you develop, tend it well. There is nothing sadder than the sight of a great brand fallen into disrepute and in need of repair:

- **Schlitz Beer:** Once the most popular brew in the nation, with a simple, clean bite and decent quality perception, the brand was acquired and then supplanted by others. It is now made by Pabst, which markets the ultra-hipster PBR, a brilliant branding story in which a pretty mediocre product becomes elevated to a proof of membership in a certain hipster milieu. Schlitz is still in the toilet, though.
- **The Republican Party:** What is it? What are its qualities now? What is it for, as opposed to what it opposes? Who are its champions? Once the party of Lincoln and Schwarzenegger, it is now associated primarily with confusion, radicalism on the right, and a countercultural, weird fringe with libertarian positions that used to be associated with the left.
- **The Left:** Good Lord. What a mess.

Brand reclamation is far from impossible. In our lifetime, it has been accomplished by many, including Elvis Presley and Bill Clinton, to name two of the more entertaining examples. Both lost weight, reformulated their act, and then held their heads up high and marketed the new product with aggressiveness. Both achieved traction and will be remembered well in the history books. In business, brand reclamation is somewhat more difficult.

All these figures have chosen to brand themselves. There are, however, some extremely important individuals who choose to have no brand at all, while still wielding significant power. Perhaps this is the smartest choice of all, who knows? Among them:

- **Chinese Rulers:** Who are they? Certainly, they hold in their hands the lives of nearly a billion people. Can you name the top guys? Nobody can. That's their brand.
- **Nonmogul Executives:** Can you think of any? This era is signified by the triumph of the faceless bureaucrat. Yes, there are a few titans who still carry the mantle once worn by Henry Ford, Howard Hughes, or Charles Revson. But even the butch boys in shirtsleeves on the covers of *Fast Company* are anonymous a few months after the stories run. That works very well as an operating strategy for those who want to take in between $5 and $5 billion per year without attracting notice.
- **You:** So far. Let's change that status.

Constructing Your Brand

To begin, think of yourself as a product, not unlike a specialty brand of detergent on a rack full of old stalwarts and forgettable off-brands.

- **What are those qualities** that make up your personal brand and differentiate you from the generic hordes? Are you tough? Funny? Smart? Wise? Witty? Daring? Determined? Demented? Impatient with failure? Ambitious? Modest? Coy? Clever? Dangerous when cornered? Addicted to detail? Sloppy but brilliant? Bon vivant? Terrific friend? Horrific enemy? Fun at a party? A killer when a deal is on the table? Who are you?

- **Who is the target audience?** Is it senior management? The folks in the field? The general public? One person in particular?

- **How does the product look?** Smell? Taste? What's it like to be with the product? Are there aspects of it that you want to stress or conceal? What are those? Do you get sharp and grouchy when criticized? Bitchy when hungry? A little too sure you're right about everything? A tight sphincter when it comes to picking up a check? Problem with authority? None of these things are good. Think about how to stow them away for future use when you become a senior officer.

- **Select all other attributes** you can put into *action*. A brand is all about what you *do*. Which of these personal attributes—plus or minus—should you build into the brand? The answer is: all of them.

Personal Attributes: Good Is Good and Bad Is Good

Beyond the few that you have targeted as wholly unacceptable until later, there are really no bad attributes. There are just the ones you possess, which make up the components of your brand.

- *Good* attributes make for solid, straightforward positioning. "This is Barb. She works hard. She plays hard. She's trustworthy and bright." That's Barb's brand.

○ *Bad* attributes can be used to sell a different kind of product. "Don't make Barb angry. She turns into a fucking monster." Not a bad brand at all, particularly if it comes bundled with other things like intelligence, ruthlessness, and charm.

Here are a few negative attributes that can be packaged as assets:

NEGATIVE PERSONAL ATTRIBUTE	POSITIVE BRAND ATTRIBUTE
Obnoxious	Aggressive
Shifty	Shrewd
Indecisive	Prudent
Insensitive	Blunt, no-nonsense
Lazy	Good delegator
Obsessive-compulsive disorder	Highly organized
Paranoid	Skeptical
No moral compass	Do just about anything for the company
Greedy	Ambitious

The first asset on that list, you will note, is "Aggressive." To one degree or another, aggression is a brand booster. Those without a strong brand (right column in the chart below) require far more aggression to work their muscle (arrow). This excessive requirement for aggression can tend to make generic products even less attractive over time and in critical situations—yet another reason to establish your brand early in your career.

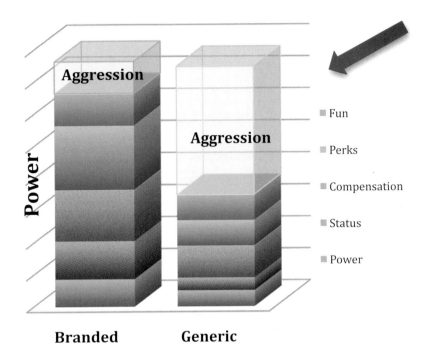

Congratulations: You've Got a Brand

Now you will require a campaign to sell the brand to your target consumer. What kind of campaign should it be?

A *long-term campaign* presumes you'll be around for a while and will have a proper chance to show the world the value of your brand.

A *short-term campaign* is sometimes necessary when dramatic opportunities show up where your brand can shine—big crises, wars, gaps that you can suddenly fill. Your senior colleague, for instance, falls ill on the eve of a big presentation. You volunteer to step in. Things go well. Huge, immediate brand recognition is achieved virtually overnight.

That is also a good example of a *positive campaign*, which works by demonstrating all the strong, effective qualities of your brand straight up, through your work.

You may also consider a *negative campaign*, which has been quite successful over a period of many years in politics, where small, questionable candidates and fringes push their brands to the top by besmirching other, more established brands by any means necessary. Those with less to offer are advised to consider this route.

Other campaign options include Positive/Negative, Pure Self-Interest, and Pet Rock.*

Takeaway

A good brand is more than hype. It must live up to its positioning every day by establishing its authenticity over and over again on the job. Ajax cleaner may say it is "stronger than dirt," but it's got to prove it in the kitchen. When you "Google" something, you expect it to be Googled, which is different than it being Binged. Brands express their identity in *action* that is consistent with prior actions. If your brand is to be thoughtful and conservative, you don't want to suddenly start throwing bombs in an open meeting. If you are branded as a swashbuckling infighter, you don't want to break down and look all grief-stricken when somebody takes a shot at you. If your brand is all about killing the people Bob hates, that's what you have to do, swiftly and professionally, because that is your brand.

Establish it. Live it. Expand it. Enjoy it. It will bring you power. Never stop working on it, expanding it, keeping it specific and maintaining its market share. Companies whose products achieve good market share must continue to build and protect their brands, adjusting them here and there without doing violence to their essential nature, fighting off challenges from competitors when necessary, and never giving up shelf space.

---

* Pet Rock was a product introduced in the 1970s, and was a marvel of branding as an end in itself, unrelated to function. The Pet Rock was, as its name makes clear, a small, oblong rock, presented as a pet that required very little upkeep and virtually no emotional investment. It sold very well to people who were convinced that some kind of benefit was derived from buying a branded rock in a package rather than simply acquiring one in their gardens or a nearby park location. The Pet Rock campaign strategy, named in honor of this branding breakthrough, consists of quietly being in the area of somebody who is actually doing something and just pleasantly keeping them company. It's a perfectly good brand, and extremely stress-free once it's established.

Crisis Management

Every meltdown has an arc—a mistake, a gestation period, a realization by the wounded party, a period marked by gossip when the situation could evaporate or metastasize, and, finally, an opportunity for apology and regeneration. Each of these phases must be confronted and managed in its own particular way. The problem is, very few people, let alone organizations, weather a crisis in the correct way. People tend to collapse under pressure; organizations tend to whitewash or dillydally. Here are just a few badly handled crises that come to mind:

- **Circa 1313 BCE:** Pharaoh (it's not quite clear which) is confronted with the exodus of the greater part of his enslaved workforce. After first granting their freedom due to a number of strategic pressures, he changes his mind, flies into a rage, and chases the slaves into the Red Sea, where he and his entire army are subsequently drowned. Crisis worsened by: **Executive Anger.**

- **1485:** Extremely unpleasant King Richard III has taken the throne by way of murder and finds himself similarly pursued. In the meantime, he succeeds in alienating even his closest allies with his bipolar attitude and the unpredictability of his loyalty, his tendency to renege on his promises, and his general viciousness and narcissism. At the loneliest point of his isolation and the height of his enemies' animosity, he goes to war to protect his ill-gotten power. His army is made up of management consultants and mercenaries. At the Battle of Bosworth Field, he finds himself without transport and is killed while yelling for his horse. He is thereafter buried in an unmarked grave that is now a parking lot. Crisis worsened by: **Bad Management of Team, Bad Logistics.**

- **1996:** Bill Clinton has a sexual dalliance with an intern at the White House, who after one such episode saves the little blue dress she was wearing at the time, which is spattered with evidence of the extramarital crime. An odious troll of a Republican operative,

Linda Tripp, becomes aware of the dress's existence, and makes the facts available to an opportunist reporter at *Newsweek*. Due to his massive lack of judgment, followed by his bungling of the matter in the public by lying about it frequently and rather pompously, the president is subsequently impeached by a jubilant Republican Congress for a crime not considered of any import in any other non-Islamic nation in the world. Crisis worsened by: **Bad Executive Impulse Control Mingled with Very Ineffective Lying.**

- **2010:** The Deepwater Horizon, a BP oil rig working the Gulf of Mexico, explodes. Many workers on the rig are killed in the spectacular inferno, which is captured on video. Tony Hayward, the executive in charge of British Petroleum, gives a host of unfortunate interviews, complaining, for instance, that the tragedy has been extremely inconvenient for him personally, and that "I want my life back." No one feels sorry for him. Subsequent investigations show that BP ignored safety regulations and warnings that the Deepwater Horizon might be at risk. Hayward loses his job and BP is forced to pay billions and billions of dollars to rectify the situation, payments that are still ongoing. Crisis worsened by: **Bad Executive Oversight/Greed/Insensitivity.**

- **2013:** Carnival Cruise Lines has a fire in the engine room of their thirteen-deck, 100,000-ton floating horizontal skyscraper, *Triumph*. The ship is stranded off Mexico with no food, electricity, or operable toilets. Stories abound of passengers sleeping on the main deck to avoid the rolling tides of excrement washing through their cabins and being provided with nothing but ketchup sandwiches to eat for days on end. The head of the cruise line is also the owner of the Miami Heat, and in the middle of the crisis he is spotted enjoying himself at a game. After more than a week of this, the *Triumph* docks in Mobile, Alabama, disgorging its 4,200 disgusted occupants. Many are put on buses going to rescue locations in adjoining states. At least one of these rescue buses itself breaks down on the way to the rescue location. Carnival is widely perceived as a disorganized, insensitive bunch of losers and is forced to cancel a dozen more trips of the ship in question, costing millions in lost revenue and nearly a dime on its earnings per share. Crisis worsened by: **Insufficient Executive Mandate/Really Lousy Organizational Response.**

In some respects history is a chronicle of all the calamities, disasters, and catastrophes that men and women, through their own ineptitude, greed, viciousness, or stupidity, have visited on themselves and their dependents. Forget about history. Every day brings stories of various self-lacerations, both in business and not. Here's how to avoid such injuries.

How Are All Crises Alike?

We see that all crises are different. A giant, morally lazy oil company is not the same as a superstar cracking up and throwing her bong out the window. And yet, in a basic sense, all crises through the entire passage of time are united by some key characteristics.

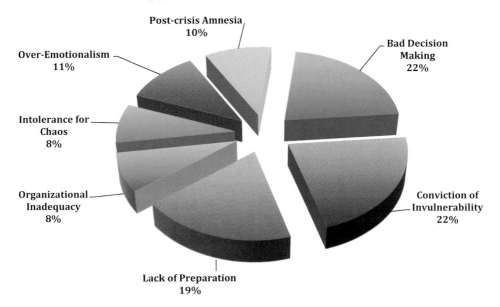

Common Attributes of All Crises

Post-crisis Amnesia 10%
Over-Emotionalism 11%
Intolerance for Chaos 8%
Organizational Inadequacy 8%
Lack of Preparation 19%
Bad Decision Making 22%
Conviction of Invulnerability 22%

Note on the Chart: The relative percentages may shift somewhat given the nature of the incident, the kind of organization that is involved, and the individuals trying to cope with it. But the constituent elements are relatively stable:

- *Bad decision making:* Crises are often avoidable, because they are the result of a mistaken policy, action, or long-term pattern of behavior. Before the BP oil spill, inattentive or arrogant management ignored repeated warnings that the Deepwater Horizon might have an accident precisely like the one it eventually did have. Bill Clinton, likewise, might have anticipated that his lifelong taste for a little action on the side would be unsustainable at his level of power and exposure to the hatred of those on the other side of the aisle.

The bottom line is that virtually all crises are self-created by the stupid things we all do. So . . . Don't be stupid?

○ *Conviction of invulnerability:* Tony Hayward never thought he would have to answer obnoxious, piddling interviewers, not even when his oil rig befouled the entire Louisiana coastline. John Boehner, the highly partisan Speaker of the House in 2012, was shocked when the Republican governor of New Jersey resented the fact that aid to his state was being held up by the usual nonsense Republicans do to punish blue states. Power brings arrogance, and the assumption that nothing will ever go wrong. Which is, you know, wrong. Everything goes wrong eventually. Crises management involves clear-eyed anticipation of that fact by those who see not only what is possible, but what is likely, and even unlikely.

○ *Lack of preparation:* A plan generally becomes necessary when it's too late. What's drawn up here is not a plan, but a reaction. The optimistic executive mind views the future like this:

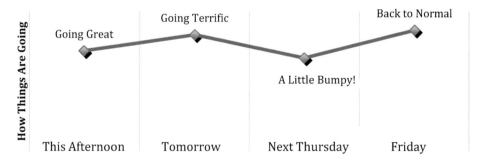

What the Future Looks Like to The Executive Mind

N.B. Everything looks pretty good here, with the possible exception of next Thursday, when there is a conference call with investors that the executive is nervous about. After that, all will go Back to Normal, a state that, when it is achieved, is even higher on the value scale than Going Terrific and Going Great. That's because both those latter categories can change in a heartbeat. Back to Normal has a tendency to stay that way for a while, which is very much appreciated. This rosy frame of mind is preserved even though *all prior experience is to the contrary.* The fact is, for just about everybody, reality is inevitably more like this:

What the Future Is Really Likely to Be

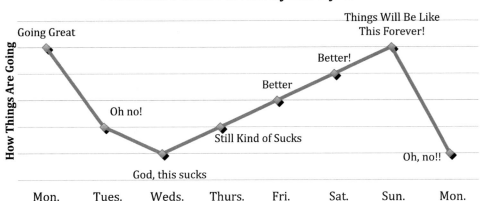

And yet people *still* don't plan for the worst. They don't even have to plan for the worst! They can just try to anticipate it a little! And yet . . . they don't.

- *Organizational inadequacy:* Companies are jammed with people who can say interesting things. Sadly, however, within most organizations there is not one single person who, in a crisis, keeps their head while everyone around them is losing theirs. And when things pop, everybody turns to the top guy in most occasions, who is seldom, unfortunately, the coolest head. That is the one time when the most senior individual really needs somebody to tell him what to do. Only there's nobody there. Which is why there are so many consultants in the world.

- *Intolerance for chaos:* Structured organizations abhor disorganization and absolutely loathe the confusion and self-doubt that accompany chaos. So they tend to overreact immediately. This intolerance for anything other than rigid order may also cause the opposite reaction in the face of a real problem—hedgehogging (that is, rolling into a little ball and waiting for things to go away).

- *Overemotionalism:* People in a crisis often find themselves gripped by powerful feelings that blind them to proper action. Common emotions (see chart, right) include:

Emotions in a Crisis

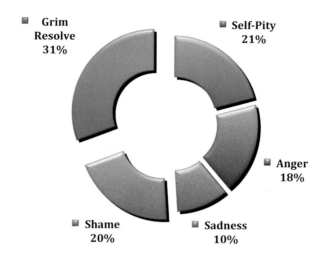

- **Self-pity:** "Why is this happening to *me*?" When in fact it's happening to everybody. Sorry to pick on Tony Hayward again, but "I'd like my life back" is a perfect example.

- **Anger:** "Whose fault is this?!" Uh-oh. Names are being taken.

- **Sadness:** "What's the point of working so hard when things like this happen? Boo hoo hoo!"

- **Shame:** "How are we going to hold our heads up after *this*?"

- **Grim resolve:** "Circle the wagons. We're going to kill those thumb-sucking bastards." People don't often make the best decisions when they're filled with smoking visions of revenge and destruction.

- *Post-crisis amnesia:* When the crisis has passed, there is a genuine need for evaluation, reflection, and adaptation. Who wants to do that? Nobody. On with the *show*! This early-onset organizational Alzheimer's is perfectly expressed in the behavior of Wall Street and its supposed regulators after the economy's collapse in 2008. The moment the sun came out afterward everybody promptly forgot any lesson ostensibly learned.

What's the alternative to all this nonsense? Consider the following a starting point for discussion.

THE FOURTEEN STEPS OF
CRISIS MANAGEMENT®

1. Examine the horizon	Crises are always preceded by a precipitating incident that doesn't look so bad. It is often something that can be ignored. It shouldn't be. On your toes!
2. Stop bad behavior	If you are a famous and admired sports figure married to a proud and beautiful woman, do you really believe that you can frequent innumerable hookers with impunity without at some point being caught? Why? Or say you're a governor known for your personal rectitude. How long do you think you can be hanging out with hookers before the state Republicans, who hate you, will find out about it?* There comes a crucial point where 95 percent of all bad situations can be avoided. Seize that moment! It may never come again!
3. Foster manageable paranoia	The good crisis manager makes sure that the decision makers realize that there may be consequences to their actions!
4. Catch it early	Sadly, most crises do not send a little note of warning that reads, "I'm coming. Hope you'll be at home." After muttering and bubbling, they simply erupt. Janet Jackson rips off her bodice to expose a nasty-lookin' piece of nipple jewelry. Your wife sees a text she shouldn't and slams you over the head with one of your golf clubs. Here's the point where most people freak out and overreact. Resist the urge. Take a step back!

* It is amazing what people think they can get away with. Studies of crazy, self-obsessed delusional egotists reveal so many examples of behavior destined to erupt into a conflagration that it is impossible to chronicle them all. Take John Edwards. Remember him? Loved his hair. Dreamed of the presidency of the United States. Whoops. There's a love child. What to do? Give it to your best friend/campaign manager and tell him to say it's his. Nobody will ever find out, right?

5. Gather information	WTF is going on, really? People will be running around like bugs surprised when the rock is turned over. Some are screaming like the sky is falling. Others are attempting to go about their daily business as if nothing out of the ordinary is happening and half their face has been blown off. As soberly and rationally as you can, find out what is going on.
6. Play Whack-A-Mole	Most crises seem to pop up, disappear for a while, then pop up again in a different place. Perch over each hole in the ground and wait. You're not going to solve this thing overnight, not these days, not with a predatory, opportunistic slander machine working 24/7 to keep its meat fresh. Whack. That. Mole.
7. No, sir, you *can't* hide.	Those responsible for the crisis or for repairing it must be on location, available, and visible. It is the tendency of all crisis creators to either 1) retreat to their caves, sipping a fine Burgundy between briefings, or 2) blissfully go about their daily business far away from the scene of the crime. If the crisis is to be neutralized, the big executive must be present to confront the fallout. Statements must be made that show awareness and compassion. Pictures must be taken that demonstrate living proof that the organization, while at fault, is not without a heart, goddamn it.
8. Accept chaos	In the midst of a calamity, everybody wants it to be over so that all the toy soldiers can once again be lined up in their proper rows. The good crisis manager allows all the false solutions, the quick fixes, the dumb, dramatic reactions to swirl around while a true and lasting course is found. Don't let this period last for too long, though. You are evaluating, permitting the tides to go in and out, not fomenting indecision.
9. Remain cool	There's no punishment for taking a few moments to think. So . . . think. Ponder the parallel futures that lie ahead.
10. Establish the plan	You have taken off your helmet and found that the air is breathable. You have some idea of what to do, the decisive act, statement, position, demonstration of will that can make this thing end and stay ended. It's not perfect. But it's the only way to go. Launch the plan!

11. Communicate	A plan is not a plan if its intent and purpose are not explained to pertinent audiences—employees, shareholders, the media. Even if the message is very, very minimal, there must be some message that tells the world that you have a story and you're sticking to it.
12. Don't apologize indiscriminately	Apologies in this society are not necessarily a solution. They are often taken as a requisition for punishment. They are not accepted. They are not appreciated. Perhaps there are rare occasions when a serious, brief, and heartfelt apology is appropriate. But most of the time the crisis is not ended by the apology. It is, in fact, extended to include a merry dance that ends in the decapitation of the apologizer.
13. Declare yourself closed for business on this stupid thing	There will now be intense pressure, mostly from the media, to advance the crisis, build it, keep it going, plumb its depths for more grist. Resist. It's time to get back to the real world. You're not playing the crisis game anymore.
14. Learn something, why don't you?	This phase is optional. Others are going to want to skip it. Try not to.

In the end, nothing can stop the crisis once it has started on a path to your door. Shit happens. That's okay. You'll live. Unless, you know, it kills you.

Takeaway

ne final point worth considering: There are times when a crisis is the result of people doing the right thing, not the wrong one.

- A supervisor decides that a flaw in the production of a train trestle is not being reported to the proper authorities and does so.

- A department executive declares that he is tired of having all these consultants around, refuses to cooperate with the next head count reduction, and produces a mutiny.

- A sales manager suddenly issues a proclamation stating that there will be no more three-hour drunken lunches unless they are approved beforehand for solid business reasons. The entire sales team then goes out to lunch for six hours in a display of solidarity.

- A few huffy middle managers refuse to make personal contributions to the CEO's favorite presidential candidate. He then makes a stupid statement saying those who continue to resist his call to political action will be fired.

This is a very special kind of crisis—the one where doing the WRONG thing may be the only way out. That's really tough. I don't envy you.

204.

Electronic Communications

Obviously, the world is better with all the stuff we have in our pockets, hands, and ears. Who could question that? In our appreciation for all things digital, however, even the most devoted of the super-connected must admit: Sometimes it's tough to tame the rolling river of electronic sludge. The issue is, how can we make the tsunami of e-mail, text messages, tweets, Instagrams, etc., work *for* us, not against us. Some of the problems we all face:

Problem #1: Too many empty communications. This chart illustrates the three basic messages that are conveyed over the bazillion-dollar superstructure that is the Internet.

Substance of Electronic Messaging

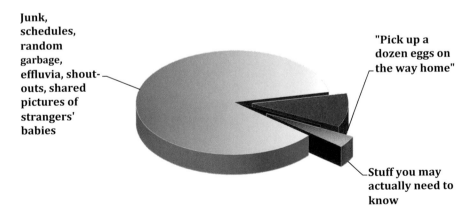

Junk, schedules, random garbage, effluvia, shout-outs, shared pictures of strangers' babies

"Pick up a dozen eggs on the way home"

Stuff you may actually need to know

There is no fighting this trend with direct action. A more Zen approach based in Not Knowing may in the end be more appropriate. If twenty-five useless messages fall into your Galaxy and nobody is around to care about it, were they sent at all?

Problem #2: People always checking their implements instead of focusing on what's going on around them, including you.

Management of the daily load of real work, both electronic and otherwise, cannot be accomplished if everybody is blinking like Morlocks into their shiny little screens all the time. The ironic thing is, there seems to be an extremely small relationship between the amount and intensity of smartphone checking and the actual importance—both potential and actual—of the communications itself. To wit:

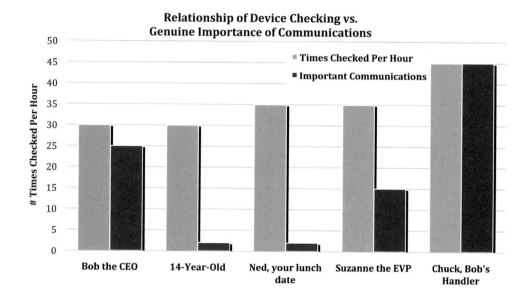

Notes on the Chart: What we ascertain from this data is that there is no relationship between the number of times an individual compulsively checks his smartphone and the value of the content conveyed in its messages.*

○ Bob the CEO, for example, checks his BlackBerry between twenty and thirty times per hour, roughly the same amount as an average fourteen-year-old. The executive receives a fair number of important messages for his rank and station, however, which may explain his hefty habit. The fourteen-year-old does not, but that doesn't stop her from checking.

---

* All data proprietary, © 2013 National Association for Serious Studies.

◦   These habits appear moderate, however, next to that of Ned, with whom you are having lunch. He fishes into his pocket and hauls out his personal digital assistant once every two minutes at least and receives the same number of critical messages as does the fourteen-year-old. One could speculate that Ned has an emotional disorder that makes the intimacy of even so formal an exercise as a business lunch intolerable to him. This is not business behavior; it is a form of incipient mental illness, driven, as so many in the workplace are, by anxiety.

The final two individuals have a somewhat different but no less instructive profile.

◦   First comes Suzanne, an executive vice president with so much on her plate that she must be in virtually constant contact with the mother ship. Her number of important messages, however, fully justifies her electronic paranoia. This is the kind of person who awakens at 2:30 a.m. for a drink of water and ends up awake for the rest of the night working on her iPad.

◦   And finally, there is Chuck, who is Bob's handler. This job entails getting Bob from place to place, making sure all his needs are anticipated and covered, and that all Bob-related headaches flow through him and out into the open ocean. He checks every ninety seconds or so. And most of what he finds is horrible. For the Chucks of the world, the smartphone has been at once an operational godsend and, at the same time, a fetishistic object whose possession sends them straight into a hell of their own making.

For the most part, the conclusion we reach here is that all this constant peering into implements, texting while walking, sexting while drunk, flaming when enraged, and other abuses are symptoms of a larger malaise that do not improve business or the lives of those who pursue it. Like all tools, electronic ones must be put into a proper framework and managed.

There are those who master this concept as they master every other aspect of their lives. And there are those who fall prey to a sorry addiction that controls them, rather than the other way around. The tragedy of these people is that they cannot enjoy electronic communications like normal people do, in a social or business situation. They have to spend each and every day looking for ways to beat the monkey that has hopped on their backs and buried its long, spiny fingers around their heads. Fortunately, there is a program for such people (see next page). And while this practice is not easy, it has worked for others, and is quite helpful in building the kind of independence of spirit and presence of mind that are useful not only in personal life but also, quixotically, in the world of business, where self-mastery is the name of the drill for student and master alike.

Electronic Freedom

A Twelve-Step Program

1. We admit we are powerless over our electronic tools and that in permanently assigning a piece of our consciousness to them our lives have become shallow, fragmented, and unmanageable.

2. We recognize the beauty and importance of nondigital thought and analog experience that is greater than any message we might receive electronically.

3. We make a decision to reconnect with our own thoughts and the actual, physical world that goes on within us and without us.

4. We give some thought to what it is about ourselves and our lives we are avoiding when we constantly drink from the electronic river.

5. We admit to those who care about us that we have a problem and beg their forgiveness for past insensitivities, particularly at dinners.

6. We remain dedicated to fighting our defects of character that drive us to be superficial slaves to our electronic devices.

7. At social occasions we either leave them at home or use them only to call a cab at the end of the night. Sometimes we even let them run down, mostly on weekends.

8. We make a list of all those who have come to rely on our electronic availability 24/7/365 and let them know that that chapter of our lives is over, apologizing in advance for our absence if and when it should occur.

9. When we backslide, we will promptly admit it to ourselves and others.

10. We ask our friends to let us know when we are sliding back, and to reward us for our good behavior in analog ways.

11. We will take a few moments every day to sit quietly and experience things without sharing them.

12. Having had a spiritual awakening as the result of these steps, we try to carry this new form of existence to those still enslaved by technology, and to practice these principles in all our affairs.

Dos and Don'ts for Electronic Communications

ome sensible guidelines to observe:

- Keep your e-mails brief.

- If you must go on and on, put all the other important information way up front. Realize I'm going to read about half of it, maybe.

- I'm going to need an action point in just about everything you send to me.*

- If you're marketing something that I didn't request, realize that the moment I receive your fucking e-mail I'm going to implement the Block Sender feature in Outlook.†

- If you have a strong opinion and want to start a discussion about it, encapsulate your thought into one sentence, followed by "Let's talk about it." Do *not* use e-mail to convey complex positions that may be misunderstood by those who can't read very well;

- With every serious and nonserious e-mail, text message, or tweet that you send, imagine it being read by somebody who is suing your corporation and has the right of discovery over your electronic communications.

- Before you hit SEND on any e-mail that contains your thoughts beyond a sentence in length, take a deep breath, count to five, and take a look at the distribution list of your e-mail. While you are at it, scroll down on the message and see how many e-mails preceded it in the chain. If you are junior to most of the addressees, make that a count to ten. If the CEO is on the list, count to twenty. *Ask yourself this one question*: Have I hit REPLY ALL when I didn't mean to?

- Do *not* use emoticons unless you are insufferably cute, 'k? ;-}‡

---

* While we're at it, let me define an action point for you. It's not something where you say to me, "So what do you think we should do?" I'm going to ignore that. What I'm going to need is a question to which I can answer "Yes," "No," or "Okay" or "NFW."

† Whoever decided that e-mail is an effective marketing and sales vehicle was a moron. On an average day, a working business person will receive between 50 and 250 e-mails. Does anyone suppose that an invitation to another webinar is welcome?

‡ Insufferably cute emoticon of a person winking with an enigmatic smile. The footnote symbol is not part of the emoticon.

- For the most part, people over the age of fifty do not understand the concept and proper way to send and receive text messages. Very often, they will want to have a brief phone call instead. Humor them.

- Do *not* send and receive messages while in business meetings unless you intend to convey to the important people around you that you don't have any respect for them. There are certain exceptions to this:

  ✔ You actually don't have any respect for them.
  ✔ You are the senior person in the room and everybody knows you're addicted to yourself.
  ✔ You are checking the stock price obsessively, an excess that is accepted in virtually all public companies.
  ✔ You are in the middle of a horrendous crisis and everybody knows that if the ball is dropped on it there will be hell to pay.
  ✔ Somebody is having a baby or has just been arrested and you have warned everybody else at the meeting of the situation.

- Don't tweet unless you have your wits about you.

- Don't tweet personal stuff on a company account or one associated with your professional-related tweets.

- Don't tweet anybody a picture of one of your body parts.

- Don't put personal stuff on your Facebook page that is not consistent with your business persona if you have a reputation to maintain and an income to protect; people will not be persuaded that it's okay that last weekend their manager of accounting services was at a bachelor/bachelorette party, smashed on hurricanes and smoking a blunt with a bunch of naked hookers, not even if it was Saturday night. And stuff on Facebook about how your boss is an asshole will have the expected impact. There is nothing private on social media.

And hey. Guys? You don't need Anthony Weiner to tell you that there is nothing private in the Twittersphere. There is nothing private on Facebook. It's possible there is nothing private anywhere anymore. Everything you do in the e-verse will reside there forever, available to somebody at some point for purposes you never anticipated. At the very least, expect the worst and moderate your electronic communications accordingly.

Takeaway

Your electronic communications are an extension of your business persona. As such, they're partly you, but not all of you. Don't be a nerd and substitute the electronic you for the real one. Twenty-five years from now people will look back at pictures of everybody madly tweeting and texting and talking into thin air and say, "What the hell were you people thinking?"

205.

Crazy People

There is a great video that will hopefully be available on YouTube forever. Google the phrase "David O. Russell Lily Tomlin" and you will find it, a great display of uncontrolled craziness not unfamiliar to anybody who has worked with a decomposing boss. It begins with the obviously surly actress behind a desk on the set of *I ♥ Huckabees*, quietly but acridly complaining about things to Mr. Russell, the director. She's grumbling, needling him about all the inconsistencies and changes going on, a classic disgruntled employee. You can hear his voice off camera a bit, cajoling, arguing, wheedling. Then, all of a sudden, from the bottom of the frame here he comes, arms flailing, hair flying. He is screaming. He is cursing. He sweeps his arm across the desk behind which Ms. Tomlin is sitting and sends its contents flying. He smashes a few things and then rampages off the set entirely. You can hear him screaming up and down the hallways off camera in this childish, aggrieved tone of voice, shrieking, howling, and then *bang*, in he comes through the stage door of the set like a demented intruder, yelling his head off, throwing things, and cursing, cursing, cursing. It's an appalling display of infantile rage comparable only to the Great Bill O'Reilly on-tape freakout of 2008, where Bill loses his wafer-thin temper and fusses like a little baby at his teleprompter operator. You can Google that, too. It's priceless.

Mr. Russell has gone on to great success, winning many awards and universal acclaim for his talent. Mr. O'Reilly remains the highest paid and most-watched presence in cable news and a best-selling author on the subject of killing people.

The realm of business often rewards those who are by any sane measure, nuts. This is because those who are bound to rigid solutions, are focused on themselves to the exclusion of others, and are irrational in pursuit of their goals, are likely to do very well in the game. In other words, in the world we're trying master, it's very useful to be a certain kind of crazy. Most helpful in a business context are:

- Toxic narcissism, which helps the crazy person feel invulnerable and destined for greatness
- Obsession, which imparts focus
- Compulsive behavior—a very good trait for accountants and other financial types
- Paranoia, which keeps a person on his or her toes

In addition to conferring power, however, craziness also comes with certain detriments. The narcissist is blind to the thoughts and feelings of other people, and tends to have a bad temper that clouds his or her brain under pressure. The obsessives are busy with their Purel when others are swinging a little looser. Paranoids are so fraidy-scared you can make them jump when you say Boo. In this way, all crazy people are not only empowered, but diminished in some way. Those who understand the nature of their craziness can manipulate, guide, and get over on them if they know how.

In this brief subunit, we will deal with several key issues on the way to mounting some entry-level and mid-career strategies that will help us in our management (and ultimate manipulation) of crazy people.

Some Key Assumptions

We will begin here with some simple but statistically verifiable assumptions:

- *There is no human being who will not act illogically under certain conditions.* Once you assume that every single person around you is subject to craziness, you won't be surprised when they do something squirrelly—become inappropriately concerned with order, fly into rages when thwarted, hide behind their doors when confronted with problems, grow so repressed they barely open their mouths when they speak, act as jolly as Santa Claus in the mornings and malevolent as Mephistopheles after lunch.

- *Many of the conditions that produce craziness are present in the daily welter of pressures, opportunities, setbacks, and challenges of business life.* At work, one must sell things to people that they do not want, manage unmanageable subordinates, take crap from people simply because they have a higher rank in the corporate food chain, accept bad decisions one knows will bring humiliation and failure to the organization, dress in a monkey suit, and shave places you don't want to shave. Over time, these various considerations begin to wear away at one's well-built sanity, exposing the hot, molten center where their violent, irrational, infantile, crazy personality lies.

○ *After adolescence, people tend to get crazier as they get older.* Most people are kind of nuts when they are in their teens. The prefrontal lobe of the brain has yet to fully develop. New life experiences are exploding on you virtually every day. From roughly the ages of twenty to thirty-five, however, most people begin to display increasingly responsible, thoughtful, mature and "sane" reactions to things. That is, they react in rational ways to difficult issues, flaring up only when demands become overwhelming.

After a time, the pressures on the human brain begin to take their toll. Business intrudes more and more, and the personality starts to disintegrate. It's like being brainwashed in a Korean prison camp, where one is awakened at odd hours, tortured for a period of time, and then allowed to go back to sleep only to be rudely awakened again by one's captors. The "sane" reaction to such treatment is to act out all at once, while attempting to maintain an even keel in general, like this:

Note: Each diamond on the chart above represents a pressure point that could well result in a crazy reaction. The individual in this case, however, manages to maintain appropriate mental composure in spite of the ongoing onslaught of triggers.

After a while, though, research indicates that even the sturdiest individual begins to display a reaction to relentless daily pressure that is all over the map:

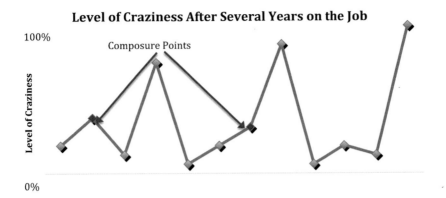

Level of Craziness After Several Years on the Job

Note: Above, the lows experienced by this individual are now reaching near-death status, with reactions to some stimuli hovering at the zero point. There is, however, still some hope for this person, as we see a successful effort being made to reestablish composure now and then (red markers). Time and experience, however, wage their war on us all, and the eventual arc of the afflicted person in their late/middle stages of career (after, say, fifteen years in) comes to look like this:

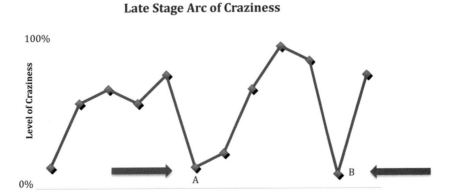

Late Stage Arc of Craziness

Note: Arrow A indicates the point where the individual got a week off. Other than during that fleeting occasion, he or she was pretty much crazy all the time. Point B reports a significant underreaction to a serious crisis that arose over a weekend, which itself is crazy behavior.

◦ *People tend to get crazier as they obtain more power.* Power doesn't always corrupt. Actually, in many cases, power doesn't corrupt much beyond a tendency to expect one's toast to be done at the same exact temperature every morning. What power does is give a formerly reasonable individual the scope to do whatever he or she would like to do without anybody raising their voice with advice or in protest. Nobody who lives without such controls over a period of time can keep their sanity. The self-confidence, coupled with the incessant granting of every wish and command, creates an overheated incubator of superego in which the once adult and tempered persona of the individual regresses into the blob of needs and incipient ill temper characterized by spoiled children.

◦ *Even the most powerful craziness makes its owner vulnerable.* Let's try to find some of those vulnerabilities as we look at the distinct kinds of crazy people you're likely to meet—and possibly work for.

The Seven Kinds of Crazy People

1. The dangerous, violent **bully** views his objectives and those of the state (or corporation) as one and the same. He is willing to do anything to get what he wants, including the heartless eradication of massive numbers of people and the murder of friends as well as enemies. Emotionally vacant and utterly without moral scruple. Whatever he does is right because he does it.

   Vulnerability: Moments of paralyzing weakness, indecision, and terror. Profound loneliness.

   Strategy: Flattery and backbone. Obsessive attention to the crazy person's moods. Proximity. Equal if not superior viciousness in the face of enemies both real and imagined. Sensitivity to his sentimental side. Awareness of when the killing mood casts him in a dark shadow, for in those moments no animal large or small is safe.

2. He or she is a charming, brisk, highly intelligent, willful **narcissist**, a big visionary with a "why not?" attitude that is hard to resist. Willing to expend—and sacrifice—unlimited human and technological resources to get what he  wants. When thwarted, a number of interesting personality distortions occur, among them self-pity and an irrational inability to face facts. Napoleon, for instance, as I mentioned earlier, stuck to his plan to invade Russia in the winter. It was his undoing. For some reason, instead of safely putting him in the ground, his enemies exiled him. Full of his own sense of manifest destiny, he escaped his exile to kill still more men in his hopeless quest for a comeback. He turned from the savior of democracy in Europe to one of the greatest tyrants and mass murderers in history. Either way, he felt pretty good about himself.

   Vulnerability: Eventually, every narcissist comes up against a hard truth that they are not perfect, not destined for all that their imagination has mapped out for them. This hurts. They are also incapable of understanding the feelings of others, which makes them tone-deaf in many management situations that require empathy or finesse. They also tend to be grandiose visionaries who have a really tough time focusing on details.

   Strategy: Don't waste time with the truth. He will kill its messenger. Be prepared for a stunning and unapologetic level of selfishness, which may be best expressed in a profound joke by Mel Brooks: "Tragedy is when I get a hangnail. Comedy is when someone else falls into an open sewer and dies." A great opportunity is presented here to those who can take vague pronouncements and turn them into action.

3. A maniac for order holds together the fraying skeins of the **paranoid mind** by keeping meticulous track of every transaction, every phone slip, every color-coded file. If something falls out of place, it must be restored. Afraid of everything—germs, for instance—he seethes invisibly about in complete chaos that no amount of rigid attention to detail can control. Very bad temper. When such an individual is in power, he inevitably displays a

variety of florid behavior that marks him as crazy and dangerous, assembling Nixonian lists of perceived enemies and looking for bogeys in every shadow and elevator bank.

Vulnerabilities: Trembling membrane that is afraid all the time. Needs constant help making sure that things are in order, fighting dragons both real and imaginary.

Strategy: Particularly susceptible to suggestion and the application of strategic pressure, this poor crazy person is lonely, isolated, and fearful. Be the *solution* to his problems, even if they are imaginary. Conveniently, imaginary problems are often easier to solve than real ones.

4. An **evil wizard** lives in a dark tower, calling up freelance Orcs from consultancies that swarm in over the horizon to slaughter, maim, and then party after sundown. You can't blame them. They are simply trying to establish their dominion over the kingdom using the tools they possess. While bullies and sociopaths can be a lot of fun when they're in a good mood, these scary people are always a bummer, conjuring winged warthogs from

the black depths. You walk around scared all the time. At trainee levels, they tend to congregate in computer security, where they invoke bad scenarios only they can solve.

Vulnerability: Defenseless against good magic.

Strategy: A coven of good witches and valiant knights of both genders is needed. Only in groups of the righteous is power against evil wizards found. It helps to have a dragon on your side, too.

5. It's incredible how a variety of businesses are dominated by **self-destructive people**. I have known men and women whose job it is to interview celebrities and other public personalities for a living who refused to pick up a phone to set up the interview. Martha Stewart, with a huge fortune and all the power in the world at her disposal, monkeyed with a small investment and had to go to jail after lying about it. Bill Clinton we also know about. Sarah Palin is pictured here not because she went rogue or would have made a disastrous vice president (let alone president!). She is here because, with only one news outlet willing to string her along as an on-air personality after her fifteen minutes in the spotlight, she chose to sour her relationship with Fox News. That is hard to do. They employed Herman Cain. But she did it, because certain types of crazy people won't be satisfied until they investigate the very depths of their heedless nature.

Vulnerability: Enormous, crushing lack of judgment.

Strategy: Advice and guidance may be offered. Like, if you were in the Oval Office one day in 1997, you could say to the president, "Bill, as your friend and advisor I would counsel you not to get that blow job. It's not going to be worth it." But it wouldn't work. Bill wanted his blow job and that was that. If you work for one of these, you will constantly be in crisis management mode. If they are your friends or colleagues, be very, very careful that you are not swept up in the insanity. There are a lot of destinies out there for you. Being collateral damage doesn't have to be one of them.

6. And then there are the **hit men**, who are truly off the rails. The people who dedicate themselves to hurting, maiming, and destroying because they work for somebody really, really bad. At left, we see Elle Driver, a member of Quentin Tarantino's fictional Deadly Viper Assassination Squad. She works for Bill, injecting people with poison when he tells her to do so, or cutting off their heads with a scimitar when necessary. Likewise Two-Face, a former do-gooder politician in Gotham City who underwent a horrid accident that disfigured him. On the right is the face he would like to present to the world. His misfortune is that on the left he now displays what his true nature dictates. If every senior officer had this affliction, the world would be a better place.

Vulnerability: Their destiny is to be assassinated by some other hit man. And they know it.

Strategy: It's tough to work for a stone-cold psycho. The challenge is that once upon a time the totally crazy mother used to be a human being. Then they changed and became a monster. And if you serve them long enough you will find you have become *their* monster.

7.   We close this discussion with the most difficult crazy person of them all. Who is this fucking guy? Do we know him? Do we know what he's going to do? Can we count on him not to flake out, burn out, flame out, sell out? No, we can't. Because he is a cipher.

Vulnerability: None known at this time.

Strategy: Whatev.

Takeaway

We have to begin with the assumption that varying levels of craziness attend daily living and afflict everybody, high and low. Each vector of pressure works on each personality in unique ways. One problem will crack a certain type of person one way. The same problem will unmoor another from the space station in a completely different way. Each is manipulable to one extent or another, depending on the intensity of their craziness:

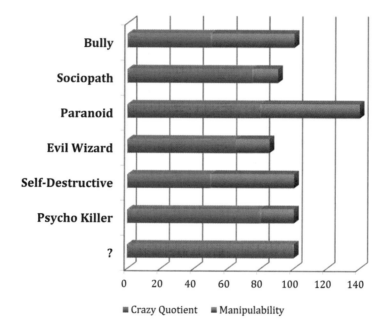

You will note that in the case of "?" it is virtually impossible to control that which you do not understand.

As for your own insanity, keep it in check for now. But it may help you to know which forms of craziness serve you best in the workplace so that when different aspects of yourself start falling apart, you can select the most productive forms of mental illness to cultivate.

Most Productive Forms of Craziness

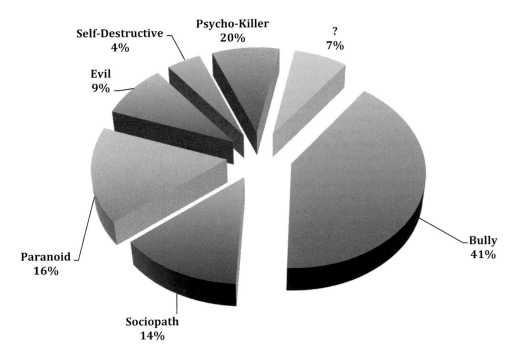

The other flavors of craziness have their places in the pantheon, to the sure. But not everybody can succeed in the more specialized realms of evil and self-destruction. While it is possible that psycho-killers are born, not made, being emotionally, physically, and spiritually inaccessible to people is tough work. Don't try it at home.

206.

Friends, Enemies, and Frenemies

Are your enemies helping you? What are your friends plotting? These are questions you will ask yourself, at one point or another, throughout your short stay on this planet.

And yet, it is a basic truism of office life that life without even lousy friends is stale, flat, and unprofitable. Well, it might be profitable. I know several very successful moguls who have no friends. No real ones, I mean. So they buy their friends instead. They dine with purchased friends. They chat on the phone with their purchased friends every day, talking about the business they do together, which is always based on the mogul's patronage, his coin. And they sleep with their purchased friends, too. After a while, if you are very powerful and very successful, you find that you can convince yourself of anything—if you think it; it must be true. And so they conveniently forget the business of how they've acquired their friends and find themselves surrounded with what they can only imagine to be genuine relationships.

In Los Angeles, for instance, it is common to hear big shots talk about each other as "my dear friend," when you know for a fact the two gentlemen or ladies hate each other. Not too long ago, for instance, Ron Meyer, the COO of Universal, sued Brad Grey, the top dog at Paramount, for a disputed $50 million. Meyer had no comment for the press. Grey defended himself through his PR person with a lightly sarcastic retort. What had the town chuckling was a small aside in the piece that appeared in the 2013 Oscars issue of the *Hollywood Reporter*. "Even though the dispute is a holdover from Grey's pre-Paramount life as a manager and producer," reported Matthew Belloni, "it's extremely rare for a top Hollywood executive to be targeted in such a way by a rival. . . . Making matters more complex, Grey and Universal Studios COO Ron Meyer are said to be close friends." That last sentence there was the funny part, and completely typical of the town. The only thing that people in Hollywood get a kick out of, right after the failure of their enemies, is the failure of their dear friends.

Of course, faux friendship and collegiality is not exclusive to show business. In fact, the ability to feign friendliness is one of the great achievements of human evolution. The proof that Congress is in atavistic frenzy came right at the turn of 2013, when Speaker of the House John Boehner, a Republican, passed Democratic Senate Majority Leader Harry Reid outside the Oval Office. "Go fuck yourself," said Boehner. Reid inquired if he had heard the Speaker correctly. "Go fuck yourself," Boehner repeated. Fortunately, they did not whip out their halberds and go to work trying to smash each other's brains in. Our ability to be appropriately insincere is a mark of our increased civilization, which now seems to be losing ground.

No, the feeling of a harmless camaraderie is necessary for the daily enjoyment of organizational life. And somewhere in that cloche of functional friends, hopefully, there are one or two or three genuine business friends who will watch your back while you are watching theirs, who will not lie to you about anything important, and who will defend your honor even when you are not in the room. In a fifty-year business career, there might be three or four individuals whose friendship will outlast your business context, not counting golf, because golf buddies don't count. Hitler could have been a decent golf buddy if he had survived the war, and gotten into virtually any country club, too, since many of them still share his views on religious affiliation and race.

It is also necessary, believe it or not, to cultivate a few enemies. In corporate life, the enemy of your enemy is your friend. So having clearly designated foes is actually a very credible way of developing not only friends but a friend *group*, which is even more important than a friend, organizationally speaking.

Who Are My Friends?

We might imagine that this would be an easy question to answer. In a business setting, unfortunately, it is not. There are many differences between a "real" friend and a "business" friend, as this chart illustrates.

"REAL" FRIENDS	BUSINESS "FRIENDS"
Make big emotional demands, with occasional annoying mooching, imposing, etc.	Clear emotional boundaries; demands are mostly for support of key projects and mutual nonaggression.
Can be very rude and get away with it	Standards of cordiality virtually always in place
Generally tell you what they think whether you want to hear it or not	Often tell you what you want to hear just because they're nice

"REAL" FRIENDS	BUSINESS "FRIENDS"
See them when you want to or they want to, but not when neither of you want to	See them all the time whether you want to or not
Don't care all that much if you always have a good time or get along very well	Extremely important that you enjoy each other's company and maintain high level of affability, even if it's somewhat false
When meeting socially, don't always get drunk together	Always get drunk together at every available opportunity
Allowed to show anger of any scale and duration, with proper cause	Displays of anger inadvisable. Pique, perhaps. Annoyance. But only with relationships of real duration, and even then, with extreme care. For instance, while you might call a "real" friend a "schmuck," you would never do so with a business friend, even if he is one.
No quid pro quo assumptions	Multiple quid pro quo assumptions; in fact, there are some durable business friendships that are based on nothing but
Not dependent on context of relationship, that is, job, location, etc.	Heavily context-dependent
Mostly not envious of their success or secretly happy when they confront difficulties	Get very jealous when they receive a promotion or earn more money than you do
Go through fire for them	Probably would do so too, unless it's a really *big* fire . . .
Last a lifetime	95 percent last the length of the job association
Probably don't do you much good, and in some cases are actually disastrous to your health and well-being	Can be important building blocks in the construction of your power base

Let's go to work.

The Seven Ways to Make and Maintain Friends in Business (The Short Course)

1. Be nice to people. They may be suspicious at first, but after a while they will come to view you as an ego-boosting safe harbor from the whips and scorns of all the nasty assholes. If you have to be reasonably insincere on occasion, go ahead. People appreciate insincerity. It's proof that you care.

2. Don't ever shame anybody in public, even when what they may be saying or doing is obnoxious and stupid. If ass must be kicked, do so in private, and always couch your negativity as a failure to understand, rather than a direct attack on them. "I don't get what you're saying, Larry. It seems counterintuitive to me" is better than "That's just about the dumbest idea I ever heard, Larry."

3. Listen to people. They have something to say even when they don't really have anything to say. People do too much talking and not enough listening. Reverse that trend and you will be appreciated as probably more sensitive than you are, and also viewed, ironically, as a good conversationalist.

4. Always say hello to people in lobbies, elevators, on the line at the deli getting coffee, whatever, no matter how lowly or insignificant their position. Entire days have been ruined when an employee doesn't receive his "Hi" from Ms. Entwhistle, who has no idea what damage she has just caused while she was thinking about her morning muffin. With peers, use their names. People hate being called "buddy," "champ," "my man," and other all-purpose name replacements. This goes double for e-mail. "I can't make that meeting, Barb" conveys an amazingly different message than "I can't make that meeting."

5. Display a *happy demeanor.* It's astonishing how many sour-looking weasels walk around surprised that people don't seek their company. Manage your face.

6. Solve problems, don't create them. A huge number of very dislikable people have this aggravating habit of either creating problems they can then solve to the acclaim of the multitudes, or blowing up the size of issues and then handing them off to others. Try to not do that.

7. Make people happy. It's possible that you don't know how to do this in "real" life, but it's a lot easier in business. Figure out what your potential friends and allies might want and then do everything you can to help them get it. If you're against what they want, work the other side as subtly as you can. No point in turning a friend into a frenemy.

Contrariwise . . .

The Eight Ways to Make and Maintain
Enemies in Business (The Short Course)

1. Be mean to people. Most of the jerks I know restrict this policy to those who are weaker and smaller than they are. The thing is, people don't always stay small. And a lot of big, important people remember when they were small and had to deal with a douche like you.

2. Make people look bad at meetings. Entire cultures are built around this one. It's a macho thing. General Electric in the 1980s and 1990s was famous for it, and I've always felt it came directly down from their founder, Thomas Edison, who was a real SOB.

3. Make clear to other people that their thoughts and opinions are boring and meaningless to you. You can do this by talking a lot and then, when others try to get a word in, checking your BlackBerry. It won't be too long before you won't have to endure their yammering anymore, because they won't be sharing anything with you at all.

4. Cultivate a superior attitude in public spaces where you may run into groundlings and Morlocks. If you don't know somebody's name, just call them "dude," or, if they are a woman, "babe." People love that.

5. Make gender an issue. Most men with brains larger than walnuts have ascertained that there is very little upside—either as an employee or a manager—to being a sexist. Aside from accepting the justice of the situation, there are simply too many disincentives in decent corporations to doing so. Ironically, it often seems to be women who are the most inhospitable, competitive, and hostile to fellow women in the organization.* Certainly, it is not a requirement for women to make their judgment in such matters gender-based. But a bit of support for one's sisters might be expected if friendship, equality in the workplace, and the elimination of the glass ceiling are considered worthy goals.

6. Display a *crusty, grouchy, unapproachable demeanor*. There are entire ranks of executives in whole companies who look like they just ate rotten cheese. I was once in an elevator with a senior officer from Westinghouse with whom I had just been in a meeting. "Hello, Mr. Oblick," I said, which was, I thought, a moderate and reasonable thing to

---

* Examples of this in private are hard to chronicle, but in the public sphere one has only to perform a cursory overview of the media surrounding, say, the elevation of Katie Couric to the anchor chair at CBS to see this to be the case. Without exception, the nastiest, most personal, most appearance-based attacks on Couric were launched by female journalists at the major newspapers of the mainstream media.

say in that context. He looked at me in dark and gloomy silence, which persisted for the entire ride down from the top floor to the lobby of the office tower. I read the other day that he is dead now, so I guess I can stop despising him. I'll miss that.

7. Let other people solve their own problems and yours as well. Dump as much crap as you can on them and if they consult you for help, let them know what you think of people who can't manage their own situations.

8. Make people feel really lousy about themselves. You know how. You do it to yourself every day.

Friend vs. Enemy Orientation

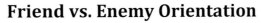

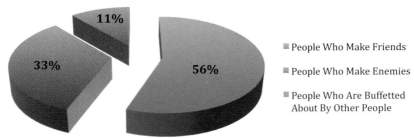

Note on Chart: People generally make a choice on how to orient themselves: acquisition and maintenance of friends (in blue, 56%) versus cultivation of a series of acrimonious relationships (in red, 33%). If you choose the blue team, you will be in the majority with all the other folks who basically want to walk around in a world of potentially benign citizens with whom they can share a steak without choking.

The real losers are those who are constantly buffeted about by others (in green, 11%). These poor souls generally end up being overly friendly to enemies and insufficiently affectionate to friends. If you find yourself anywhere in that vicinity, do everything you can to get out of that zone as fast as you can. On the other hand, that's not usually an easy switch to make. It's more of a destiny kind of thing.

If you choose to be in the red zone of people who would rather make enemies, you will be in good company. Most moguls are comfortable in that group.

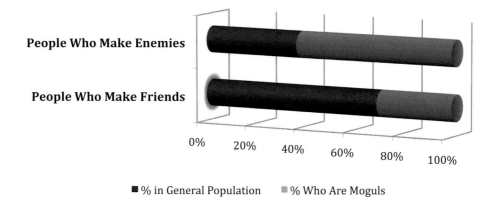

Note on the Chart: As you can see from this data, the majority of regular people try to make friends, and even some moguls do, too. A minority of the general population, but a majority of moguls, go the route of enemy acquisition.

Frenemies: When the Enemy Is a Friend, and Vice Versa

Our final discussion in this emotionally complex arena touches on the significant group of peers, subordinates, and superiors who are neither friends nor enemies but situational associates who, at one time or another, are neither or both.

Frenemies

Frenemy relationships abound in many fields, making the wise, unsentimental, and basically unemotional management of them a necessity. These include:

➤ Politics, most obviously, which notoriously makes strange bedfellows. Until recently, this field was well populated by frenemies who disagreed with each other but could still eat, drink, go to social events, and even marry each other now and then. Now everybody just hates each other.

➤ Organized crime, where there seems to be a lot of slobbery cheek kissing between men who are fully prepared to draw down and kill each other at the drop of a toupee.

➤ Show business, where the line between who is your friend and who is your enemy is constantly shifting as people alternatively embrace each other and then fuck each other over.

Close study of this latter issue shows an interesting phenomenon, most prevalent in show business but also reported quite frequently in other professions filled with frenemies, a fascinating behavior pattern that we can report on for the very first time.* It can be best expressed quite simply as: *The number and duration of hugs between associates in show business is inversely proportional to the actual affection that exists between the two individuals.*† Expressed mathematically:

$$A = BS / d^2$$

Or, the amount of Actual Affection (A) is equal to the number of insincere back slaps (BS), divided by the duration of the hug, squared. Thus, in Case 1, two moguls who actually like each other meet and enjoy a one-second hug featuring one measly pat on the back.‡ Or:

$$A = 1/1 = 1$$

This yields a strong Affection index of 1. In Case 2, let's observe two agents who engage in a virtually romantic embrace of six (6) seconds and exchange a flurry of no fewer than five (5) lusty pats on the back.

---

* "Hugging as a Meaningless Expression of Faux Affection in the Entertainment Business," Schwartz et al. © 2011–2013, National Association for Serious Studies.

† One extremely powerful television executive is known for being a very big hugger. A personal story may be permitted to illustrate this point. The first time I met the individual in question, the man put his arm around my shoulder and gave me the kind of embrace I usually reserve for friends I haven't seen since high school. Even though I had heard about his predilection for this kind of thing, I was still so surprised that I actually blurted out something candid. "Peter," I said. "I don't know you. I mean, we just met. Why are you hugging me?" He looked at me for a moment, himself a bit startled, and said, "That's what I do. I'm a hugger." I said, "That's nice." We've been hugging ever since.

‡ In some venues, a shoulder squeeze or chest bump is substituted for the traditional back pat. The significance of this alteration has yet to achieve sufficient attention quite yet, so this aspect of the phenomenon is not factored into our calculations at this point.

$$A = 5/62 \approx .14$$

Employing these metrics, we achieve an Actual Affection index of .13888889, which is a revealing sign of their actual low level of mutual regard.

Efforts to quantify evanescent phenomena such as this are ongoing and will be reported both online at the website of the National Association for Serious Studies and in subsequent editions of this Curriculum. In this case, the issue of counterfeit expressions of emotion are closely associated with the unit on insincerity that immediately follows this one.

Takeaway

We have taken perhaps a somewhat bloodless approach to this issue. That was by design. Friendship, enemies, the confusing bridge between the two—these are highly emotional issues. Those who handle them with too much raw, unmanaged emotion run the risk of overpersonalizing their relationships. Friendship is necessary. But it's not business. Keep the distinction in mind. So:

✔ Maintain your friends and treat them like the precious treasure they are. Even when your interests and theirs do not coincide, handle the differences with delicacy, strategic care, and the assumption that the long-term relationship is just as important as any short-term gains one might achieve at their expense.

✔ Take equal care of your enemies; always look for ways your interests and theirs might intersect. Pay close attention to the question of who also considers your enemies their enemies as well as who might consider your enemies their friends.

✔ Use your frenemies as you would a hammer or a personal digital assistant, tools that will help you get your job done. When they get old, replace them with new ones.

In Defense of Insincerity

Of all the business arts, the ability to be credibly and honorably insincere is perhaps the most misunderstood and undervalued. There are several disciplines built on the art of high insincerity, including the entire field of diplomacy and high-level mergers-and-acquisitions work, where two parties constantly discuss mutual benefit when the real matter under discussion is conquest and surrender. The insincerity involved helps make the process more tolerable for everybody.

Insincerity is also at the center of many of our most essential social institutions, including but not limited to marriage, child-rearing, and successful post-divorce relations with former spouses.

Let us begin with some short multiple-choice questions. Don't worry. No student has correctly answered them all on the first try. But together they help us to understand the magic of an insincere mien, a mien that will help you to negotiate many a craggy and seemingly impassible predicament.

1. What is the proper rejoinder to this question: "Do you think Larry likes me?"

    a. Of course he does. You're one of his most valued soldiers.
    b. No. It's quite obvious he doesn't. Haven't you noticed that he leaves the room every time you come into it?
    c. What? I'm sorry. I was texting my lunch order for sushi. If they don't get it by 11 a.m. you might as well just forget it.
    d. Hey, who does Larry like, really? The most important thing is that I love ya. Now get outta here, you big chucklehead.

The correct answer is d), because it demonstrates the engine that moves so much of the valuable insincerity that makes the workplace tolerable.

2. What is the proper rejoinder to this question: "Did I do okay on that board presentation?"

    a.   It was okay, I guess. I mean, you didn't spit up on yourself.

    b.   It was terrific, Barb! Outstanding. I never saw a better one. You were brilliant. Bo-yah!

    c.   What? I'm sorry. I was just listening to my messages.

    d.   I really enjoyed it, Barb. You were very much on point, and very poised all the way through. Loved the graphics, too. Who did them?

Once again, the properly insincere answer is d). But this time the issues are somewhat more complicated, and the choices slightly less clear. Answer a) is honest, but of the kind of honesty that is of little utility in civilized society. It is truth used as a bludgeon, and deserves a response in kind. If a subordinate gave me that response to my question after a crucial presentation to the board, I would say "thank you" and immediately target him for lengthy daily torture and eventual defenestration.

Answer b) is so unctuous, so obviously over-the-top that its recipient can only feel that the actual situation was so dire that an overly sweet concoction of prodigious dimensions was necessary to offset her performance. It would have the opposite result of what was intended—that is, it wouldn't be believed. It is remarkable how many of those who wish to be properly insincere fall prey to this kind of overstatement and egregious slime.

Answer c) is neither sincere nor insincere. It is certainly a choice, but not one that will endear you to anyone who is on the receiving end. If interactions in life are opportunities in disguise, this reply, in effect, is like leaving 90 percent of the pot on the table at the end of a poker game.

Answer d) prevails because, first of all, it bears some relation (however gentle) to the truth, yet it also shows that the responder was listening, that he or she is in touch with Barb's desires and fears and properly attuned to some of the technical and professional issues that were met and surmounted by the presentation (interest in the graphics). It is neither excessive nor greasy, but sufficiently in touch with the needs expressed by the question and she who posed it. It embodies, in short, the second aspect of successful insincerity:

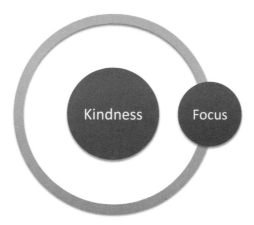

Quality insincerity is *focused*. It recognizes the context of the exchange, homes in on the potential reality of the situation, and lobs the shuttlecock into the air for additional targeted conversation.

3. *What is the proper rejoinder to this question:* "I don't understand it. I went in there and pitched that proposal with everything I had and they gave it to the other guys. Why?"

    a.   Well, Bob, if you really want to know, I just think their proposal was a lot stronger than ours. When you get right down to it, we just don't have the horses that they do on a project of that size.

    b.   The whole thing was fixed from the very beginning, Bob! We didn't have a chance! We should go to the SEC! We were robbed! You kicked *ass*!

    c.   I hate postmortems. Let's move on, okay?

    d.   Things just sometimes happen, you know? That project would have been a fucking headache anyhow. We're better off. Now let's get out of here. Drinks are on me. And by that I mean, it's on you, but we'll use my card and you can sign my expense report.

I don't know about you, but I'm really starting to get a good, solid hate on the excessively honest, insensitive Mr. a). He consistently tells the truth, of course, so there's that. But the kind of truth he dispenses just makes people feel bad and does nothing to help get things back on track. If I worked with the guy, I'd have him transferred to Petaluma, except I hear people are nice in Petaluma.

As for Ms. b), you can see her trying to make things better, she's just so *bad* at it. When facing a reversal or disappointment, you don't want somebody grinning and thumping you on the back as if you just won something. You need some recognition of the reality of the situation. Also, for insincerity to function as it should, the practitioner should not essentially have a big sign around his or her neck that says I MAY BE INSINCERE, BUT I MEAN IT! We can do better than that, can't we?

And again, c) just won't do. There's no emotional bite.

Let's examine why d) continues to prosper in the insincerity sweepstakes. First, it engages the disappointed Bob on an emotional level. Second, it doesn't ignore the negatives that are hanging in the air; the reply recognizes that something has gone wrong. It doesn't overpraise Bob's performance, either, since no matter how good it was, they didn't win, did they? Best of all, perhaps, it offers a rationalization that minimizes the objective and makes its loss less relevant over time. "I didn't want that toy/job/girl-boy anyway," could possibly be the oldest and most childish of boo-boo ointments. Finally, d) holds out the daring offer of companionship, even intimacy, in the face of an angry, upset, thwarted person. When most citizens would be running *away* from the potential nuclear blast, this player is running *toward it* with a martini glass in hand. It offers us a third element of insincerity:

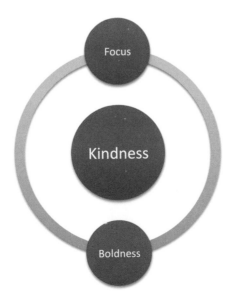

4. *What is the proper rejoinder to this question:* "Hey, this is great! Jerry is leaving and that means his position is open! I'm going to pitch Bob for it! Do you think I've got a shot?"

- a. Actually, no, Hannah. I really don't. I'm not trying to be rude, but I think they'll probably go for somebody with more experience.
- b. Maybe. Hey, come to think of it, I may go for it myself. Why not? I'm as qualified as you are!
- c. I don't know. Sure.
- d. Of course you do, Hannah. But it's going to take a serious campaign. These kind of things don't fall into people's laps. Let's get some coffee and talk about it.

For purposes of our conversation, we're going to assume that a) is probably correct. There are a million variables in the selection of Jerry's replacement. It could go any number of ways. They could choose Ned because Bob likes his putter. They could choose Betty because she's got seniority. They could go out of house and select that guy from Yahoo who had everybody bamboozled at the last IT meeting. Anything could happen. But Hannah needs to feel like she has a shot. And maybe she needs to be treated with a reasonable level of insincerity in order to feel good about herself, the organization, and life in general. And since we like Hannah, we'd like her to feel that way. So answer a) continues to be of little value to anybody, lacking as it is in any respectable level of insincerity.

Answer b) is totally wrong, too, but interesting. This guy has been sucking up to Bob with nauseating intensity since the beginning of this unit. Now that a peer, Hannah, is involved, he's dropped his nice-guy thing and has turned into a total jerk. He's insensitive, selfish, and baldly opportunistic. This is what lies underneath sycophantic losers like this one. They give insincerity a bad name.

I don't know about you, but I still don't like c). There's very little that can be said about him except that if he were an elderly Eskimo, it might be fun to put him on an ice floe and send him out to die on the open sea.

The thing about d) that continues to earn our approval is a totally new dimension of ongoing insincerity:

Like every other successful business tactic, effective insincerity requires *skill*. Before we are done, an impressive array of skills will be brought to bear by responder d) in the effort to help Hannah gain a decent shot at the promotion:

All very important skills—put to service in pursuit of professional-grade insincerity!

And while the aims, the assumptions, the motivation, the reality of the total exercise of insincerity itself may be completely and utterly hollow—after all, Hannah is a long shot for the job—there is something about the endeavor that is not: The feeling behind it is not insincere. It is founded in the conviction that the very best kind of insincerity, the kind that no civilized society can do without, is the power that makes even corporate life worth living, and that makes the world go around:

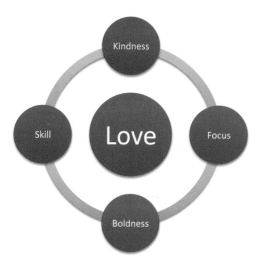

Takeaway

We come, at the end of this key topic, to the issue that we've been dancing around throughout the conversation: What about the Truth? As in, Truth with a capital *T*? In any exercise in which politeness and pleasant insincerity is the goal, you eventually come close to the line that, once crossed, makes you a liar. Nobody wants that in boldface on their internal resume. On the other hand, many worthwhile lies have been told in pursuit of a decent objective. This is a thorny problem. In pursuit of some guidance, perhaps it would be fruitful to pose some rather Socratic questions:

- What is the truth? Is it the same for each person?
- What is a liar? Are all liars bad people all the time?
- Are all of those who always and without exception tell what they consider to be the truth good people?
- How many wars have been started by good people who couldn't live without imposing their versions of the truth on those who didn't quite see it their way?

- How much happiness and satisfaction has been created by big fat liars who told other people what they wanted to hear?
- Which is worse—insincerity or cruelty? Insincerity or failure?
- Are there certain circumstances in which it is absolutely incumbent upon every human being to tell the truth without exception?

Of course there are. The earth is not flat, even though there were once those who believed it to be so. It is always wrong to put poison in pet food and the paint that coats children's toys, even though China is the Wild West and we shouldn't judge them. Subprime mortgages should not be given to unemployed people or those making 10 percent of the value of their loans, even though somewhere I'm sure there are bunch of bank officers militating to get that great little sector of the banking business going again.

So yes, there is occasion for truth. One should always be where one says one is going to be, traffic permitting, when one says one is going to be there. Expense accounts should primarily be used for legitimate business purposes. Thou shalt not kill, also. That's a good one.

Beyond that? There's a lot that's open for discussion. Good luck with it. And have I mentioned that you look very nice in that new outfit? Where'd you get it? Have you lost weight?

208.
The Zen of Cosmic Boredom

Perhaps all stages of life involve crushing boredom. None, however, represents as significant a challenge as boredom in business. This is because there are many boring people you will come across every day whom you can't avoid while fulfilling your responsibilities (and earning your paycheck) at the same time. Your livelihood depends on mastering the boredom that threatens to overwhelm you.

It's easy to resent the boring. But many are, in fact, blameless and cannot help their boringness. Others use it as a tool and must be severely punished. Here are some:

1. *Bosses.* As a group, bosses may be aggravating, fearsome, exciting, demanding, and more, but the quality and level of boredom they inflict tends to be less intense than most of the other boring people you will encounter. This is because, while time spent with them can be boring, to be sure, often it's much more varied than pure tedium:

Why Boss Time Is Less Boring

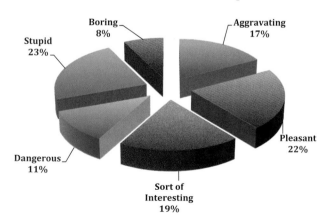

Note: This unpredictable mix renders time spent with bosses less prone to unpleasant levels of boredom. It's still there, though (in orange).

At higher levels of management, somewhat ironically, there is more boredom, but also a more acute level of danger and excitement that banishes it.

Really Big Boss Time

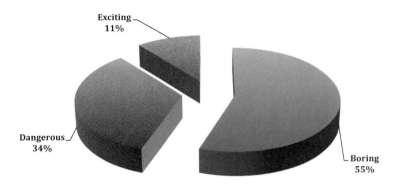

Exciting
11%

Dangerous
34%

Boring
55%

Note: Time spent with very big bosses differs from any other time spent on the job, being partitioned into much more distinct elements. Boredom level may be significant at times (high-level managers love to expostulate) but the investment in time is well justified by the charge of higher excitement and a certain level of danger that always exists in the presence of great beasts.

2. *Management consultants.* Management consultants are hired to torture employees and then kill them. The torture is the boring part, in which the consultants make people sit through long, generally upbeat PowerPoint presentations on why they are about to be executed and why that's good for everybody. Then they march them off to their doom.

3. *Wimps.* These are all the people who didn't do anything particularly good or particularly bad. They don't oppose anything or embrace anything. They impose boring meetings on others.

4. *Golfers (except to other golfers).* They're not alone in their need to impose powerfully boring anecdotes about their enthusiasm. I once had dinner with a guy who spent the entire meal talking about the variety of apples that are grown in his home state of Washington. Seriously. I kept thinking it would be over soon and he would change the subject. But he didn't.

5. *People who talk all about their deals/start-ups/how much money they made.* Is there anything less interesting in the world than having to sit and listen to how rich somebody got on a deal you had no part in?

6. *Cheap bastards who never took out their credit cards while ordering the most expensive thing on the menu.* See, this is what I mean about boredom being a function of repressed emotion—in this case, rage.

7. *Relentlessly angry assholes.* Speaking of which, there are many successful people who are for some reason always pissed-off. There are two theories about this. First, they are angry because they are frightened of losing status, and this terror transforms itself into rage. The second theory is that the more generally pissed-off you are, the more you are suited to business, and in this way the system itself selects angry people to be its leaders.

8. *Bankers.* They hide behind a veil of boredom while they do all sorts of things that are nasty to other people. And they're so happy with themselves!

9. *Meeting addicts.* These have meetings to plan meetings to plan meetings to plan meetings in which meetings will be planned. Damn them!

10. *Inelegant suck-ups.* Listen to them wheeze and pander. It's gross. If you were doing it, it would be much more elegant.

11. *Corporate politicians.* Their paranoia and pointless gamesmanship trap their colleagues in a limbo of suspicion and ill-feelings; hypocrites, time-wasters, and organizers of events honoring executives who have either already been honored way too much or should never be honored at all.

12. *You.* That's right. Look in the mirror. How boring are *you*? To yourself, I mean. Because if you're boring to yourself you will be boring to other people. And then they will be boring to you. And there you are.

Understanding Boredom

As we have discovered, boredom is not a neutral, disinterested state. It is, in fact, a highly emotional one, featuring a rainbow of negativity. What follows is a chart that chronicles the arc of intense tedium that attended a recent budget review meeting at a large multinational corporation.* During that time, the individual, a midlevel manager required to attend solely to

---

* This is by no means a unique occasion. Anyone who has to work for a living may find themselves subject to something like it. A friend writes: "When I was a teenager, I got a summer job working for security at a golf course that was holding a tournament. It's possible they hired too many people. One day they took me out to the middle of a huge field at the edge of the property. And they put a chair in the middle of the field. And they told me to sit in the chair for my shift. I had a twelve-hour shift, 7:00 a.m. to 7:00 p.m. They didn't tell me what I was going to be doing, so I didn't bring a book. At noon, somebody came out with a sandwich and a bottle of water. They went away and I was alone again. After I had sung every song I ever knew . . . and danced around the chair. . . . I cried awhile . . . and after twelve hours they came by and picked me up. And I never went back again."

beef up his department's side of the table, experienced, in this order and in growing intensity, a stunning range of emotional events:

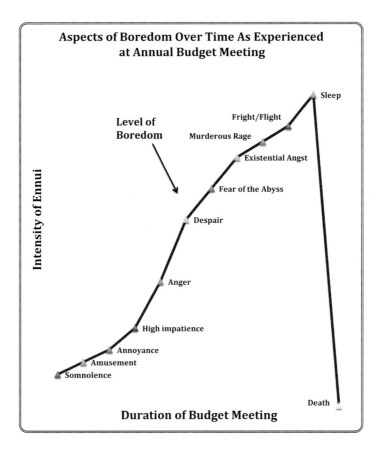

Notes on the Chart: This sad journey into tedium ended in death-by-boredom of the unfortunate subject. These things happen. The sufferer, at the last limit of tolerance, simply expires when his or her heart stops beating from a profound lack of interest in continuing to do so. Along the way, at various points in the budget review, the subject experienced:

- **Somnolence:** The meeting began with a dozy sense of comfort, with little hint of the horrors that loomed ahead.
- **Amusement:** At this point, the group began to discuss formatting of line items, and the subject had to stifle several impulses to giggle.

- **Annoyance:** Now really, he thought. What the hell. Couldn't we do this whole thing in about fifteen minutes if Bob over there would stop trying to impress everybody with his goddamn thoroughness?
- **High impatience:** At this point, the subject actually broke a pencil he had been chewing on and had to spit out several splinters and some graphite.
- **Anger:** Boredom and anger now were present in almost equal measure. His thoughts began to turn philosophical.
- **Despair:** He slipped into a deep funk . . .
- **Fear of the Abyss:** . . . followed by an overwhelming dread at his own mortality and the inexorable passage of time . . .
- **Existential Angst:** . . . followed by a deep conviction that life itself had no meaning.
- **Murderous Rage**: Rebelling against this subtle but effective form of torture, the subject, now caught in the hypnogogic state* that precedes deep REM sleep, explodes in virtually uncontrollable fury that can't be expressed.
- **Fright/Flight**: Where can he go? What can he do?
- **Sleep:** The subject now spirals down into the uncontrollable urge to simply shut his eyes for a few moments. When he opens them again, several people are looking at him strangely and there is drool on his chin.
- **Death:** He is found after the meeting slumped in his chair, at peace at last.

There is no boredom in death. This is perhaps the point that despicable Nazi-sympathizer-philosopher Martin Heidegger was making when he wrote:

> Profound boredom, drifting here and there in the abysses of our existence like a muffling fog, removes all things and men and oneself along with it into a remarkable indifference. This boredom reveals Being as a whole.

Heidegger did his best work on boredom. He devoted a hundred pages of his oeuvre to exclusive consideration of it, in fact. Two inferences that we may draw from his work:

- He embraced boredom as a writer. His essays are a massive, impenetrable iceberg of Teutonic tedium. Nobody can really understand what he meant, although students of

---

* The terms *hypnagogic* and *hypnagogia* refer to mental phenomena that occur during the "threshold consciousness" phase that immediately precedes sleep. These may include dreams that present as reality, hallucinations, and sleep paralysis (the terrifying conviction that although one is awake, one cannot move).

philosophy are forced to read him and pretend to understand him. And boring? Unbelievable. Worse than *Beowulf.*

- He got the Zen of boredom.

If one is to survive, one must master that Zen, the sense of pleasant emptiness that comes when one has mastered meditation. Interestingly, the practice of Zen meditation is remarkably congenial to the experience of attending a meeting:

- In Zen, as in a meeting, you assume a comfortable position and simply sit. Sitting is at the heart of meeting as it is in Zen.

- In Zen, as in a meeting, you empty your mind, breathe evenly and deeply, and listen to the thoughts that pass around and through you; you do not try to think, or to hold on to any specific thought; you simply sit and breathe and let the river flow.

- In Zen, as in a meeting, you eventually lose any sense of self and of the passage of time. You rise at the end, refreshed, lighter, and prepared to meet whatever comes next.

. . . but nothing in the end will extricate you from all boredom. Only Zen will do that. "A remarkable indifference," is how Heidegger described it. In that remarkable indifference, if achieved with perfection, a higher state of consciousness is reached. Yogis and monks work a lifetime to achieve that state. You are fortunate to be offered the opportunity to get there every day, another perk of a life in business.

Obviously, reaching this Yoda-like plane of nonconsciousness takes practice and dedication. It's hard to do. As you develop your Zen chops, you may be excused for employing a variety of stratagems:

1. *Schedule your own meetings, whenever you can.* You can't be in two places at once. And something you organize yourself will automatically be more interesting to you, if not to anybody else.*

2. *Keep meetings on track.* All should begin with small pleasantries, no longer than five

---

* Naturally, not everyone can simply organize their own meetings, particularly ones that make going to a more important meeting led by senior officers unnecessary. But a good, solid, low-level meeting in pursuit of your boss's larger goals may be a more persuasive alternative than the third meeting of the subcommittee investigating sites for next year's sales conference.

minutes. The meeting itself, unless it has a varied and tasty plateful of agendas,* should be no more than thirty minutes. The milling and mutual backslapping after the meeting is the counterpart of the five-minute pleasantry phase that began the gathering. The sense of *moving forward through time* should never be relinquished. Time, we now know, is relative. Interesting things move along faster than boring ones.†

3.   *Victimize boring people.* Do what you can to exact punishment on those who insist on boring you. Use your wits. Use your humor. Use that throat-clearing thing you do that annoys other people. But don't let them get away with it! Fight the fight! Never give up!

4.   *Master yourself.* People in solitary confinement have to do it. Hospital patients who have broken some portion of their bodies have to do it as they lie in bed in traction. Students taking a course in wave theory have to do it. Boredom is everywhere. To achieve anything meaningful, there will be times that one has to punch through the malaise and get to the bright side of the road.

In short, to master boredom one must master oneself. And that, young grasshopper, is what the Zen we speak of is all about.

Takeaway

If you work very hard and achieve a great deal, and your career spans many decades, and is jammed with wonderful challenges and triumphs, you will still face, almost on a daily basis, a variety of situations that will be heavy with the crushing weight of intense boredom. You will not succeed if you cannot tolerate this aspect of business life. You will find something else to do, because the fear of boredom will poleaxe your ambitions and distort your daily strategy for getting the job done.

Yet even if everybody around you is as action-packed and intellectually evocative as it is possible for human beings to be, there is one person who you'll have to be with every day who can be very, very boring to you.

---

* Agendas came in platefuls between the late 1980s and the early part of the twenty-first century. The measurement is being used in this venue in an attempt to reinstitute its amusing usage.

† Einstein's theory of relativity states that people traveling on a spaceship near the speed of light feel time in a normal way, but are in fact moving through time much more quickly in absolute terms than those on the ground. People in the spaceship will age a couple of years while hundreds of years may pass on earth. This is because sitting in a spaceship is very boring. Life on earth is more interesting, so time moves a lot quicker.

You.

How many days will there be when you sit at your desk, workstation, in your office by yourself, waiting for something to happen? There are no boring tasks to perform. You are between things. Nobody is around to laugh or scratch with. Your onscreen game of Fairway Solitaire is not alluring. There's nobody to call. Nobody to write. You've watched YouTube long enough. You've Googled. You've Tweeted. You've gone on Amazon and bought socks. You've visited eBay and bid on a bourbon decanter that looks like Elvis. And now there are . . . five hours left before quitting time.

You're going to have to find a solution that's right for you. Me, I like to go out and take a walk. I know a lot of folks who take a nap in the afternoon. Big, successful folks. Of course, they have a door. So work hard until you get a door. If there are no doors in your corporation? I feel sorry for you. Perhaps there's an empty office on your floor? A broom closet? I know a corporate lawyer who used to take a like-minded colleague into an equipment room that was piled high with boxes. They would emerge a little while later and head in opposite directions with serious demeanors. They didn't look one bit bored.

209.

Insensitivity Training

Business sometimes means making difficult decisions that have a negative impact on other people. Many idealistic, ethical, or cowardly business people find this aspect of achieving success scary. Others, who attend "real" business schools, find it far too easy to bend, spindle, and mutilate other people after their multiyear curriculum in dehumanization.* This course attempts to establish a middle ground between oversensitivity and undersensitivity that is very much worth finding.

There are two types of businesspeople:

1. People who are overly wrapped up in the basic decency of other people, who may be too sensitive when they have to take actions against those other people's interests, even inadvertently;
2. People who have a negative opinion of people (and probably of themselves), who find it overly easy to hurt others and sometimes actually enjoy doing so.

These exercises are for them.

Desensitizing Exercises

These brief exercises are designed for those who are simply too sensitive to be successful in a business environment.

---

* I am hastily assured, when I make this "dehumanization" point to graduates of B-schools like Wharton and Harvard, that their school has "a huge emphasis on business ethics" to correct for the other courses of study in which students are immersed.

EXERCISE	FREQUENCY	PURPOSE
Go to the top of a building and look down on all the people below	Every day for six months	See how small we all are in the vast scheme of things
Find most obnoxious, lazy person in your working environment; spend at least fifteen minutes observing their complete uselessness and vacuity	Once a week for twenty-six weeks	Realize that many people are not worth saving while they jeopardize the success of the rest
Gain admittance to process-oriented meetings	Once a week until process is complete	See how much of success in business is defined by hard, objective metrics
Study the business news; find instances of corporate divestitures and layoffs; note effect on stock price	Every day for one year or until point is made	Learn how companies are rewarded for insensitive (and sometimes destructive) behavior by Wall Street
Get hammered after work with senior officers with neck sizes larger than twenty-two inches	Once a week for 104 weeks	Come face-to-face with guys who really don't give a shit about other people a lot of the time; see how they are rewarded
Seek out the biggest asshole in the corporation to whom you have access	Every day for as long as you can stand it	Develop the ability to imagine the destruction of others
Read your Company's 8K, 10K, and annual report filings with the SEC	When they are issued	Come face-to-face with how little you are making compared to the guys and girls who know the score
Go to the animal rescue shelter; do not leave with an animal	Every Saturday for three months	Learn that you can't save everybody
Go skiing	Once per winter, if it is not your sport	Note how many people actually shouldn't be doing something so dangerous and complicated and how they would probably be better off if they were home watching it on TV; imagine putting them there
Go golfing	Once per season, if it is not your sport	Recognize that you would actually be happy if somebody would put you out of your misery
Sit in on a budget review meeting	Once per quarter	Note how many finance people are at the table advising other people to cut their budgets; speculate how much cheaper it would be to run things if there were half that number

EXERCISE	FREQUENCY	PURPOSE
Have dinner at a very expensive restaurant and pay for it yourself	Once per year	Come to grips with the fact that you would be a lot happier if spending $850 on dinner didn't matter to you
Do something you're ashamed of; go out in the evening and drink until you don't care anymore	Once a week, then twice a week, then with increasing frequency until you can't even tell how often	Get over yourself

Sensitizing Exercises

These brief exercises are designed for those who are currently too insensitive to live with themselves and others and want to do better.

EXERCISE	FREQUENCY	PURPOSE
Fire somebody face-to-face*	Once every quarter, until you can no longer stand to do so	See if you can connect the action of terminating somebody with the pain that it causes
Go to work wearing a pair of underpants that's three sizes too small	Every day for a week	Feel what it's like to be uncomfortable around other people.
Alternatively, wear two socks of different colors, rip a large hole in your stocking, or shave only one side of your face. Go to work like that.	Once a week for a month	Live in fear that others will make fun of you
Get an invitation to a planning meeting. Every time someone suggests something cruel, stab yourself in the palm with a pin.	At least once a month, twice a month at budget time	Introduce physical pain into what would otherwise be a wholly intellectual exercise for you

---

* You might be surprised to know that the majority of officers who routinely eliminate people never do so face-to-face. If they had to do that, there might be fewer management consultancies in the world.

EXERCISE	FREQUENCY	PURPOSE
Go to a cheesy bar in a working-class section of the city in the middle of the day. Look at what it's like to not have a job.	Once a month for six months to two years, or however long it takes you to get the point	Associate consequences with your actions
Find the person in your department or area who is least liked and admired by everybody else. Take them to lunch.	Once a quarter	Just to be kind
Tell somebody mean that they're a schmuck	As the need arises	Going public with your alternative persona; exposing yourself to the risk of not being a schmuck in an environment filled with schmucks
Say hello to everybody for the entire day	Every day for a month, then see if you want to continue	Puncture the bubble that separates you from other people
Perform one act of random kindness every day	Three months, or until you stop nauseating yourself	Learn that there are different ways to treat people than what you've been used to
Celebrate Christmas every day of the year	Okay, that's enough of that	You don't want to lose your edge, do you?

Takeaway

Oh, and then there are a very few gifted souls who were born without sympathy for others. They usually become lonely deadbeats of one kind or another, ruthless criminals, or successful business moguls. Sometimes you get an individual who merges all these destinies and you end up with Bernard Madoff. Other times people actually evolve. Take Bill Gates, once a powerful mogul with a hunger to eradicate all competition and now a hugely admirable philanthropist who, with his wife, Melinda, actually makes a difference in the world.

Most of us, however, try to walk a middle line between being a heartless sociopath or an heir to Mother Teresa.

The majority of those studying this Curriculum will need to toughen up a bit. The rest will have to let some sunshine into their leaden, gray interiors. Either way, the goal is to achieve a proper level of daily insensitivity to others, on both a micro and a macro scale, one that allows you to operate without crushing internal conflicts or deterioration of all personal decency.

210.

A Short Course in Ethics

Ethics is a very annoying subject to a lot of people, and I take a huge risk in presenting it to you at the end of your Advanced Studies. It is classically the last thing they teach you in established business academies, where the subject is preceded by the widest variety of ways to fuck people over.

Why do we need to take the risk, then, of waylaying you along your merry course to Mastery of the Business Arts, pausing for a moment to consider the question? I don't know. Maybe it just feels right to do it. And that, my friends and students, is the whole deal about ethics. It shouldn't matter. Most of the time, it doesn't matter. Sometimes people will kill you dead if you mention the subject. And yet . . . for some reason . . . we like to feel good about what we do. And each of us has a line that we can't cross without feeling like it wasn't worth it. No matter how big the payday . . . it wasn't worth it. Naturally, history teems with businesspeople big and small who didn't suffer under any such ethical burden, including:

Roman emperors: Some were okay, but even a cursory look reveals a loony bunch of hedonistic, heedless idiots possibly poisoned by the lead in their water and empowered to do any nutty thing that came into their heads.

The Inquisition: Beware of mean people who think God is on their side.

Vlad the Impaler: Didn't lose a wink of sleep after impaling people.

Andrew Carnegie: Sometimes you have to show the workers who's boss, which means shooting some of them.

Imelda Marcos: You don't want the people getting in the way of your acquisition of that new pair of shoes.

Robber barons of the 1990s: Not going to mention them by name. The ones who are still alive are all big philanthropists now and I may need their medical wings some day.

Michael Bloomberg: He almost succeeded in eliminating giant sugary drinks! What a bastard!

This is obviously just a cursory list. Throughout the history of government, business, indeed all human enterprises, there were great leaders who had a serious problem reconciling their high ethical positions with their daily life. Thomas Jefferson was a champion of the freedom of all men whose record on the issue of slavery will keep historians busy for the next several centuries. Today, every banker whom you meet at a cocktail party has a stated position on ethics that he has to ignore when he goes to meetings at his place of business. Maybe not all the time, of course. Just when it's required.

The problem is, ethics are very easy to have until you need to exercise them. Then it's kind of amazing how many of them can be discussed rationally and modified. Like this:

Note that the circle begins again after the latest progression. Lots of people have a variety of reasons they'd be willing to bend the rules to make a little money, or a lot of money, while still maintaining their belief that it's wrong to steal . . . or for *other* people to steal . . . depending on what you think "steal" means . . . or whatever.

For some, though, there are some ethics that are nonnegotiable. Morrissey, the poet and musician, refused to go on the Jimmy Kimmel show with the *Duck Dynasty* beardoes, because he considered them "animal serial killers."* You may think he's silly, but that's an ethical position. Even people in business have to take one now and then. A few years ago, a trader at Goldman Sachs quit because he felt the firm was running its business to enrich its senior management at the expense of their customers. That was a personal ethical stance in an environment where very little of that is expected. Your bar may be higher or lower than the one of those around you. For instance, if you work for a company that puts antifreeze into kids' toothpaste, you may have to quit if you have a strong ethical problem with that. If you don't, you will remain. This is why companies that do bad things have so many bad people in them.

Each organization has a body of moral principles that govern a culture, whether each individual goes along with that culture or not. For instance, in our culture it is an ethical given that it is wrong to kill people. Everybody accepts that ethic, even though as a group, and sometimes individually, we kill people all the time, and many of our heroes kill dozens of them with impunity in movies dedicated to that activity. This is because underneath the stated ethos—which usually involves such things as honor, loyalty, honesty, and courtesy, among other attributes—there is always an accompanying unspoken ethos that gives individuals (and organized groups) the right to kill people who are doing something inconvenient. Whatever the stated ethic, by the way, the overriding, unspoken one in most business societies is success.

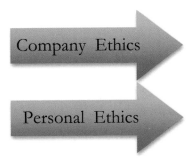

Figure #1: Optimal synthesis between
organizational and individual value systems

At the beginning of a career span, there may be an optimal synthesis between the values of the job and one's own personal value system (Figure 1). The employee wants to work hard, keep his or her nose clean, and perform his or her job as well as they can. That general framework is acceptable to the company as well.

---

* Their entire raison d'être being the killing of ducks.

Over time, however, the pressure to succeed—and by extension to make money, friends, and achievements of one kind or another—has a way of distorting the entire subject. Research reveals that ethical concerns are immediately affected by the introduction of the entire issue of money.

This is not to say that everybody who makes a lot of money will fudge the numbers. It is, however, easier for them to rationalize doing so. Rationalizations are at the heart of ethics moderation. Popular ones include:

- Everybody does this kind of thing.
- Nobody ever gave me a break, now I'm taking care of Number One.
- This is chickenfeed in comparison to what the big boys do.
- I was so naïve back then! Now I know the score.
- My family comes first, not the frickin' SEC.
- God, that feels good.

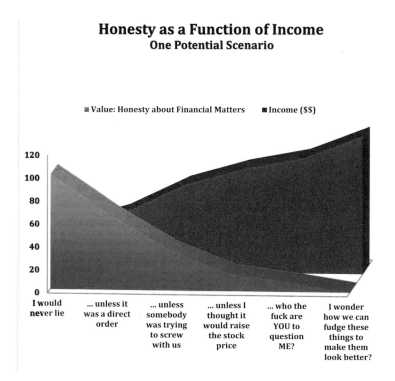

Honesty as a Function of Income
One Potential Scenario

These are only a few workable rationalizations. It's remarkable what people can come up with when they're working hard to get around doing the thing they feel to be right. And the subject doesn't have to be financial. You can pick a topic at random. During the course of a career—as money, responsibilities, power, and possessions accumulate—the values that deteriorate at one point or another may include:

- Loyalty to former partners/bosses
- Fidelity to spouse
- Attitude to pilfering company equipment and materials (pens, notebooks, champagne, hats, jackets, etc.)
- Attitude toward monkeying slightly with expense account (limos, food for friends, in-room movies)
- Insider trading

This is what you might see even if the company itself had the highest moral and ethical standards. Some do. They instruct their people not to bribe foreign governments, even when exhorted to do so by local elected officials; to avoid demanding sex in exchange for promotions even when they are tempted to do so; and to keep just one set of reliable books. In this case, when a company is kind of good and so are you, you will note that the organization's value system very slowly transcends and encompasses your own (Figure 2). This is not necessarily a bad thing, up to and until the day when you leave the enterprise, at which point you may find you have no value system whatsoever. This is quite common in Silicon Valley, where people who have become Googled or Facebooked go back into the real world and find themselves devoid of opinions that are not related to those of their former orthodoxies on such important issues as piracy, privacy, conflict of interest, hacking, leaking, and whether venture capitalists are good or bad guys.

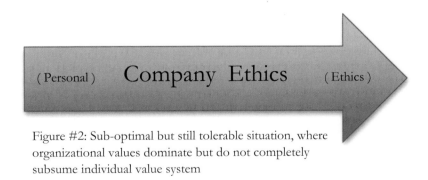

Figure #2: Sub-optimal but still tolerable situation, where organizational values dominate but do not completely subsume individual value system

Unfortunately, many corporations have ethics sequestered into a tiny room with the kiddie toys while the real business goes on elsewhere. Remember when you used to go to big Thanksgiving dinners and the children were seated in a small table in another part of the dining room? That's where they put ethics. You get the same food as the big table, but it's not always on the same china and flatware, and you're not always with the people who make the big bucks.

The culture inside a big investment bank in the first years of this century was not conducive to ethical (or at times even legal) behavior, and there was no reward offered to those who played by the rules. The primary ethic at that time seemed to be to avoid getting caught while you were gambling with other people's money.

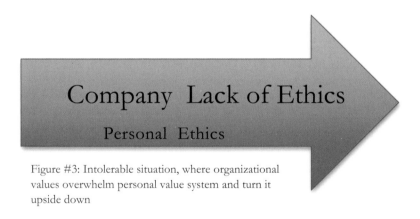

Company Lack of Ethics

Personal Ethics

Figure #3: Intolerable situation, where organizational values overwhelm personal value system and turn it upside down

In a situation like that one—when the business environment is rotten to the core—the individual trying to live up to certain standards may feel turned upside down (Figure 3). The goal then is twofold:

1. Get right with what's wrong and learn to live with it.
2. Get out.

Option 2 is, it goes without saying, very difficult, and as one gets older, almost impossible. The only thing telling you to leave is your bad feeling about something the company is doing. Except for that, you have a million reasons to stay, including all your responsibilities to yourself and your family, the friends you have made, the time you have put in, and how hard it is to replicate or improve upon your current job status. This is why you have former hipsters now extolling the virtues of nuclear power and erstwhile slackers who used to Take It To The Man now following behind gray-suited elephants with a broom and a dustpan. A high ethical standard is so much easier to maintain after people have all the money they need.

Our brief is *to be as ethical as we can be* on a day-to-day basis, even if the solutions we reach are not perfect, and we do not succeed in guiding matters always to the beginning, middle, and end we might have wished. In any complex situation, with decisions on the line, the general layout of individual behavior within the closed environment of the business ecosystem is likely to be as variegated as a hummingbird's wing.*

---

* "Individual Choice Within Complex Ethical Situations: A Quick Look at a Deep Subject," by Bing and Schwartz, © 2013, National Association for Serious Studies.

Ethical Options

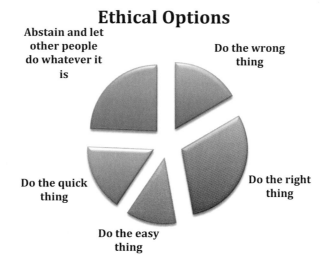

Abstain and let other people do whatever it is

Do the wrong thing

Do the right thing

Do the easy thing

Do the quick thing

Takeaway

Finally, it is simply important to know that matters of ethics and morality are not easy for the organization, either. What may seem complex but comprehensible to the individual may pose an impossible conundrum for the larger entity. There's a cost for "doing the right things" as well as the wrong ones. What if the decent thing to do will send the stock into a swoon? What's good for you may not be good for the company, and vice versa.

In short, you, your peers, and your organization are all in this together. The company is juggling regulatory questions, the threat of bad publicity, and the immediate punishment that Wall Street may inflict on any corporation that does a right thing that doesn't return immediate gratification to the almighty investors and their representatives. You, on the other hand, have to wrestle with your own ambitions, and the expectations of those who rely on you.

Finding your way to some ethical comfort level as you go about your business life will be one of the great challenges you will face going forward. Good luck with it. Don't expect perfection unless you become a rock star of one kind or another with all the time and money in the world.

300.

Tutorials and Electives

Beyond the powerful tools assembled in the Core Curriculum and the Advanced Curriculum you have just completed, there are a number of Tutorials and Electives that students may now select for further contemplation and study of issues that will pertain to latter phases of a successful career. Nobody need consider all of them as mandatory. But attention to these extremely terse, hard-hitting subjects will prepare the student for the moment where their mortarboard comes down and the rubber soles hit the road.

Tutorials

301. Care (and Feeding) of Senior Officers

A lifetime of attention must be paid to the ongoing issue of how to manage, and discreetly lead, those in charge of the big picture—an extension from the equally challenging topic of simple upward boss management. Senior officers are wholly unlike the simpler middle management from which they have sprung. It's the pressure. A brief study of marine biology yields a fair example of what pressure can do to an animal. Here is a fish that lives under normal pressure near the surface of its habitat:

Following is one of the denizens of the deepest part of the ocean, where the pressure of its atmosphere has helped to shape a number of interesting adaptations:

That is not a cartoon, ladies and gentlemen. That animal actually exists, in the very deepest part of the ocean. He has a little lantern on the end of a stalk that Mr. Darwin has given him to combat the darkness. And enormous teeth.

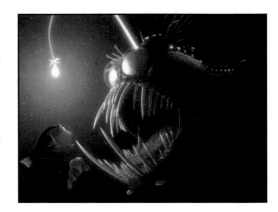

The implications are clear for those who wish to manage these creatures of the deep, the ones who live in darkness, with the force of six gravities pressing down on them.

- They are probably smarter.
- They are tougher.
- They have all the faults humanity is heir to on a much grander scale.
- They need more help and do less actual work. But everything they do feels very important.
- They are never wrong.
- They are less sensitive to others and more sensitive about themselves.
- They don't like to do their own killing.
- They reward their friends with tremendous generosity, because they can.
- They treasure their enemies above all else. They tend them well, until the moment they harvest and eat them.

Qualities that one must develop when seeking the big responsibility, big challenge, and much bigger money involved in serving the deepwater fish:

- Listen harder
- Wait longer
- Display greater courage, and . . .
- Eagerness, and . . .
- Calmness
- Be forever flexible
- Love the unlovable

In no way does a list like this minimize the challenge of dealing with everyday bosses. In many cases, they are equally if not more difficult. In terms of pettiness, for example, small, relatively powerless low middle managers will reign supreme. People who have a little bit of power are often the worst in keeping it in some modicum of control. And there is nothing more dangerous than a teeny-weeny ego puffed up for occasional industrial use. Extensive research over a thirty-year period reveals these interesting variances between the run-of-the-mill boss and the larger kahuna:

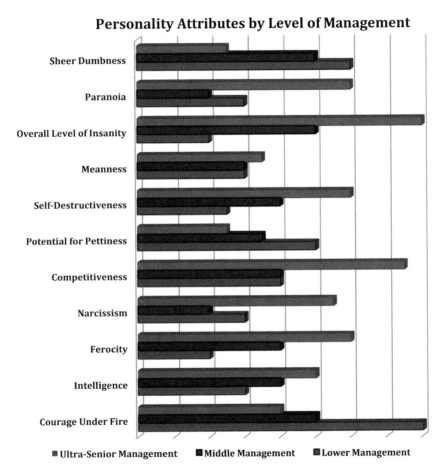

Personality Attributes by Level of Management

■ Ultra-Senior Management   ■ Middle Management   ■ Lower Management

Points of Interest on the Chart: All levels of management display an above average intelligence and capacity to be mean. Potential for pettiness is highest among those with the least power, while ultra-senior management dominates in the fields of narcissism, competitiveness, general ferocity on the job and overall level of insanity, showing, it is believed, how the demands of the job play on their psyches. For courage under fire and sheer dumbness, however, nobody beats your low-level boss. In most regards, middle management has earned its designation of being in the middle of everything. And in paranoia, ultra-senior management again dominates.

Students are referred to earlier units on management and power for suggestions on how to incorporate this data into their daily workflow. But as always, any strategic plan, no matter how dumb or uninviting, is better than none.

302. Town Car Management

Title is good. Money is better. But the best thing of all is perhaps the most elusive: a good, reliable car service.

Here are the three ruses, dodges, and lies told by despicable drivers who are not where they are supposed to be. In the first case, the driver is nowhere near the site. There are no "cops who made me go around the block." He's all the way across town driving as fast as he can to get to his client, who is standing in a rainy alcove at midnight with a heavy suitcase in the seediest part of town. In the second lie, the driver will not "be there in five minutes." He will be there in thirty-five minutes, because he overslept and is still on the freeway somewhere. The third instance is the most disgraceful. The client is precisely where he or she is supposed to be. The driver is about three blocks away, stuck in traffic because he stopped for coffee and misjudged the time. He is not "there" because the client is "there," wondering how two people can be "there" at the same time when one of them is clearly "not there."

Until this issue is solved, every trip is accompanied by anxiety. Will I get to the airport on time? What if the car doesn't show up and I need to get a taxi? It's raining, I'll never get one. I'll miss the plane! I'll miss my meeting. When I return, will the guy be there to pick me up? Will he be in the right place? Will he flake out altogether, leaving me to wait on a cab line that stretches around the block after my six-hour flight? I won't get home until 2 a.m.! And I have to be back at the office the next morning for a 7:30 breakfast with Bob!

That's just one imaginary but not unlikely scenario.

So the first criteria for success in car services is *reliability*, which is made up of two elements: punctuality and location. Both are important.

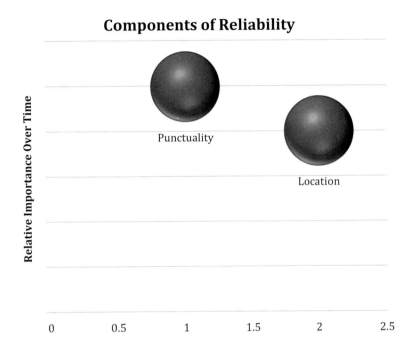

Components of Reliability

The issue of location is slightly trumped by the benefits of being on time. If the driver is actually there when he said he would be, a little mistake in placement may be forgiven. When you're late, you're late.

Criteria #2 is *the Driver*. Associated points:

- *Health:* Hacking and wheezing, sneezing, excessive nose blowing, clearing of throat in manner that suggests contagious respiratory illness, flatulence;*

---

* Sorry to be gross. But have you ever been in a car whose driver pulls over to urinate in a glass milk bottle as the interior of the vehicle fills with steam? I have.

- *Mental status:* Matters of concern include egregious displays of hostility, moody sur-liness, inappropriate merriment or disassociated ravings about UFOs, nutrition, who killed Kennedy, etc.;

- *Talking/Not talking:* A nice brief chat at 4:30 a.m. is always welcome, but a full one-hour conversation may not be; conversely, a driver who does not speak when spoken to is actually quite unsettling;

- *Route management:* Needs instructions to obvious places; eccentric choices end up taking twice the acceptable time; won't take directions when client offers them, even when obviously lost;

- *Commitment to safety:* Rollicking down the highway on Mr. Toad's wild ride; road rage leads to driver/driver confrontation on city streets with no means of escape; condition of car deteriorates before reaching destination.

Criteria #3 is *the Experience.* Of far less import than questions 1 and 2, the experience essentially boils down to the service Being There and Getting You There. But a good car service makes you feel like you're important to them. You want to be recognized when you call. You want, potentially, to have the same guys pick you up over a period of months and years. You want the cars to smell nice and not be falling apart. All of those things count. You have a right to them. You have a right not to be left screaming by the side of the road somewhere when your car fails to show. You have the right to have a cordial person driving you who is sober and doesn't want to kill both of you in a ball of fire because he's so depressed.

Oh, and don't cheat on your limo rides. They're as bad as in-room movies when it comes to scrutiny. The one thing controllers look for is waiting time, by the way. You can get away with a lot in terms of cars used for legit purposes . . . but one minute of questionable waiting time will get you thrown into the brig for sure.

303. Giving an Effective Presentation

I will take this opportunity to tell a little story at my own expense that illustrates what an ineffective presentation can do to a business audience. In this case, I was the audience, and a high official at the National Aeronautics and Space Administration (NASA) was the offending presenter. This took place a while ago, so the technology of presenting was slightly different than it is today. But the essentials of the tale are timeless, I think.

At the time, my company was obsessed with Quality. Not quality. Quality—with a capital Q. There's a difference.* Small-*q* quality is a real thing that attaches itself to products and services that make customers happy. Big-*Q* Quality is a productivity movement that's been torturing employees for nearly a hundred years under various guises. My company's version that year took us to Disney College at Walt Disney World in Orlando, Florida. At this august institution, the study of Quality and how to achieve it in a workforce went on 24/7, with workshops, lectures, and demonstrations interrupted by meals and nights of revelry. One night our entire management group went off campus for dinner and festivities. I don't remember much of it, except that we got in at 3:30 a.m. and were required to be up, bright-eyed and bushy-tailed, at 7 a.m. for breakfast. Then there was a bus ride of some duration, followed by a fabulous tour of the NASA Quality facility, which had yet to suffer its tragic loss of face after the explosion of the space shuttle Challenger.

I believe we went to Cape Canaveral, which is due east of Disney. I woke up there in a chair, surrounded by my colleagues, extremely hungover, very tired. The room darkened. A guy in a uniform walked in with a stack of overheads under his arm.† "Good morning," he said, and put the first graphic up on the projector. The next thing I recall was the very sharp elbow of my friend Mark, the president of one of our operating divisions, jamming into my ribs. "Hey!" he whispered in my ear, so close I could feel the heat of his mint-drenched breath. "Wake up, you stupid motherfucker." I sat up and thrust a sharpened pencil into my palm. The officer was talking, ironically, about O-rings, the part of the shuttle that failed a year or so later. "These are the production specifications of this important piece of equipment," he said, and changed the graphic to one featuring a cross section of the item. The next thing I remember, the heel of Mark's casual footwear was digging into the top of my arch. It hurt. "Hey," he said, looking forward as if he were paying attention to the presentation but with his eyes boring into me with something approaching total contempt. "Come on, man," he said. "If you're going to sleep, at least don't fucking snore."

---

* For further definition of this term, see the Glossary of Key Vocabulary.

† Overheads were a technology of presentation that preceded computer projection. They were about 8.5"x11" transparencies, quite beautiful when done correctly, that were displayed on a light table known as an "overhead projector," which illuminated their images and threw them up on an old fashioned screen. They were very expensive to produce and colored ones were considered the absolute state of the art in presentation graphics until around the turn of the twenty-first century.

I had been snoring, you see. Several people around me in the audience seemed to be laughing their asses off and doing their best not to let it show, snorting into their hands, shaking uncontrollably, that kind of thing. At that point, I got up and walked out. Washed my face. Got a breath of air. Went back in. For the next hour, the routine was repeated. I sat. I lost consciousness in the boredom that immediately precedes brain death. The NASA guy slowly worked his way inexorably in the darkened room through ten, twenty, fifty, one hundred overheads. And then they woke me from my final coma and we all went home.

I never want to go through anything like that again. And I never want to impose an experience like that on anybody, either. Which is why students are encouraged to observe the following rules when it comes to presentations of all kinds, even financial ones.

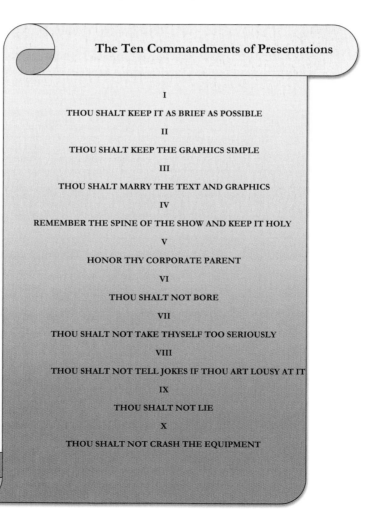

The Ten Commandments of Presentations

I

THOU SHALT KEEP IT AS BRIEF AS POSSIBLE

II

THOU SHALT KEEP THE GRAPHICS SIMPLE

III

THOU SHALT MARRY THE TEXT AND GRAPHICS

IV

REMEMBER THE SPINE OF THE SHOW AND KEEP IT HOLY

V

HONOR THY CORPORATE PARENT

VI

THOU SHALT NOT BORE

VII

THOU SHALT NOT TAKE THYSELF TOO SERIOUSLY

VIII

THOU SHALT NOT TELL JOKES IF THOU ART LOUSY AT IT

IX

THOU SHALT NOT LIE

X

THOU SHALT NOT CRASH THE EQUIPMENT

These would seem to be simple commandments, but they are often broken. The multitudes still worship at the Golden Calf of too much PowerPoint, in true belief that a big dog-and-pony show with all the trimmings will wow people instead of actually putting them to sleep or despair.

Just know this: The vast majority of us can now focus on any one thing for about twenty minutes, if we try very hard.

304. Consultants

All organizations have gaps in their operating efficiency. They do a variety of things to plug them. If a small town in the Old West had a crime problem, they first looked around for a fellow citizen to step in. If none was to be had, they hired a gunslinger. The gunslinger would come in and kill whoever needed killing. After that, he might even become the new sheriff, even if his entire prior career had been as an outlaw.

When a crime family needed to hit an enemy in their jurisdiction but had nobody who could later claim deniability, they called in a hit man from Chicago or St. Louis who got the job done and left town on the next train.

When Richard III couldn't muster enough men to fight those who opposed his move on the throne, he summoned mercenaries from all over Europe to swell his ranks. The same was true of George Washington, who needed seasoned fighting men, as opposed to farmers with muskets. So he called Germany, and brought in a bunch of Hessians. For years, if any baseball team needed a guy who could hit for high on-base percentage and steal bases at a record pace, they called Rickey Henderson, who worked for them until everybody got sick of him again.

Business organizations do the same thing. The law department is great at contracts but has no one dedicated to full-time litigation. They hire an outside counsel. Finance doesn't have the hands to evaluate a proposed acquisition. They hire a few investment banks who immediately begin to generate fees for themselves while they do some due diligence. They don't trust their PR department with heavy lifting in a crisis. They call in Edelman or Kekst or Rubenstein or Abernathy MacGregor or, if they're really in trouble, they call Matthew Hiltzik. Google him and you'll see what I mean.

If the need is less crisis-driven and reputational and more about "achieving productivity," "doing more with less," or "creating operating efficiencies," however, they call in a hit team from Chicago. No, wait. That was the mobsters. In business, they call in Bain or McKinsey or what is called a "management consultant." It is possible that such firms do something other than fire people—but in the end their solutions are geared to end up with fewer people and lower costs. Then they leave town on the next train.

What this means is that 1) it is most often best for existing employees if organic internal solutions are found; 2) when they can't, consultants should come in with very focused briefs in which of their areas of expertise are needed to complete a specific task; and 3) beyond that, management consultants must be avoided at all cost.

There are excellent reasons why management hires them, though:

- They don't know what else to do.

- Their bosses are breathing down their necks.

- They don't really care about the business. They're here to boost their careers.

- Occasionally, consultants have areas of expertise that may actually help.

This last consideration is undeniably true in certain cases. But even when that's the case, the benefit is not economic.

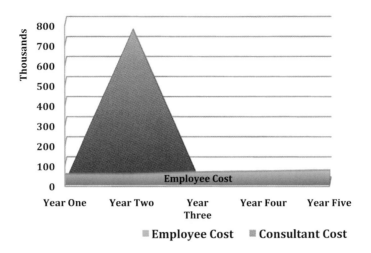

According to these estimates, the dedicated single employee, who is also tasked to figure out ways of operating cheaper and more productively, will equal the cost of the consultant in the twenty-fifth year of his tenure.

There are a few things to think about as you pursue this important line of study throughout your career.

- There will be consultants; some may even be useful.

- To oppose the consultant publicly is to fly in the face of senior management, which has a crush on him/her/it. The appearance of cooperation is better.

- No consultant will ever recommend the ouster or humiliation of the person or persons who pay their fee, so the closer you are to that entity the safer you are.

- The consultant will eventually go away. They're like toys. After a while, those who hired it become impatient for one reason or another and find another toy to play with.

The time to stop a management consultant is *before* it is hired. Therefore, always push for internal solutions to a gap in the organization. Sometimes you will succeed. Remember that a comfortable, confident senior management with a staff it trusts has no need for consultants. If your boss or bosses feels squirrelly around the edges, in the end you have nobody to blame but yourself.

305. Business Metaphor

There are several sectors of industry that have contributed their lingo to ours over time.

- Farm and Field
  - ✔ The dog won't hunt.
  - ✔ We've got to get our ducks in a row.
  - ✔ We can't put all our eggs in one basket.
  - ✔ The chickens are coming home to roost.
  - ✔ What a horse's ass.

- Radio, Television, and Electronics
  - ✔ That really turned me on.
  - ✔ He's not on my wavelength.
  - ✔ She's really plugged in.
  - ✔ Stop giving me static.

- Military
  - ✔ Run it up the flagpole and see if anybody salutes.
  - ✔ Fly in tighter circles.
  - ✔ Field-strip it and get it ready for battle.
  - ✔ Take a bullet for your buddy.
  - ✔ Fall on a grenade for the team.
  - ✔ Murphy's got the con.
  - ✔ Let's drop the big one.

- Sports
  - ✔ Let's huddle up.
  - ✔ We're gonna have to punt.
  - ✔ We can get it into the red zone but nobody around here can punch it across the goal line.
  - ✔ We're gonna call an audible.
  - ✔ We're great at the blocking and tackling but our air game sucks.
  - ✔ Okay, Bob. You're up.

✔ The stock has done a six-bagger since 2012.*
✔ He struck out with the bases loaded.
✔ She popped up to the pitcher.
✔ I can't do the job if you take the bat out of my hands.
✔ He's okay off the tee, but he's got a lousy short game.
✔ Let's just lob it in there and see if anybody can return it.
✔ Goooooooooooooooal!

○ Computer Programming
   ✔ I'm not interfacing with your scenario, babe.
   ✔ I don't have the bandwidth for that today.
   ✔ It's a robust idea, but not scalable.
   ✔ I'm going to take this offline with the guys and get back to you.
   ✔ We need to upgrade PR.
   ✔ It's not a cliché, Ed. It's a meme.

○ Psychology
   ✔ Let's not get hung up with statistics.
   ✔ I'm getting pretty sick of his ego trips.
   ✔ You'll have to excuse my yawning. I've got ADD.
   ✔ You'll have to excuse my hostility. I've got ADHD.
   ✔ You have to excuse Bob's behavior. He's a sociopath.

○ Organized Crime
   ✔ We'll make him an offer he can't refuse.
   ✔ Bob doesn't want to whack him. Bob wants you to whack him.
   ✔ I'm a retired businessman living on a pension.
   ✔ This is the life we've chosen for ourselves.
   ✔ It's business. It's not personal.

○ Surfing
   ✔ Dude!

---

* Sextupled its value. A stock that has gone from $5 to $30 has performed a "six-bagger."

✔ Gnarly quarter, bro.

✔ I'm sick of his bogus projections.

✔ Last year's bonus was a bummer. This year's was more bitchin' 'cause we maxed out of the grid.*

✔ The entire M&A team is stoked about this acquisition.

These are obviously just a few. Each world has contributed far more and the list is growing—and shrinking—daily. It is the wise student who keeps his list pruned and updated regularly, and notes the trends expressed by senior management. You want to be new, but not too new. And you certainly don't want to be caught thinking you're cool when the phrase you've used is totally bogus because it jumped the shark so last century ago.

---

* Translation: Last year's bonus was really terrible. This year's was better because we exceeded the requirements on the performance grid established by the board's Compensation Committee.

306. Sex at the Office

The subject of sex at the office is immensely complex, freighted with moral and even religious baggage. It is included here because no matter how far you go and far you get, sex will always be an issue, if not for you, then for somebody who works for you, somebody you work for, who has either been tempted by sex, exalted by sex, or—more likely—destroyed by sex. Here are some thought problems for those trying to make generalizations or create some form of personal policy in these matters:

AFFAIR/RELATIONSHIP	OUTCOME	FORESEEABILITY %
The head of sales for a major manufacturing company with a well-known record of assistant-lechery initiates an affair with a blond, synthetic assistant who has a record of serial liaisons with executives. It goes on for some time until she quits and sues the company for sexual harassment and establishing an unfriendly work environment.	She gets a payout of several million dollars and is now living somewhere in the beautiful Southwest. He is now a top executive at another company.	100%
An internationally famous, married executive meets an editor at a world-renowned business publication. She is newly married to someone else. Still, romance ensues between the mogul and the editor, then divorce for them both. His is particularly acrimonious and reveals many aspects of his deal with his company and his personal finances as well.	The mogul and the editor are married. Both reputations remain robust and unsullied and each is highly regarded as an organizational philosopher of the first order.	37%

AFFAIR/RELATIONSHIP	OUTCOME	FORESEEABILITY %
A middle manager in a huge global insurance company where gray is the dominant color adopts his assistant as a mentee, bringing her along in the organization, helping her extricate herself from a long-term abusive relationship, selling her his used car for a pittance, and otherwise making her life better. She is a flamboyant, impulsive, dramatic individual who dresses in bright colors and otherwise provides a bit of sunshine in the life of the office. She is also, unbeknownst to her colleagues, suffering from bipolar 1 disorder, which, in its more florid phases, subjects her to both auditory and visual hallucinations. No sexual activity of any kind occurs during the life of this relationship, although there is much affection and communication.		
Her hallucinations having reached epic proportions, the assistant begins holding religious meetings in empty offices of the corporation. She sees employees walking about in "raiments soaked in blood" around their private parts, and imagines all conversations are sexual in nature and pertain to her. The quality of her work declines. The HR department takes matters into its own hands and terminates her. She sues for sexual harassment. She loses at the EEOC level and then sues at a civil level. She loses there, too.	In spite of the discrediting of her case, her former mentor is eased out of his position at the corporation and forced to "retire" at the age of forty-eight. He is currently unemployed.	23%

AFFAIR/RELATIONSHIP	OUTCOME	FORESEEABILITY %
She is a very senior executive at an advertising agency. He is her subordinate, although a player in his own right. One day she meets the man of her dreams and gets married. Her former lover retains his position in the company, but seethes, dreams of the old days, drags himself around in mourning. One night there is a party. She is there with her new husband. Her former lover is there, too, alone. He gets drunk off his ass, more drunk than he has ever been before, and suddenly decides that now is the time to air all his grievances. In public. Much screaming ensues and everybody is horrendously humiliated.	Nothing. Everybody continues as before. To fire anybody would lead to even more public embarrassments, not to mention the possibility of legal action. So things go on as they were. Years go by. And after a while, everything is forgotten, all is forgiven, and everybody is the best of friends.	8%
Oliver and Julia have known each other for years. He is her boss in the research department of a large corporation. He is married and lives on the West Coast. She is unmarried and lives on the East Coast. While he is her superior, she has a fine title and large responsibilities and in a real sense they are colleagues. His marriage is not happy. Long nights, he sits in his upholstered den in the San Fernando Valley bedroom community, where he and his wife have raised their three boys, all of whom are now in college or out in the world. He is very lonely.		

AFFAIR/RELATIONSHIP	OUTCOME	FORESEEABILITY %
Increasingly, his duties take him to the East Coast, where he and Julia continue to work amicably in close but platonic proximity. Oliver turns fifty. One day, suddenly, after years of close association and increasingly affectionate conversation—at the office, over drinks, over dinner— Oliver and Julia realize that they have fallen in love. After a period of secrecy, they confess their situation to the CEO of the company, who wishes them well and takes them both out to dinner.	Oliver and Julia now live together in a nice apartment in Manhattan. They are quiet about their relationship. There are no public displays of affection. But their status is well known to their colleagues, who are happy for them both.	.027%

These examples are offered as evidence that when it comes to these matters, Chuck Berry had it right: "C'est la vie, say the old folks," the poet wrote. "It goes to show you never can tell."

The problem for students who wish to dabble or plunge into this form of life experience is that this profound and inexorable uncertainty is the antithesis of the clear-eyed, strategic approach that this Curriculum stands for.

There are times, however, when, in pursuit of happiness, or wealth, or both, the most sensible thing is to abandon sensible things, say what the hell to yourself, and jump.

307. Drunkenness and Other Maladies

Management of personal excess is a key issue for a long and successful business career. Leading forms of maladjustment now proven to be permissible within a business enterprise include:

◦ *Alcoholism*, as long as one shows up on time and is capable of comporting oneself with dignity in all daytime situations.

◦ *Use of drugs.* Cocaine has always been the business drug of choice in the music business, and the occasional appearance of weed among sixtyish ex-hippies now in high senior management has also been noted. Use of legal prescription drugs, of course, is assumed, including Lunesta, Prozac, Lexapro, and Zoloft, all of them usually mixed with vodka.

⊙ *Work addiction.* Not only tolerated but encouraged.

⊙ *Insomnia.* As long as one doesn't compensate for sleep deprivation by napping in open meetings.*

⊙ *Rampant personality disorders*, such as displays of high temper, depression, paranoid attacks of anxiety, etc., most of which are identified as management styles.

Conversely, there is associated punishment for failing to indulge in some of these areas of abuse:

⊙ *Alcohol:* Some people don't drink. They suffer several annoying consequences:

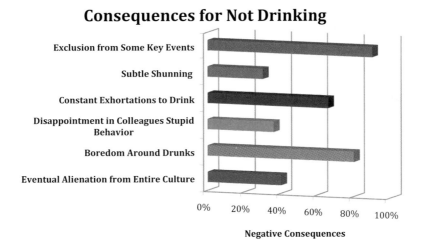

Consequences for Not Drinking

There are no punishments for not taking drugs, although one may be excluded from dubious activities.

---

* Exceptions are made for those held in great affection, who attain mascot status when they obviously attempt to fight their overwhelming meeting narcolepsy, and for elderly CEOs, chairmen, and board members, who can drool as much as they want.

In some cultures there is heavy weather indeed, however, for those who are not afflicted with work addiction. Those who seek to avoid nighttime stress fests, weekend circle jerks, and destruction of holidays may have to find other employment in some organizations. A large percentage of senior managers find the statement "If you don't come in Saturday, don't bother to come in Sunday" amusing. It isn't.

We have spent some time during this curriculum in discussion of various forms of mental illness that are rewarded in business life—brutality, narcissism, bossiness, the inability to see other people as real entities whose lives have equal value to one's own. As society changes, as our technology and our standards of living change, these factors shift and mutate as well. In the late twentieth century, for example, mean, tough sadists and narcissists held sway in a lot of corporations and were celebrated in the slavish business media for their "tough, no-nonsense" ways and their "take-no-prisoners" attitudes.

Today, a form of unemotional, stunted autism is more the norm, as electronics fill our empty heads and those afflicted with terminal weirdness ascend to the billionaires list. Whatever the pathology du jour, it will require management.

308. Going off the Grid

As recently as the late twentieth century, it was possible to differentiate the working day from its counterpart. One arrived at the workplace at a certain time. There was, perhaps, an hour in the middle of the day that one might take for oneself (sometimes less, for genuine slaves of the system; sometimes more, for those who ran it), then it was back to whatever passed for work until quitting time.

At all other times, it was possible to be "off." You would wake up after a night of sleep uninterrupted by messages and demands from work. You would perhaps read the paper or listen to the radio while you ate your breakfast. Then you would go to work. When you left that establishment, it was to repair to a bar where all talk of the job was verboten unless it involved ragging on the powers that be. After that, you could go out to dinner without being disrupted by someone rushing in and demanding your attention over some ostensibly pressing matter (unless something was actually burning down). After dinner, you would go home, kiss your spouse, kick the dog, and go to sleep. There was a possibility, in those days, before time as we know it collapsed into one festering rain forest of tweeting and buzzing, that you could wake at 3 a.m., filled with apprehension and anxiety about the day to come. But there was nothing to occupy and perpetuate the anxiety right away. Nothing to feed your disquiet. And so, after a few moments of tossing and turning, you could think, "Aw, fuck it." And go back to sleep.

Today, things are so very different. If you are on the West Coast, that 3 a.m. waking may have been caused by the silent light of your iPhone going off as the first east coast e-mails start coming in. Many people I know, when they wake for a glass of water in the middle of the night, compulsively reach for their digital assistant, the antidote to sleep. After scanning a handful (or a host) of aggravating stuff, they fall into a fitful doze at dawn, only to be awakened fifteen minutes later by their ringtone alarm. They dress while peering into the device. Nobody eats breakfast at home anymore; there are too many issues that must be addressed first thing. Besides, breakfast would just involve the entire family sitting at the same table having their brains sucked out through their little machines.

At the office, thanks to the immediacy of digital communications, there is no lag time between event and reaction. At lunch, a lot of stuff can happen while you're away. Bob could call. There could be e-mails or text messages that need to be responded to immediately. Maybe if you're really powerful and resolute, you can put your device away long enough to eat your salad and have a little chat with whomever you're with. After work . . . well, there is no after work.

Hours When Worst Crises Occur

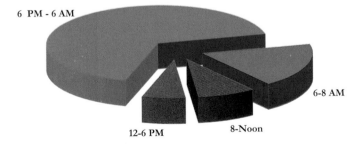

Research replete with genuine experiential data indicates that, since the advent of digital ubiquity, by far the worst situations develop either late at night or in the very early morning, with the preponderance of trouble popping up after 9 p.m., when just about everybody has been thinking and drinking.* A plethora of crazy things can happen at dinner. Later on, as the hours stretch toward midnight, senior management—left alone without subordinates for too long—plunges into a vat of apprehension. The only way to ease that is to start sending messages. The same is true of the hours immediately after waking, when the morning blogs and other forms of pseudo-intelligence make themselves known.

There exists an X factor about these things that is not explainable by any rational means. The planning and labor required to fix the problems may take place during working hours. But the intrusion of the dramatic crisis into the lives of those it affects most often takes place during the hours that used to be considered "off."

All of this demands that the long-term player now and then escape completely. This is known as "going off the grid."

A successful strategy for "going off the grid" takes a lifetime to develop, maintain, and grow. But the essence of it lies in *preparation for the break* with those whose own working patterns have come to depend on yours. Of secondary but almost equal importance is the selection of a place to go that is not wholly dependent on your willpower. Some have already been discussed. Personally, I have found that a remote corner of the Julian Alps somewhere in the no-man's-land between Austria and Slovenia is a highly effective choice. There are portions of the South Pacific that also serve, but one may still be eaten there by a swarm of bloodsucking correspondence. Choose well. For no matter how hard you try, no matter how determined you are to lay in your strategy of breaking away, *they will try to get to you.*

As for preparation, you must assume a certain irrational reaction on the part of those who rely on you. They will seem prepared emotionally for your departure. But they are not, really. Let's look at one example from our files:

This case is by no means atypical. The individual in question prepared her boss well for her ten-day hike in the Amazon. Two months out, awareness that she would be unavailable for exploitation began to penetrate, along with marginal preparation for that situation. One month out, things were looking good, and there was a crescendo of awareness and readiness a week before the date when she would go off the grid. The day before, however, the executive to whom she reports had a total relapse, apparently forgetting that she had any plan to go away and professing shock and dismay that she would be unavailable for a very big project that had suddenly appeared. Armed with the knowledge that this was to be expected, however, the employee did what

---

* "During Dinner and Immediately Afterward: An Investigation into the Timing of Serious Organizational Crises," © 2013, National Association for Serious Studies.

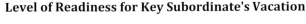

Level of Readiness for Key Subordinate's Vacation

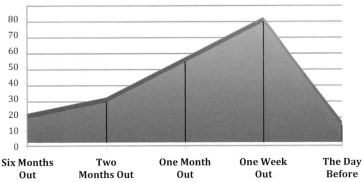

this course of study should now have prepared you to do: She left, having not only prepared her boss but her colleagues for her departure as well. The work was covered. The boss, after a time, stopped hyperventilating. And she got off the grid for just about as long as she could stand it, and was only too happy to get back to work.

309. Leveraging Without a Lever

here are times when you don't have power at all, others where you only have a little. This doesn't mean you don't need to get things done the way you want to. For the most part, this would involve "leveraging" your little bit of power to move objects and tasks bigger than you. Traditional business metaphor would invoke the use of a lever:

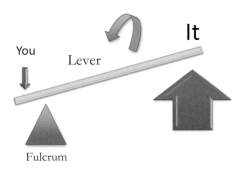

Traditional levers may include ...

- Sheer force
- Mutual need
- Guilt
- Affection
- Quid pro quo assumptions
- Possibility of reward/punishment
- Imposition of paranoia/fear
- Perception of debt
- Aggression

Without one of these, the party seeking to leverage is left without a lever:

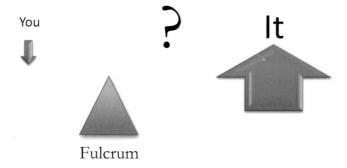

Fulcrum

This is indeed a sorry situation. All you have at this point is:

- You
- It
- The fulcrum
- A lot of dead space between you and It

What is to be done? Upon reflection, the answer is quite obvious. To move It, you must tip the fulcrum over on its side and wedge it underneath the objective to be moved, like this:

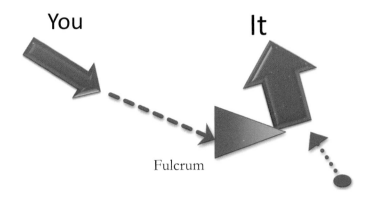

You It

Fulcrum

Two outcomes are rendered obvious by this:

- "It" is moved, but not optimally and in a funky direction, and;
- With no lever at hand, the fulcrum attains greater prominence, and must be acted upon directly by "you."

What, then, is this fulcrum that was formerly nothing more than an inanimate object placed beneath your lever, rendering that lever capable, as Archimedes said, of "moving the world," now transformed into an active agent in your behalf?

The fulcrum is variously defined as:

- An agent through which vital powers are exercised;
- A thing that plays a central or essential role in an activity, event, or situation;
- Any prop or support;
- One that supplies capability for an action;
- A spinelike scale occurring in rows along the anterior edge of the fins in primitive bony fishes such as the sturgeon.

I believe we may safely discard the last definition. This leaves us with a very clear strategy. When you need to move a heavy object with no lever on hand to help you do so, you must instead rely on:

- An agent through which your vital powers are exercised;
- A thing that plays a central or essential role in the activity, event, or situation you want to take place;
- Any support you can obtain for your goals . . .
- . . . in the form of a person who can "supply capability for an action."

What does this mean? It means it's time to ask for help. I suggest starting with your boss. If your boss can't do anything for you, stick a fulcrum under his butt and get him to ask his boss to do it. Leveraging without a lever is simply another form of managing up.

And while you're at it, go out and get a lever. If everybody is going to continue leveraging everything, you really can't leave home without one.

310. Is There Anything You Won't Do?

We dealt with this issue a bit in our final discussion of the Advanced Curriculum, the one on ethics. Of course, on first blush you will say "Yes, for sure, there are many things I wouldn't do." And then the time comes and oops, there you go. Here, for purposes of discussion, are some delicate things that may come up. Ask yourself:

Would you neglect to tell a colleague about a meeting with Bob that she should probably attend, so you could take the meeting by yourself?

Would you tell your husband that the five-hundred-dollar cash withdrawal you drunkenly made from the ATM at Dixxxie Dudes in New Orleans took place when you popped into that establishment for a moment to grab some cash for your dinner with the finance department?

Would you try to get the company to pay for the macadamia nuts you had from the hotel honor bar in your room, even though you know that anything you get from that area is absolutely not considered a legitimate expense?

Would you pass along a rumor about an upcoming deal to a friend who could trade on the information? What if *everybody* was doing it?

Would you sell a mortgage-backed security instrument, even though you knew that at another part of your firm there were guys who were making huge investment bets against that very same product? What if *everybody* was doing it?

Would you grant loans to people who clearly did not fit any definition of a good risk? What if that was the only way to get new business and, you know, *everybody* was doing it?

Would you foreclose on the mortgage later, in order to make a profit on the situation, even though you knew that the foreclosure was illegal? (Of course you wouldn't. But then, you're not a banker yet.)

Would you tell your boss you were "working from home" when really what you were doing was going skiing?

Would you send private e-mails to your friends and family from your company e-mail on your office computer? Did you know there were policy regulations forbidding that?

How many regulations, when you come down to it, do you consider demeaning, counterproductive, impossible to live up to, nonsensical, and arbitrary? Does that give you the right to flaunt them? Of course it does. But which?

Would you sit at a meeting where an enormous and nonstrategic divestiture was decided upon and say nothing? Even if you knew that the move was being made to protect the bonuses of the guys who were making the decision?

Would you cross a picket line, even though your dad was a union shop steward? Did you know that most of the anti-labor lawyers I have known had parents who were union men and women, some of them important organizers?

Would you sit around a big boardroom table while ancient trolls and ogres cackle over a succession of racist and sexist jokes? They're the bosses of your bosses of your bosses! Would you speak up?

Would you order a $500 bottle of wine for you and your legitimate business dinner companion and put it on the company? Why not the $250 bottle? How about a $2,500 bottle? If you could get away with it?

Would you have a clandestine affair with an attractive colleague? How about an attractive subordinate? How about several? Why not? You're not married. Oh, wait. You are?

Would you gossip about the things your bosses reveal about themselves when they are in their cups? Who would you gossip to? A reporter? If you were completely and 100 percent off the record?

Would you order the firing of a whistle-blower who seems to have found a problem in the new pharmaceutical your company just got past the FDA?

Would you quash a report that indicated there was an electrical problem with the most important new aircraft your company had produced in thirty years?

Would you ignore reports of sexual harassment in one of your field operations because it would be embarrassing? How about reports of child abuse in a sports program sponsored by your company? What if that kind of thing had been going on for a hundred years, as it was in the Boy Scouts? Would you put the reputation of the organization ahead of the safety of the children? Remember! You love the Boy Scouts!

Would you backdate stock options to make sure they were profitable for you and the guys whom you reward them with? It was common practice a few years ago. You wait until the stock gets to a certain number, then you issue options to buy that stock at the much lower price it was a few years ago, dated appropriately. Hundreds of firms were doing it, mostly on the Internet. Fewer than twenty people have been successfully prosecuted for it. Now you probably couldn't get away with it. But back then? Would you have done it?

Would you send dissidents to Siberia when they got on your nerves? How about to the sales office in Fresno, California?

Would you sell baby formula you knew did not pass U.S. standards to third-world countries, as Nestlé did a few years ago?

Would you put poison in pet food and distribute it internationally, like Chinese manufacturers have done? How about that toothpaste for kids that they put ethylene glycol in for flavoring? Would you do that in order to make your numbers? What about the toys covered with the poisoned paint? You've got revenue projections to hit. Would you do something like that to hit them?

What would you do if you wouldn't? Would you quit? What if everybody is doing whatever it is you don't want to do? Is your welfare and that of your family less important than your fussy scruples?

You'd do everything to protect your home, your well-being, your standing in the world, your kids' education, that trip to Kauai you've got planned for Christmas.

Is there anything you wouldn't do?

You don't need to answer right now. You'll get a chance, when the time comes.

311. Losing Your Mojo

It's been a long day. It's been a long, long day in the middle of a long, long week. And that long, long week is floating on a vast lake in a chain of weeks in the middle of a long, long year that is simply a tributary of the ocean of years, it seems, that you have been alive.

When was the last time you had a promotion? When was the last time you had a raise that was more than 3 percent? They want you to say thanks for the 3 percent, too, don't they.

In the morning, you sit in the same car you've had for the last couple of years and wait for the light to change. Or you stand in the middle of a weird, sleepy crowd, each person with coffee cup in hand, hanging on by a hook in the ceiling, and stare into the middle distance to make sure you don't meet anybody's eyes, as your subway waits between stations, leaking air. Or you perch quietly on the cracked plastic seat of the commuter train as the sun begins to rise, trying to filter out the obnoxious noise of the idiots who will talk on their cell phones while everybody else is trying to sleep, or read, or simply wink out of consciousness.

And you think to yourself, "How long is this going to go on?"

It's going to go on for another couple of decades. You're in business. The job doesn't only mean loving the smell of napalm in the morning, the clang of battle as cascades of adversaries clash on the open field, the late-night wassails after the fight is done. There's that, of course. But that's not even the tough part.

It means doing it on the days where there's nothing doing. It means answering to an asshole for a couple of years. It means waiting for the old to die and the dangerous enemies to fall on their own sword, as they so often do. The company sells your subsidiary, merges your department with another. Decides to move everybody to Des Moines, maybe. Des Moines is not so bad. You move to Des Moines for a few years. After a while, you think, "How do I get back to San Francisco?" And yet you do not go. You hold on and see what's going to happen for a while.

And during one of those times, you lose your mojo.

It's only natural. Mojo is a delicate compound:

- ▪ Pride
- ▪ Forward Momentum
- ▪ Power
- ▪ Money
- ▪ Sexual Energy
- ▪ Hope

MOJO COMPONENTS

Any one element can grow and overwhelm the others. If you get a bunch of new money, for instance, you can do without enormous influxes of sexual energy or power for a while. If you achieve some cool attribute that speaks to your power, you may even be able to forgo your customary interest in new money. If you know that you are capable of dominating your own sex and alluring the opposite (or the same, as the case may be), you may find the other requirements diminishing in importance. In the end, though, you need a little of all these things. Most of all, hope. You need hope.

Roger is now a senior officer in a large multinational corporation. He has, at the age of sixty, achieved something close to the fuck-you money for which he has worked a lifetime. He has a good family life, is in love with his wife, has a few grandkids on the way. In short, he has it made. You would think this was because, over a career that spanned thirty years, he had exuded mojo over long periods of time, and sustained his level of the stuff with the great consistency that be-speaks success in business. Au contraire. Here is a true look at his mojo over the years in which he was achieving his various dreams and objectives:

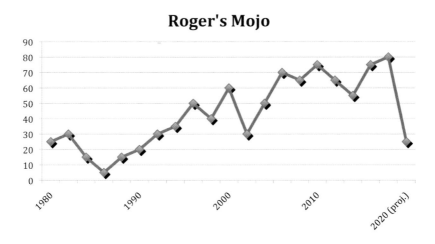

Sometime after 1980, Roger did not get a promotion he was anticipating. It was given to some-one who spent most of his time drinking and crying on the phone to his lawyer behind closed doors about his impending divorce. At that point, Roger lost almost all of his mojo. He spent the next few years building it back. In the mid-1990s, thanks to a good internal mojo production ca-pacity, he achieved liftoff, sustaining another setback in the mid-1990s when his corporation was merged with another, but rallying to hit career highs thereafter (except for a rough patch when he appeared to realize he would never reach the absolute top of his pyramid). The 2020 projection is based on an estimate of when Roger will not require the kind of mojo that fuels a functional business career. Too much mojo is as bad, in some cases, as too little.

Mojo is produced internally, using fuel from both inside and outside sources. One can never take it for granted. And although it is difficult to operate without it over time, it must be assumed that this important asset will come and go, depending on personal and professional circumstances, and must be monitored and replenished as needed. Sustained lack of mojo should not be viewed with alarm but rather as an indication that something fundamental is in need of upgrade, removal, or regeneration.

312. Maintaining Mental Fitness

Once you have mastered the Curriculum, you will still be annoyed by crazy people. There are two highly advanced strategies going forward to deal with this.

The first is to establish yourself as apparently every bit as pathological, unpredictable, and dangerous as the most demented around you. This group of exercises may be helpful:

➤ *Pull-To's:* Grasp the crazy person firmly by both shoulders and *pull* them to you, with an exclamation like "Fantastic!" Release. Repeat until the crazy person remembers he or she had something else to do and goes away.

➤ *Push-Aways:* In the middle of someone else's rant or insane bloviation, *push* the crazy person away from you, hard, with an exclamation like "No way!" If they get close enough again, repeat.

➤ *Downward Dogma:* Likewise, when you encounter a crazy person who can't stop espousing an obnoxious, doctrinaire position with which you disagree, drop to your knees and stretch out lengthwise, examining the carpet with both hands and muttering to yourself, "I know I dropped them around here somewhere."

➤ *Vertical Sit-ups:* If the crazy behavior is taking place at a meeting, raise yourself as high as you can in your chair and maintain an isometric alert position for fifteen seconds. Relax. Repeat until the end of the meeting or somebody asks you what's wrong.

➤ *Chair Lifts:* Many conference room chairs have little levers on their sides that raise and lower the height of the chair. When craziness breaks out, hit this lever so your chair goes down to its lowest position, and then raise it to its highest. Repeat until somebody tells you to stop.

➤ *Jumping Jackoffs:* Leap from your seat and rush from the room with an air of severe alarm. Reenter the room with an air of mild concern. Regain your seat. Three minutes later, repeat. Continue exercise until you return to an empty room.

➤ *Sprints:* Find yourself a floor full of crazy people—usually the executive floor. Bring a sheaf of papers to hold in one hand. Then run as fast as you can around the circumference of the floor, head down, looking intently at the paper. If you choose, you may run directly to the elevator, ride it down to the ground floor, ride it back up, and resume running. Keep each sprint going for three rounds of the workspace. To be accomplished once in the very early morning and once late at night, when only workaholics are around. In time, people will come to the conclusion that you are "crazy busy," which will redound to your credit.

➤ *Long-Distance Brain Rinse:* Imagine yourself on the moon. These are moon people. You do not speak their language, so you must be silent. But you are interested in their movements, these moon people. So you . . . observe. My, isn't that interesting. Good thing it has nothing to do with you! Maintain the exercise until you are no longer aggravated by what's going on.

➤ *Squats:* If crazy people are in your office, pick a moment to push your chair away, fall to your knees, and root around under your desk as if you are looking for something. Continue the exercise for thirty seconds. Then pop back up, regain your seat, and say, "Where were we?" Repeat until you are alone again.

➤ *Tai Chi Nonresponsiveness:* In a gathering or one-on-one discussion with a crazy person, bring one hand up to your chin very . . . slowly. Appear to think deeply until the silence is deafening . . . then very . . . slowly . . . say, "Well, hmm . . ." or possibly, "Ah . . ." and move your hand from your chin to the back of your head. Scratch thoughtfully. Repeat these and other extremely . . . slow . . . movements and utterances. . . . until they are no longer necessary.

➤ *Kundalini Stretch:* This is the precise opposite of the prior drill. When required, twist your arm around the back of your head and touch the opposite shoulder. Keep it there. Raise your right leg until it is fully bent and place it behind your left knee. Hold that position as long as you can. Return to your posture of rest. Then repeat the exercise with the other arm and leg. Keep going until desired results are achieved.

➤ *Tantric Bop:* In this discipline, one must dedicate oneself to hours of intense engagement with the crazy person, screwing with them until they become exhausted and subsequently avoid seeing you again under any circumstances. This is an extremely radical exercise not recommended for those who can't keep it up for hours.

This exercise regimen, taken seriously and performed assiduously over time, will succeed in keeping crazy people at bay in most circumstances. Like all programs of its type, it carries with it certain risks if overdone, most particularly the possibility of becoming one of those people you are trying to avoid. It's also very difficult to perform this workout around ultra-senior management.

313. Dealing with Feelings of Overwhelming Entitlement

Going forward, business will carry with it a variety of perks and emoluments that people become used to. These include things like

➤ free coffee in the morning

➤ perhaps a fridge at the end of the hall with water and beverages

➤ a big buffet at lunch*

➤ credit cards you can use for fun stuff marginally associated with business

➤ people to answer your phones so you never have to talk to anybody you don't want to

➤ Town Cars and other conveyances available for use by even low middle management, within certain policy guidelines

➤ Access to business-class flights, which really are much nicer than coach

➤ Trips to romantic cities around the world where one is treated like a visiting dignitary

➤ Incredible hotels, resorts, and spas

---

* At some point in the last ten years, a variety of managements have had the stunning insight that if you give people free food at lunch, they will stay on location, take a shorter break, and be back at the treadmill in record time with a good feeling about the company.

➤ Flights on twenty-first-century private jets that cut through the night like a scimitar and where food and booze flow like a mountain stream bursting from the side of a mountain

➤ And a whole lot more

Plus there is a general assumption that you are a supreme entity in the cosmos, one who must be scurried after by those dedicated to your happiness. All of this—*all*—is attached to your status as a person in business with a certain rank and position. It is a short leap, psychologically, between the receipt of all this cool stuff and the idea that you *deserve* it because of who you are. And perhaps you do. The problem is, what happens when you are not who you are anymore? When you go into a restaurant that has always seated you at the front with the heavy hitters but now ushers you to a very nice table in the garden room with the rest of the tourists? When your room at the hotel is a "junior suite," which is a bedroom with a couch in it, rather than the three-room monster with the hot tub and the view of the eighteenth green that you're used to? When you have to fly coach, because a business-class seat on your own nickel costs more than three thousand dollars? Where you need to stand in the rain to hail a cab, rather than hop into that nice warm Mercedes S550 limousine that was always purring at the corner waiting just for you?

Even if all you rate are the low-end enjoyments of a business life, you come to rely on them. So does your family. I know a kid who is now six years old, the daughter of a New York City hedge-fund type. She has never flown commercial. What's she going to do when she gets a little bit older and suddenly gets on a plane with . . . *strangers on it*?!

The more successful you become, the more entitled you become, and the less satisfied with each small thing that is done simply to make your life better and your job easier. The stuff you used to savor is now a source of distress if it is not just *so*. This explains the mogul who, flying in his private G5, is served a lobster not to his satisfaction . . . and throws it at the flight attendant in a fit of pique. As well as the group of senior managers who, drunk on their butts, turn over a table at one of Manhattan's most exclusive restaurants and almost end up in the pokey.

Several things happen to a person who becomes spoiled by success:

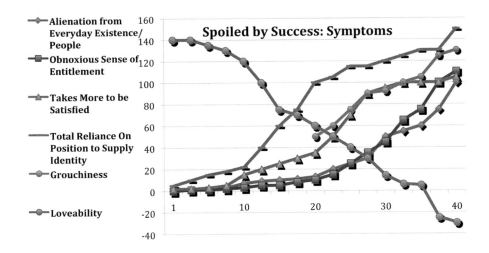

Don't let it happen to you.

Now if you'll excuse me. The kitchen has just brought up my luncheon and I hate to be disturbed when I eat.

314. Basic Wine and Whiskey Talk, and a Brief Word on Cigars

The ability to hold one's own on the subject of wine and whiskey remains an important arrow in the quiver of corporate respectability among the rich and ostentatious. Those who choose to compete in this area should heed these bits of advice:

- *How to talk about anything as if you know something.* The same basic techniques one has employed for years about financial and managerial matters will serve well here, although a *light* overlay of cultivation and élan is a necessary addition to the basic skill package.

- *The vocabulary of wine:* The key insight to be explored here is that, unbeknownst to the uninitiated, *there is no descriptive adjective that is off-limits when describing a wine.* Legitimate words in common usage are:

➤ Chocolate

➤ Velvet

➤ Wood (oak in particular)

➤ Rubber

➤ Asphalt

➤ Raspberry

➤ Strawberry

➤ Loganberry

➤ Any kind of berry

➤ Perfume

➤ Spice

➤ Cinnamon

➤ Syrup

➤ Porridge

➤ Leather

➤ Smoke

Any combination of these, or other olfactory nouns that come to your mind while you are describing the wine, is acceptable, particularly if you employ your hands thoughtfully as you do so. Made-up sensations, ambiguous adverbs, and infelicitous comparisons are also useful. Examples:

➤ "It's got lovely chocolate notes, with a slight afterburn of tar and leather."

➤ "I'm getting a little strawberry, with a lovely hint of cinnamon and oak."

➤ "It's a bit moody, with bright, musical highlights that remind me of Mozart or Timberlake."

You will note that in the last instance, both emotional and musical descriptors have been hauled out for use. If people laugh at you, so much the better. Pretend you were kidding. Making fun of wine pretention is an art unto itself. Here are some basic things you can know about wine:

• Nobody who knows about wine will think less of you if you ask for their recommendation.

• The only real faux-pas in the world of wine is to pretend that you know something when you don't.

- If you like red wine and not like white wine, drink red wine with any damn dish you have ordered.

- If you like white wine and do not like red wine, drink your white wine and be happy.

- Wine is for happiness, not for all the other uses to which status seekers put it.

- And if you should happen to find a really knowledgeable person—as opposed to a wine snob—take the time to learn a little from them about the subject. It's a lot more interesting than stamps.

○ *The simpler world of brown drinks:* When it comes to whiskey, the palette of images, issues, and similes is much smaller. Two observations will keep you on safe ground where scotch is concerned:

➤ *Whether it is single malt or a blend.* Single malts are distilled from one batch of whiskey. They are often strong and have a decided aroma, bite, and texture. Single malts from the Hebrides, off Scotland, for instance, taste like a mouthful of peaty moss. Once you're used to them, you won't drink anything else for a while. Blends are just that. They take a number of usually excellent scotches and put them together into one nectar. Some blends are the best brown drinks in the world.* Whiskey drinkers are less prickly than oenophiles, by the way, less clubby, more expansive, and usually more drunk more quickly, and have nothing against ushering a new student into the ranks of enthusiasts.

➤ *Where it was made.* There is no law against looking at the bottle. A lusty discussion may then ensue about whether the product from Islay is superior to that from Mull and so on and so forth and blah blah blah. The talk will go on, as will the drinking.

Whereas there are many crazy adjectives that can be brought to bear when wine is on the table, all you have to know about scotch are a few that pertain to dirt. Feel free to mention:

➤ Peat
➤ Loam, and

---

* Just because a scotch is a blend, by the way, doesn't mean it's not excellent. There are those who prefer a staunch blend like Johnnie Walker Black to any of the more demanding single malts reeking of soil and shrubbery.

➤ Moss . . .

    . . . while staying away from actual dirt-related terms like *mud, soil,* or, of course, the word *dirt* itself.

◦ *Other beverages . . .* have their own somewhat less complex language, too. A few notes:

➤ Jack Daniel's is the champagne of bottled American whiskeys. There are those who like other brands, but Jack is like what they used to say about IBM—nobody ever got fired for ordering it. Never put Coke in it, by the way, unless you want to be hooted at by those who honor this nectar that is sweeter and heavier than scotch, which because of its higher sugar content will very likely make you feel like you were hit in the head with an anvil when you wake up in the morning.

➤ Rye whiskey is now firmly entrenched as a quality option for whiskey drinkers, where before it was used solely in Manhattans for grandma. This is perhaps due to the influence of the 1950s culture of simple alcoholism brought back by *Mad Men*, but it doesn't matter. Long after that show is off the air we will be able to enjoy the smooth, inoffensive tang of a good, solid American or Canadian rye, which needs no adjectives to get the job done.

➤ Tequila is currently rebranding itself as the next big whiskey, not simply for use in icy concoctions when the chips are on the table. It comes in several age levels, the oldest of which is extra a*nejo,* which has been held in barrels for a whopping three years. Mezcal is a somewhat rougher form of tequila and often comes with a worm at the bottom of the bottle. Unless you have some specific business reason for doing so, *do not eat the worm.* Later on it may invalidate your efforts to create the impression that you are a serious person.

➤ Beer is always an acceptable choice in a business setting. Do not smash the can on your head when you are done with your beverage.

➤ The cocktails and mixed drinks that you may consume without fear of reputational decay are martinis, Manhattans (which was the original martini, created back in the nineteenth century at the dawn of mixology), Cosmopolitans (mostly for women), perhaps a vodka with a mixer, and a festive margarita (a clever, high-calorie means of consuming tequila). Mojitos are good, too, but only if they are strong enough (don't be cozened by a tall glass full of nothing but mixer and mint). *Note:* Grown men and women do not order brandy Alexanders or whiskey sours. Screwdrivers and Bloody

Marys are always welcome, but only in the morning, if everybody is having them, and a nice nap at the morning meeting is a possibility.

Finally, although it was once a prime topic for pointless and enjoyable discussion by people who had nothing else to talk about, the need for knowledge of cigars has abated in recent years, although there are usually one or more individuals, primarily men, who will sneak out a stogie at the end of a long dinner almost as furtively as if they were presenting a blunt and ask you if you'd like to share in their illicit enthusiasm. Go ahead and join them. But for God's sake, don't inhale. Unless, you know, it really is a blunt.

Electives

315. Hotel Living

We begin at the bottom, with entry-level hotels that feature a variety of insufficient amenities—free breakfasts with no bacon and do-it-yourself toasters, beds and bedding of uncertain provenance, soap the size of dominos, towels that do not fit around even the smallest midsection, honor bars with bottom-shelf liquor, bad TV. We then move on to the study of midrange hotels and inns dedicated to the business traveler, which are far more tolerable but by no means luxurious and confer no sense of status on the visitor other than the accurate perception that he or she is simply a cog in the machine with predictable tastes and needs. At the highest levels of study will be the Ritzes, Four Seasons, and other spectacular hotels, most with spas and extensive workout facilities as well as golf courses and swimming pools, often in sumptuous locations, that the true business achiever may come to call home during the high point in any given year. How each can be legitimately enjoyed to its maximum without fear of censure or reprisal will form the core of this extensive and quite pleasurable elective.

316. Boondoggles and Other Opportunities for Public Humiliation

A boondoggle is not what those in Silicon Valley refer to as an "off-site," in which one sits in a closed conference room and fights off sleep while pretentious guys with open collars play with empty concepts on a whiteboard. Nor is it a three-day stay at a convention where one works the floor during the day and gets dangerously hammered at night. Although some conventions, for some participants, can be boondoggles, most boondoggles do not take place at conventions.

The classic boondoggle is an organized excuse by senior management to indoctrinate middle and senior management, forge a common identity, make people happy about who they work for, and incidentally have a little fun along the way. There are meetings, always in the morning, always intended to be somewhat mind-expanding or out of the run of daily business. In the afternoon, there is sometimes golf or tennis. For those not athletically inclined, there are trips into the desert to fire semiautomatic weapons, or to the ocean to enjoy some hang gliding or, in super-macho cultures, life-threatening group activities in which people are sometimes injured. At certain times during the three-to-five-day boondoggle, there will be entire group events designed to forge unity of spirit and enhanced morale among those who perhaps need some.*

Places where these occasions have occurred over the past several decades are a what's-what of great, sybaritic locations across the nation:

- Inn at Sanibel Island, Sanibel Island, Florida
- Ritz-Carlton, Fort Myers, Florida
- Mohonk Mountain Lodge, New Paltz, New York
- Stein Eriksen Lodge, Park City, Utah
- Telluride Inn, Telluride, Colorado

---

* At one boondoggle studied by the National Association for Serious Studies, the entire middle management cadre of a Westinghouse subsidiary were instructed to appear at the beach of the Hotel del Coronado in San Diego. There, the three hundred pudgy, pasty executives were split into groups of ten and told to make sand art that reflected the values of their division. One guy stayed there until three in the morning fashioning the company's logo. He was widely derided, but kindly. Others made a castle with a toothbrush shoved into it. Forty-five minutes into the exercise, there wasn't a sober person on the beach. The next day it rained and the entire mile-long display was washed away along with the plans for the day. The three hundred then were summoned to the gym of the hotel, where a lusty game of gang basketball was played that included all senior officers, including the very top brass, most of whom nobody had seen out of pinstripe, ever. At giant gatherings in the afternoon, awards were given to top performers, with much cheering and singing of an anthem that everybody had to learn especially for the occasion, titled "We're Building the Best." In the evenings, there was a pub at which everyone was expected to show up and poison themselves as much as possible. It was here that many serious individuals disgraced themselves by comporting themselves insanely, drooling conspicuously over members of the opposite sex, and otherwise failing to remember that not everything that is done at a boondoggle stays at a boondoggle.

- Scottsdale Inn, Scotsdale, Arizona
- La Costa Resort, La Costa, California
- Winged Foot Country Club, Mamaroneck, New York
- Ritz-Carlton Half Moon Bay, Half Moon Bay, California
- Beverly Hills Hotel, Beverly Hills, California
- Four Seasons on Doheny, Beverly Hills, California

Those are just a few. There used to be others, but some are for some reason quite difficult to remember.

It should be noted that boondoggles are fewer and farther between at this writing. But as the economy improves, and senior managements get too bored staying at home, the boondoggle will pop up again for those who are doing well, and certain understanding of the opportunities and dangers involved will be essential to those who wish to avoid personal destruction. The elective begins with a look at the consequences sustained by those who choose to dance with a tie around their heads and goes on from there.

317. Yelling and Screaming

There are always those who will allow the tops of their heads to blow off. Those on the receiving end must consider many aspects of being yelled at:

➤ Does the person have the power to yell at you? Do you have to take it? Some peers with bad impulse control may suddenly erupt at you as if you were theirs to push around at will. You may then tell them to take it someplace else. Telling the wrong person to go fuck themselves may be inadvisable, however. Even small fry who have the capacity to lose it may be dangerous to you.

➤ What time of day is it? Yelling in the morning is unconscionable. Yelling at the end of the day when everybody is tired and things aren't going well is different. You wouldn't be mad at a baby who needs a nap, would you?

➤ Is it yelling or screaming? Yelling is loud but somewhat modulated. Screaming rises to a level where the voice breaks and Hitleresque stomping may follow, a borderline personality disorder that must be met with a reaction ranging from immediate departure to stone-faced silence.

➤   Has the yeller/screamer been drinking? This invalidates all displays of infantile pique, but at the same time makes the situation more potentially combustible.

➤   Do you care? A lot of the time, if you really study the situation, you may find that for one reason or another, you really don't care why this person is yelling at you.

Crucial to the ongoing investigation in this elective is the ability to *remove yourself from the situation*, either physically or, more probable, emotionally. In these cases, a look into the eradication of self through the study of Zen is advised.*

If, on the other hand, you are a yeller, be aware that every time you use your power to yell at people, they hate you a little bit. There are occasions, of course, where a person or persons must be yelled at, deserve to be yelled at, *would even benefit from being yelled at.* So go ahead. Yell.

318. Basic Bullshitting

A full review of the extensive literature on this subject begins this essential elective, a subject that will continue to accompany you throughout your career: producing, managing, and responding to bullshit. In its lower forms, bullshitting is an absolutely crucial skill that is highly respected by all serious players. It mostly consists of the following:

➤   Telling people what they want to hear;

➤   Engaging people's interest in something that inherently deserves none;

➤   Spinning stupid stories to keep people entertained while you are picking their pockets;

➤   Explaining the inexplicable;

➤   Making stuff up because you don't know the answer;

➤   Lying (a little bit), sometimes for excellent business or personal reasons;†

➤   Disguising the truth.

---

* See *Throwing the Elephant: Zen and the Art of Managing Up*, by Stanley Bing (HarperCollins, 2002).

† Bullshit lying must be distinguished from actual lying. When you tell somebody they look great and they don't, that's bullshit. When you tell them they've got the job and then give it to somebody else, that's lying. The ability to tell the difference is what distinguishes highly respected bullshitters from liars, whom nobody but other liars can stand to be with.

All of these skills take a tremendous amount of practice, and those who wish to become expert at bullshitting have to do a bit of it every day, just to keep in practice. Those who overindulge, however, run the risk of turning into a flatulent machine in every possible situation, like a wayward appliance that won't turn itself off. Such people are avoided even by other bullshitters.

319. Advanced Bullshitting

This elective may only be taken by those who have completed Unit 318. It is a highly hazardous investigation into the rarefied atmosphere inhabited by those who make a living bullshitting themselves. There are multiple perils involved and also some tremendous benefits. One can very quickly lose the ability to tell fact from fiction, entering a zone where the bullshit one is spinning has the feel of truth.

320. Killing People

You are very far along now, either at the top of the monkey bars or working for somebody who is. And occasionally, sometimes without warning, you are required to expunge another person from the organization. Perhaps they are simply not doing the job and are taking up space that could be occupied by a better person. Perhaps they pissed off the wrong person. Perhaps that wrong person is you. Perhaps they have shown themselves to be an enemy, and a long-term campaign must be cooked and served cold. Perhaps it's something that must be done today. Life is precious. But some lives are more precious than others. Yours, for instance. And yet it's not easy. It shouldn't be. People who have no problem killing other people are the scariest mothers on the block:

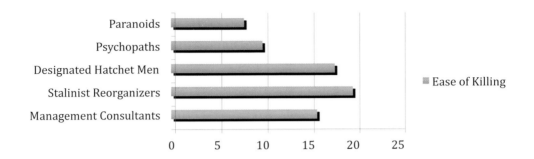

Bulk casualties are easier. The elimination of a single life-form before one's eyes takes a different level of cold blood. Even Stalin himself observed that "a million deaths are a statistic, a single death is a tragedy."

There is such a thing as an enemy that must be destabilized, undermined, and eventually crushed, hopefully by somebody else when the time comes. This designated hit person doing your dirty work for you can be either a superior who has been convinced of the rectitude of the hit or a subordinate who can't avoid following your orders. All proper steps must be taken to make sure the execution is legal and will not generate undue notice either internally or publicly. The state can often be generous, too, in certain cases, as it was in Rome when a senator agreed to make it easy on everybody and open his veins in the bath.

Extra credit goes to those who work for a person who requires an enemy in order to operate properly. They perform poorly without one. Give them an enemy and they swing into action like a champ, however. If you work for such a one, you may need to become a better killer than you might like.

321. Global Business and Other Culture Shocks

We haven't spent a great deal of time talking about the world as a playing field. You may have to go to China. You may have to go to France. You may have to go to the International Space Station to sell hydroponic gardens, if you are reading this fifty years hence. Bring clean underwear. Don't forget some business cards. When you get there, listen more than you talk. If you receive a food test—which is likely in Japan—you must pass it. Other than that, pretend you are in Sheboygan. Unless you're from Sheboygan. In that case, pretend you are in Brooklyn.

322. Fear and Its Relation to Business Performance

Along the way, you will be afraid. You will be very afraid. Not always. But some days? Some days are totally given over to fear. The kind that grips you from gut to sphincter and won't let go . . . all day.

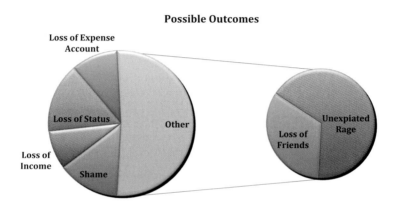

Possible Outcomes

You will have to live through days like that. I hope you do. Most of the time, you should know, things work out all right. The worst of your fears are not realized. Only sometimes they are.

323. Rationalization & Denial (R&D)

You may elect to spend several hours per day in R&D. A tenured senior advisor is required.

324. What About Love?

You are a human being. Human beings cannot continue in a social environment without in some way forming friendships, resentments, jealousy, heartache, brother- and sisterhood, grief, anger, disaffection, and the desire, someday, to move away. In short, it's a family, whatever that means to you. And in the end, after a while, it can mean a lot. Long enough, and it may mean everything. An online support group for those in need of a little love may be found at www.stanleybing.com.

325. No Guts, No Glory

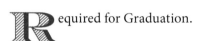equired for Graduation.

GLOSSARY OF
Key Vocabulary

Words may mean different things in the workplace than they do elsewhere. That does not mean their meanings are any less precise. Well, actually, in our context, they often are, because business thrives on certain imprecision when it suits the occasion. This makes the attempt to define operating terminology even more crucial, so that one may understand what is being obscured in addition to what is being said.

What follows is a partial listing of some of the words it would serve any student well to know. The general study of business verbiage, however slippery and challenging, is extremely rewarding for those who believe that it is sometimes important to understand what other people are saying.

Acquisition could mean one of two things.

1. Your company is gobbling up a lesser entity. This is an opportunity for you, if you choose to seize it.
2. You're the ones being acquired. That's bad. For a discussion on who will survive and who won't, see **Mergers**.

Administrative assistant is the slave and master of senior management. Though all the trappings of everyday work are there—the computer, the phone bank, the piles of incoming and outgoing paper—the real function of the job is to grant or block access and, in dramatic cases, to determine who is In with Bob and who is Not In with Bob. If you can't see Bob, it's impossible to be In with Bob. More than any other player in the infrastructure, the AAs are both high and low. They feel this status acutely. Treat them as the power brokers they are and they will sometimes respond in kind. Treat them as functionaries and you will slowly be expunged from the face of the planet.

Agenda is either the formal rundown of a meeting, luncheon, or long weekend in Scottsdale with three hundred drunk sales managers, or a hidden, dark thing, secret to all but a few. Written agendas are fine, as they go, but people who rely on them too much can be boring. The really interesting stuff takes place in the hidden agenda, a complicated amalgam of needs, demands, and dreams that make all conversations, even in business, human.

Aggravation, see **Assholes**.

Aggression is the primal drive to go on the offensive. It may be impolitic to be impatient, high-pressure, obnoxious, but at a Los Angeles agency, for instance, if you're not obnoxious enough you will fail. Keep in mind that one form of aggression is unacceptable in any culture: territorial encroachment.

Allies are not friends, who are necessary for another purpose. Allies do more than just say "Great idea" when you say something; they make you an indispensable part of the **team**.

Without allies, corporate life is solitary and, for all but the heartiest, will breed paranoia and failure. But be careful. You can't abuse your allies as you would your friends.

Alpha dogs are as large as a mastiff, but most of the time, for reasons worthy of further investigation, they are as small as affenpinschers.

Altruism is when one party does something for another party without expectation of reward. It is rarely genuine and should be eyed warily.

Ambition is an ugly thing when displayed nakedly, but a valuable tool when disguised for the good of the **corporation**. You can't evince too much of that, so knock yourself out.

Anger can be good for you. Those who are never infuriated aren't paying attention. But an excess of anger demonstrates bad self-control. A general schematic on the issue of permissibility might look like this:

Acceptable but annoying   Marginal   Thoroughly Unacceptable

Angry birds, see **Games (casual)**.

App, short for *applet*, is a way you can use your corporate digital implement to make believe you're working.

Apple, a corporation that has brought untold joy to millions of its acolytes. Long may it wave.

Appointments are made to be kept, except, perhaps, with friends, who can be offended without fear of reprisal. The problem is that one's enthusiasm for an upcoming appointment often ends precisely three hours before it's to occur. So be frugal in making your appointments. And if you have to break one, don't be afraid to lie. People appreciate the effort, up to a point, which research shows is usually three cancellations.

Arrivals and departures. Upon an arrival, make people sort of happy to see you.

➤ Greet the group
➤ Fist-bump or shoulder-squeeze selected individuals, when appropriate. If not, just take your fruit salad/cookie/bottle of water and sit down.
➤ Settle in. Rustle your stuff a bit.
➤ See what's shaking around the table.
➤ Appear to have something to do.

Upon departure, take advantage of the unstructured feeling in the room. Now is the time to poke the membrane of the group and see where the soft spots are.

Ass-covering is a craft, not an art. There's nothing pretty about it. In a corporate setting, the tools are:

➤   Paper, produced before, not after, the fact. Make a habit of documenting situations that have a scent of peril about them. Cc the lawyers.
➤   When somebody tries to pin something on your ass, make your ass unavailable, either by total absence or by simply refusing to offer it for kicking.
➤   Don't apologize for anything. Apologies are the antithesis of ass-covering.

Assholes come in an assortment of sizes and varieties, and each must be dealt with properly.

◦   *Jerks* generally stand in your way more out of stupidity than malice, but aggressive dumbness doesn't have to be malicious to be a pain in the neck.
◦   *Schmucks* are slightly more nasty jerks. In certain situations, you could be one, too. You can be nice to schmucks, or you can be mean to them. They take it either way. Why not? They're schmucks.
◦   *Pricks* are a notch up from schmucks in the asshole org chart. If most of them are not your allies, you're probably in trouble. When a prick is on your side, you know your chances of survival just went up.

It is impossible to get rid of every asshole in your life. That's okay. Some of them make pretty good friends.

Ass-kissing is addictive, and, like junkies, ass-kissers are often found in packs, nodding. They also tend to attach themselves to guys whose egos needs constant fueling. A more boring and fearful occupation is unknown to man or woman.

Assistants are the guts that hold the whole damn thing together. In rain and snow, sleet and rain, weekdays and weekends, summer, winter, fall or spring, they imagine how they could make the life of he or she whom they serve better, more comfortable, more congenial to the business that must be done. Cultivate them! Befriend them! Support them when they get wacky. Because, Lord, how they do get wacky. And still, life is impossible without them. God bless them.

B

Backstabbers can be neutralized only after they are identified. This may be harder than it appears. They are usually behind you. On the other hand, they do drop little turds in their path as they go. He's the one who's usually in the process of trashing somebody else. Today, it's the vice president of finance. Tomorrow it may be you. Protect yourself with a thick armor of friends and spies. When all else fails, invite the backstabber to your office and make him stab you in the face.

Bandwidth is the amount of digital space in the universe that has to hold the transmissions of all the electronic paraphernalia with which we now are all equipped. As time goes on, one or two really big companies will own all the bandwidth, and eventually control everything that goes into our ears, eyes, and minds by making us accept electronic implants in our craniums.

Bcc: A very cool feature ("blind cc") embedded in e-mail by which you can inform somebody else with secrecy what you're communicating to other people. But Bcc's must be handled with care. You can easily blow your cover by forgetting you're not supposed to be on the chain. See **Reply all**.

Bean counters are the invisible men who crank out the numbers and take the money to the bank. They see revenue, profit, depreciation, amortization, and taxes not as inert lines on green paper, but as the throbbing heart of the enterprise. They're right. And don't be too snooty with them just because they dress like moderately successful undertakers and converse about mundane subjects like golf and the time of their commute. They may be keeping score, as usual. Thousands of corporate fireflies have perished in their wake.

Benefits are a relic of the time when people thought a company should take care of its employees. Oh, most places still provide some medical, dental, and life insurance and even psychiatric coverage, but things like pensions seem to have gone out with jodhpurs. This, of course, is better for shareholders, whose interests are very often at total odds with those of the people who work for the **corporation**.

Bing is an also-ran search engine that poached the enormous goodwill and brand value of the Bing name as handed down by generations of Bings, including this one. Out of all the brand names in the universe, they chose . . . Bing. I don't know any other Bings out there, but I'm pretty sure they feel the same as we do.

BlackBerry, Blackberry thumb, BlackBerry nostalgia: Once there was a whole culture built around pride of BlackBerry. Then the mighty BlackBerry fell, because it is not an iPhone, full of video, audio, and a zillion **apps**, and frankly it does nothing really well except communicate via **e-mail**. Still, to be smart, you need to be on your BlackBerry. By the time you read this, the BlackBerry, which once tore the cartilage in every serious business person's thumb, may be a thing of the past. And we will all be just a little more incoherent.

Blame is a collect call from a bad place. Sometimes you have to accept it even when you don't know who's on the other end of the line. Other times you can pretend you're not home and let them leave a message you can pretend you never got. If blame attaches itself to you and you find you have to apologize for something, you are liable to be punished. Apologies at this stage of organizational development seem to be a requisition for punishment. Silence in the face of blame often works better.

Blog is a periodic dump of unedited human thoughts. Refer to www.stanleybing.com for an excellent example.

Boardroom is the most beautiful, formal, and powerful place in the corporation, the site of its most hallowed rituals. Dress for it, when you go.

Boonies are any town smaller than yours. It's natural for corporate types to feel a little supercilious about the people there; folks dress differently, seldom use terms like *interface* and *excellence*, and consistently spend less than thirty dollars for lunch. Resist the temptation to look down your nose at the boonies, however. There isn't a product (except, perhaps, for pastrami) that isn't sold there, and the people are a lot tougher than the limousine lizards of the big city who come to show them how it's done.

Boss is the person you report to, but your boss's boss is also your boss, as is your boss's boss's boss. With all those bosses around, life can get confusing, so focus your energies on your immediate boss. He's the master of your ship. Your light that guides your days. You must walk in his path until the very end.

Well, maybe not the very end. When your boss is whirling in concentric circles down the corporate drain, you are permitted to swim as fast as you can in the opposite direction.

Bottom line is the last line in the balance sheet. After all the expressions of revenue and operating expenses, tax, amortization, depreciation, goodwill, and other creations of accounting genius, there is how much money you have made, what you get to take home. In another sense, it's the point you reach when you travel beyond **bullshit**.

Brainstorming is an older term that now includes spitballing and whiteboarding. It is a highly valued activity, especially in fields where ideas are commodities that can be passed around like a joint at a party.

A real bond is forged between good brainstormers and a lot of fun can be had. After a while, they may even extrude something valuable. Then they all get crazy rich and lose the ability to collaborate with anybody.

Bogus brainstorming, on the other hand, occurs when good, hardworking folks with no ideas at all are called together to share them. Those can be a colossal waste of time. Be particularly suspicious of formal **meetings** on Big Topics where an appointed "facilitator" is there to "capture" the beauty of everybody's thoughts on the whiteboard or, worse, on big sheaves of paper that they post on the walls as the meeting progresses. In the end, those sheets are collected and what is on them is circulated for a "follow-up" that everyone knows will never happen. Of course, make really sure you are always invited to such meetings.

Breakfast is a low-risk start to a high-risk day and primarily a marvelous opportunity to have free bacon. It should not be burdened with too much weight—or grease. Beware of men eating too many berries and women who order the egg-white omelet made with no butter. They're no fun. The real agenda of the breakfast is friendship. Nobody but hard-bellied moguls has breakfast with people they don't like.

Briefcase (see **Handbag**) marks you as a wonk. It's like wearing an ostentatious pocket hankie, or suspenders, or too much scent. The only people who can get away with them are lawyers, and not the big lawyers, either, but rather the poor, grunting slaves who follow their master's or mistress's voice every day, carrying around these enormous steamer trunks of documentation when every single page of that load could fit on one pocket dongle. Pick a nice backpack or gym bag and keep it with you at all times. Let somebody else take care of the excess baggage. Oh, and don't even think about that snappy attaché case, either, unless it's holding a loaded Beretta you plan to use on Dr. No.

Brushing off persistent suitors can be an unavoidable corollary of your **power** and success. If you can, have somebody else do it. If not, there are a number of ways that get the job done and do not brand one as an inveterate prick:

- *Rescheduling:* Everything has remained jocular, and the pretense of future intercourse survives. Once you've been unable to nail down that informal drinks date for two years, the guy should get the message. If not:
- *Total absence:* Calls cease. Pleasantries dry up. The pretense of the intention to get together is dropped. And yet there he is again on your call sheet. It is clear something truly rude and terminal is required.
- *The kiss-off:* The guy can't take a hint. Tell him to fuck off.

But remember. That guy trying to get the pointy end of his shoe in the door could be you one day.

Budgeting is an exercise in creative writing. Don't let all the dry columns and numbers fool you: Behind the façade of scientific organization, it's nothing more or less than an assertion of priorities.

A good budget contains both room for activity and growth and the illusion of leanness. As such, it should have many discrete entries, each pared down to a reasonable size, each expendable only at great peril to the well-being of the guys doing the budget review. If it's a bad year, get with the program and prepare to ream out the small stuff (stopping just short of your expense account, of course). When the ship is going down, it's stupid to try to save any of the deck chairs except the one you are sitting on.

Bullshit comes in all sizes, textures, and varieties. But not all shit is bullshit.

Rabbit shit comes in little pellets. It may be strewn in your path or hidden in the underbrush. It's relatively inoffensive and rabbits can't help producing it.

Goose shit is supplied by those who do nothing but eat and shit. It has no value and messes up fields where others want to play. To get rid of goose shit, you have to get rid of geese.

Monkey shit is really bad stuff that monkeys have no problem throwing at other people when they're mad. If you can't get rid of the monkeys, don't get them mad.

Dog shit is worthless but dogs are not. Let them out now and then and you shouldn't have a problem.

Sheep shit has no business purpose whatsoever.

Bullshit is that material in its highest form. It may be tosseed, slung, heaved or pitched, and sometimes even enjoyed. Makes excellent fertilizer, too.

These distinctions may seem frivolous at times, or even unpleasant to some, but the investigation is not without value. Business can operate without the shit of rabbits, geese, monkeys, dogs, sheep, and other animals of the farm or jungle not named in this list, nor should such shit be tolerated if it becomes inconvenient. But business cannot operate without bullshit, which itself is as variegated as the size and nature of the beasts who generate it and the circumstances under which it is created. Business without it withers and dies, deprived of sufficient nutrients for underlying growth.

➤ Low-level bullshit is the stuff that's produced pretty much by everybody, every day. You can step around it and continue on your way.

➤ High-grade bullshit must be attended to. The bull may believe it is extruding something more important than it appears.

➤ Pure bullshit must be respected. You don't encounter it except at the very highest levels of organizational life and it is almost always more valuable than the grass and shrubs surrounding it.

Business is what we all do for a living. Whatever you do to make money, that is your business. Running a gas station is business. Selling lemonade on the street is business. Writing for an online publisher that pays a penny a word is not business. It's stupid.

Business cards should be carried at all times, but don't overuse or overvalue them unless you are in Japan, where they seem to be the cornerstone of human credibility. Never go to Japan without them. When you meet people there, offer them faceup, with your thumbs on top of each corner and your index fingers beneath. Bow slightly as you do so. You are now a serious businessperson in Japan.

Buzzer: Something on your desk phone that interrupts and annoys you when you're in the middle of something. On the West Coast, mostly in show business, they have these elaborate mechanisms that convey not only interruptions via beeps but also transmit a little message, like "Your three p.m. kale salad is here." To which the annoyed **executive**, almost always behind a closed door, may reply by pushing a button designated for a certain response, like "Thanks, I'll be out in a minute" or "Don't bother me." This is either less or more irritating than the simple buzzer of years past. It is, however, a symbol of status and so fulfills an additional function unrelated to buzzing.

Buzzwords are culture-specific terms whose use confers instant membership in whatever club is using them.* Suppose one's business is concerned with providing the tiny chromium nipples that connect hydroelectric transformers. When these objects wear out, they are said to "spear." One Friday, a senior officer says, "Boy, I'm speared," at the end of a long meeting. By next Monday, it's being used through the firm, and one person uses it in an interview with a trade publication. It is immediately tweeted and then read by all the journalists, bloggers, and hangers-on who are members of the masturbatory circle jerk that is the professional Twittersphere. Shortly thereafter, several hundred people with nothing else to do make **YouTube** videos featuring tired people being speared with sharp implements. All are super-hilarious. One goes viral and reaches 150 million people in six days. A buzzword has been born and it either will live as does the mayfly, appearing and disappearing like a summer breeze, or, in some cases, will outlive those who inadvertently invented it. For a discussion of the magnificent and more permanent language of which buzzwords are merely a part, see **Jargon**.

---

* A buzzword could be a meme, but isn't one, exactly, since there's nothing exact about a meme. For a discussion of memes, see **meme**, although by the time you read this, lack of interest in memes may have itself become a meme and vanished into the place where memes go to die, mercifully.

C

Capital is any form of wealth that's utilized to produce more wealth, any asset the corporation calls its own (including you).

Capitalism is an economic system in which the means of production are owned by private individuals and corporations (and their stockholders). These relatively few individuals share in "profits" and employ the majority of citizens, retaining their services for "wages." Profits seem to mount a lot faster than wages. Thus, capitalism appears to come most highly recommended by those at the top.

Company car, see **Perks**.

Competition is a pain in the neck. The entire drift of American business is a slow slide to consolidation. That effort will never be entirely successful, though. So in the end there will be ten or twelve massive government-sized conglomerates determined to wipe each other from the face of the earth. In that environment, one has every right to go out there and rip out the throats of one's adversaries and, in Los Angeles, your friends.

Compromise is good, as long as you're the one getting the 52 percent.

Conformity is often wrongly viewed as gray, lifeless, tedious. Yet it can lead you to all kinds of extreme stuff you might never have done if you weren't a conformist. During a business career, conforming may involve hard drinking, white-water rafting, extreme skiing, long nights in alien nightclub environments of an unspoken nature, bar fights, participation in professional vendettas, dealing with death, grief, defeat, and victory. Nonconformists are cool, too. They generally tend to hang together and conform to their own standards.

Consultants are very, very, very dangerous to have around. If you find one in your midst, do the obvious—take him to **lunch** and let him consult. Plumb his hidden agenda. A consultant always plugs a hole. Make sure it's not yours.

Consumer is the term that has replaced the older *customer*, a more accurate word to describe someone who utilizes the *custom* of the provider, that is, makes the decision to purchase something offered for sale. Both may soon be superseded by terms employed in the digital cosmos, where the **user** is **unique**.

Content is a fancy piece of terminology for movies, television, plays, video games, books, magazines, newspapers, or any other form of news, information, or entertainment that people consume with any of their sensory organs other than their taste buds. Soup, for example, is not content. A video of soup, however, is. Unlike the actual bowl of soup, which has physical reality beyond its role in the sales cycle, the video of soup is a marketable product, one that cascades down a chain that includes, perhaps, an original **YouTube** clip that makes its way to the Twittersphere, producing a potential television series that is then syndicated worldwide, subsequently throwing off a clothing and perfume line.

Contracts work both ways. At first, they seem to promise a bunch of goodies from the goody machine. But if you really read them, they're nothing more than the terms of your required apprenticeship, just like in the Middle Ages. An excellent contract is actually your exit package if and when they decide to fire you.

Conventions are gatherings of people with a similar business or personal interest who get together at regular intervals to do a little business and get wasted. They run on a fine mix of booze, food, and the possibility of crazy adventure, away from home in strange surroundings to say the least, since conventions are often held in big cities with lots of bad things to offer. N.B.: There is no more restful and productive place than an office where everybody has gone to the fair but you.

Convergence is the process by which all technological tools and toys eventually meld into one massive, overwhelming überdevice that satisfies all conceivable user purposes—communication, entertainment, news, traffic, weather, restaurant recommendations, and data about your current heart rate, stress level, horoscope, and requirement for a limousine immediately.

Conversation is the background noise of business. Most of it is nugatory. But be on the lookout for what are referred to as "key" conversations. A conversation is key when it provides you with an opportunity to:

- Make money;
- Get an assignment you want;
- Slough off an assignment you don't want;
- Find out if you're in trouble for something you either did or didn't do;
- Make time with powerful people who could do you good;
- Make time with powerful people who could hurt you.

Conversation is different than small talk, gossip, bullshitting, and hobnobbing, although it may at times involve all those and more. Remember that people who do a lot of listening are generally considered great conversationalists.

Corporate communications, see **Public relations**.

Corporate culture was first discovered in large, complex organizations like the postal service and General Motors. Enthused anthropologists subsequently found it lurking in business structures large and small, and now no **corporation** can be without one. A company's culture is, in fact, nothing more than the experience of working there. When analyzing your own culture, and securing your position in it, look at a variety of factors. These include: costume; working hours; requisite **jargon**; attitudes toward alcohol and drugs; and many, many others. If you are not with the culture, however, you will eventually be extruded from the oyster of the corporation like a grain of sand whose presence it can no longer tolerate in its sensitive inner parts.

Corporate tree is the vertical reporting structure that defines your business hierarchy. It's a metaphor for how management sees things. Like a tree, it is thickest at its base, reaching upward in ever-narrowing tendrils until it culminates at the luxuriant flowers way up top. No part of the trunk, no single branch is dispensable, and decay of any one level endangers the life of the entire organism. The following hierarchy is typical, if not absolute:

- *Submanagement* toils at the phone, the word processor, the open cubicle. Sometimes they are actors, abstract expressionists, opera singers—dreamers who remain happy and apart. Others are professionals, fiercely proud of the hold they have on the men and women they serve. They do not make policy and they do not make money.
- *Manager* status, in some organizations, means tremendous responsibility and a gaggle of underlings. In others, it means a pile of work, no recognition, and a salary that is dwarfed by the senior assistants who serve the top echelon of the tree.
- *Directors* are former managers whom nobody wants to make a vice president yet.
- *Vice presidents* are starting to get somewhere. In recent years, however, there are so many vice presidents around they might as well be directors. At this point, most everyone can become a vice president somewhere. In fact, you should expect to, and not settle for less.
- *Senior vice president:* Here's where you start getting serious **plastic**. You can fly business class without asking permission. You probably get a nice bonus. Many of your meals are free. You still have a lot of people barking at you, though.
- *Executive vice president:* Now you're talking. A very, very good title. Perched right below the most powerful tiers of ultra-senior management, without the cares and travails of those at the top, EVPs are the go-to guys, of which, coincidentally, I am one.
- *President* is another devalued concept in many organizations, where there are a frightening number of them floating around. Many presidents in large corporations are junior to the corporate EVPs who more freely associate with the chief operating officers and CEOs who actually run things. Presidents have numbers they have to hit. That means there is a bar code on their butts with a sell-by date on it. They are the first occupants on the tree to be provided with a substantial parachute when their branch is sawed off.

- *Chief operating officer* is often the president of the entire show. That's different than an operating president. The COO is either the supreme nabob in charge of anything that moves or the limping Igor to the CEO's Dr. Frankenstein.
- *Chief executive officer* is supposed to be the Man, the Dude, He Who Must Not Be Named. He must have command of the corporate gestalt in all its wonderful and terrifying complexity, managing people, resources, and projects—above all, making money. Like priests or actors, chief executives totally cede their lives to their work. They do it not for money, which they give to their nominal families, but for love: of power, of achievement, of combat. They also love the money.
- *Chairman* is sometimes CEO. When he's not, he's probably there because he founded the place and cannot be ousted. Sort of like Queen Elizabeth—the highest title, the greatest pomp, the smallest power. When, however, the chairman is the CEO, it may be useful to remember what a 650-pound gorilla eats for **breakfast**: whatever he wants. Maybe you.

Corporation is a legal entity that governs your little business-based nation-state. It has its own regulations, power structure, defenses, and mythology. Recently, a legal idea has flourished, thanks to the Supreme Court of the United States, that views the corporation as the legal equivalent of a person. This is essentially a comic **meme** that has yet to be worked out fully in the entertainment media. The mental image of a corporation going shopping at Costco for the really big packages of potato chips and frozen chicken wings comes to mind, although it seems far-fetched. The notion of a horny, avaricious corporation screwing everybody in sight, however, seems far more credible.

Correspondence, like shaving, should be done first thing in the morning. Don't forget to erase all meaningless e-mail every day, and freely utilize the Block Sender feature on Outlook. Block Sender is like weeding, only easier on the back. There are days when my Deleted folder bloats up with hundreds of messages I don't have to think about or answer because I never even see them.

Cost center is part of the organization that produces nothing but work. It generally sows not; nor does it reap. But that doesn't mean it's not important. When it carries out its assigned function, a cost center—strategic planning, accounting, **public relations**, human resources (or, for those who speak English, personnel) all the way up to the uttermost and costliest tippy-top of senior management itself—supports the segments of the corporate body that keep the *pengar* floating. No animal can hunt on sheer instinct. Eyes, ears, and a passable imitation of a brain are also a necessity.

Cost cutters do a lot of things under various euphemistic names, but what they really do is fire people. Corporations, like bourgeoisie, tend to gain weight with each passing year, stretching a little more about the middle out of sheer indolence. Enter the cost cutter, who may find a load of things to ream out of everyone's hide. That's okay. Cutting out a manager's business-class perk is better than cutting his throat. Sometimes, however, cost cutters are called in expressly to organize and administer mass executions. These individuals are the lowest form of corporate life. For further discussion, see **Hit man**.

Costume, see **Style**.

Creativity is one of the few big concepts that has not descended into jargon in the mouth of business, perhaps because, unlike *commitment* and *excellence*, which have disappeared into the mists of past buzzwordery, it will never go out of style. Ideas in this world are always in short supply—even bad ones. Don't be afraid to put your ideas across, no matter how dumb you may suspect them to be.

Credenza is the thigh-level hutch in which files, reports, and other office paraphernalia are housed and, when necessary, hidden. It is a conceptual object that does not exist outside the contemporary workplace, a totem of executive status and pretention. Your credenza, if you achieve one, will be as organized as the inside of your brain. Good luck.

Cross-platform was a new concept once with plenty of spin and cultural drizzle. Now it's pretty much the way we consume everything but cheese. You can listen to your tune or watch your TV episode on the computer, on the iPad, iPod, PlayStation, Xbox, Roku, on all digital platforms available to you.

Crowdsourcing, a term coined in 2006 at the height of the explosion of **bullshit** that attended the second **Internet** boom, is a word whose definition takes more than six hundred words on **Wikipedia**. As far as I can tell, it means bringing a bunch of like-minded people together to fund, research, or execute a project of some kind. It is made possible by the capacity of the Internet to galvanize temporary communities of individuals who never need to meet each other in person.

Cubicle is a tiny space imposed on powerless workers to take away their individuality and crush them into the role of anonymous cog in a machine run by somebody, somewhere who has access to a door behind which they can take a nap or eat their lunch in peace.

Cutback is a snappy euphemism used by management to announce layoffs, wholesale retirements, and mass (or targeted) executions. Develop sensitive antennae and listen for the distant whisper of the term. It is often announced by a cheerful memo introducing the staff from the good people of McKinsey or Bain who most certainly *aren't* there to fire anybody. Perish the thought! If you should make it through unscathed, or improve your position in the new, leaner organization, try not to indulge in too much survivor guilt. Business belongs to the not yet dead.

D

Decentralization is the corporate excuse for firing **headquarters** personnel and thinning out the head count. For example: A company has been holding down the national accounting function in Dallas with a team of fifteen highly qualified, experienced personnel. One day, after much self-examination and waves of apocalyptic rumor, the ax falls. Two headquarters accountants are retained, left to slave over the former duties of the multitudes; six are immediately laid off, with apologies. The final six are offered splendid posts in the decentralized structure. Unfortunately for them, these generous opportunities are located in Salt Lake City, Walla Walla, Petaluma, Fort Myers, Toledo, and Scranton. All decline, and local people are hired at lower salaries to fill the new regional positions. Net effect: head count down by six, pay levels down by 340 percent. The impression of fiscal control has been created at incalculable cost to the central brain stem function of the company.

Delegating is the ability to transform the requirement for personal labor into the work of other people. Great delegators view every task as one that rightfully belongs to someone else. After the task is passed along formally, the delegator then keeps an eye on the project so that later he can claim he had a hand in its success. Develop this art and you, too, will be targeted as talented management. Delegation is broken down into four discrete phases:

- *Evaluation:* In which the job is received and analyzed, and the determination made that it need not be done personally.
- *Assignment:* In which the lucky subordinate or gullible peer is targeted, evaluated, and informed of the good news.
- *Supervision:* In which guidance is offered and progress charted. Remember that the finished object must come from you, the delegator, since it was to your office that the request originally came.
- *Credit:* In which your subordinate is accorded all due kudos, and you receive points for having managed the project to a successful completion.

Some people skip the "subordinate gets some of the credit" part. As the boss, that's up to you. An ungenerous nature in that regard will eventually rise up to bite you in the ass, though. Just perhaps not right away.

Desk is an external expression of the inside of your brain. It is also the visible expression of what's going on in there. There are generally standards for what you may be permitted to show. You may enjoy twelve-inch-high action figures of semi-nude buxom female superheroes from the Batman universe. Your female colleagues might not share your appreciation. Your collection of Smurfs or wall-to-wall display of your child's artwork might also be considered a distraction. Within the lines, though, you have a lot of discretion. There's no need to keep your desk overly neat, by the way. An employee whose desk is clear at three p.m. may not be organized. He or she might simply be getting set for quitting time two hours early.

Digital nomads are people who claim to be working from home, from coffee shops or other remote locations. Many are **crowdsourcing**, in addition to drinking their coffee. Most are assumed to be independently wealthy or living off the largesse of somebody who is actually working.

Diversity is a policy mandating the hiring of women and minorities. If there is no such policy, there will be very few women or minorities in positions of any importance in your organization, since white people are brilliant at rationalizing why the Caucasian they chose to hire was more qualified. Next time, though, they'll be sure to give the matter proper consideration.

Divestiture is the surgical removal (by sale) of an unwanted organ from the corporate body. Hopefully, it is vestigial and not an integral part of the circulation, nervous, or digestive system. If your operation is the one being divested, it generally means you're toast. It is possible in certain cases, however, for you to jump to some other portion of the corpus. For a discussion, see **Mergers**.

Dog and pony show is a very special kind of presentation, one in which **style** is every bit as important as substance. There used to be a lot of ways to do this. Now God has descended in the form of Bill Gates, and we all have to use PowerPoint. See Unit 303, Giving an Effective Presentation for a more complete look at this subject.

Doodling is one form of cognition, and some of the deepest thinkers are the most active doodlers. So don't think that because someone is doodling, he isn't 100 percent tuned in. He may be listening with an inner ear. Doodling is also one of the best means of staying awake at a meeting one considers useless.

Door is your portal to freedom. Behind a closed door, you can think, write, dream, hang upside down with your feet on your desk, and stare off into space like a sloth. A man or woman without a door is a slave. That is why totalitarian autocrats love doorless cubicles. Don't be fooled by the democratic jargon, either. The open cubicle is not a great leveler. It's an oppressor.

Downside is all the bad things that could result from a specific action. As in: "Before we bless that plan we'll have to consider the downside implications." Or "The downside, Jack, is that we're transferring you to Sri Lanka." It's a good idea to spend some time looking at the downside of every situation, lest it become more than mere speculation. On the other hand, every downside supports its opposite. For a discussion, see **Upside**.

Drinks are one of the most venerated institutions in business life, the glue that bonds gray multinational robots to slick sharks in Hawaiian shirts. Drinks are the opportunity to hear the worst **jokes** in human history and enjoy them, to share the story about the time Norman Bostack appeared at Nancy Nowacki's hotel door in his bathrobe holding two bottles of Veuve Clicquot* to enjoy a moment of comradeship.

Fortunately, most industries have a wild variety of excuses for drinking together, from the random whim of the two chummy executives to the mass drunking of seven hundred middle managers. And where the liquor flows, and even the female vice presidents have their ties off, there is no fear, no danger, and no **agenda**. But there's the rub. It's quite possible that, when drinking with corporate pros, one may spill red wine on the chairman's tie. Try not to.

Drugs are illegal, and, worse, mostly out of style. Business is for the most part straight now. So just drink until you hallucinate, okay? Nobody you work with is as cool as you think they are or, for that matter, they think they are.

E

Eating well is a sacred ritual or a total desecration. There are only three acceptable forms of fueling up on company time:

- *Eating with friends:* Usually not acceptable to Accounting but probably the best lunch you're going to have.
- *Eating for a good business reason:* You are out there pitching at a time in which you could be relaxing, or taking a break from other people in your face. That deserves a reward. Try the prime rib.
- *Meals at your desk:* A solitary tuna on toast can be a lot more soothing than a four-course force-feeding with some **asshole** who finally nabbed you after two cancellations.

Eccentricity is any expression of excessive personality. Keep it wrapped pretty tight unless you're the big **boss**. Eccentricity is tolerated in organizations that value **creativity**. Insanity is frowned upon almost everywhere.

Eco-friendly is green stuff. If your corporation has some of it, there are large funds that will invest in you. It's also nice for employees who care about these things. If you want to test how eco-friendly people really are, try to ask them to do without water in plastic bottles. And good luck on that.

---

* She said, "Go back to your room, Norman."

E-mail has replaced all other forms of communication between people, including speech, in-person visits, dates, and heavy petting. Very slowly, however, texting is now replacing e-mail as a means of talking to people in real time one-to-one, as human beings lose the power to express themselves at any length. For brief, impersonal ejaculations directed at a mass audience, **Twitter** is now also taking the place of more extensive electronic communications.

Enemies are the product of **success**. That doesn't mean it's advisable to collect them. Whether an enemy is powerful, wise, stupid, venal, or misguided, he can torpedo you at any time, and will, probably when you least expect it. As long as he's viable, that is, has at least one friend in senior management, an enemy is a time bomb waiting to go off in your face. If you can't eliminate an enemy by guile or muscle, try cordiality, and a little discreet support of his objectives. This policy of live-and-let-live, while easy with friends, is even more advisable with enemies. Once he or she understands that you are prepared to cultivate a slow and enduring hatred, rather than a hot and murderous resolution, the enemy may be content to remain a thorn in your side rather than a knife in your heart.

Entrepreneurial spirit comes in two flavors:

1. *The Inventor* comes up with the great ideas, tinkers around with them, and puts them into action. Big money ensues. Examples: Thomas Edison, George Westinghouse, Richard Branson, Ted Turner, the Google Guys, 50 Cent.*

2. *The Appreciative Marketer* sees the potential in the work of other people and, recasting it and marketing it brilliantly, puts it out there and reaps the reputational and financial rewards. Examples: Henry Ford (commoditizes all prior ideas on car manufacture into the Model T), Bill Gates (PC-DOS becomes MS-DOS, the Apple Desktop becomes Windows), Steve Jobs (visits Xerox and sees their new pointer system, conjures the vision of the mouse and executes it), Mark Zuckerberg (appropriates interesting Harvard dating service and turns it into **Facebook**).

It seems that with the arrival of the computer culture in the late twentieth century, one no longer needs an original technology or idea to be a great entrepreneur. This is good news for most of us, although not everybody has the audacity to purloin other people's stuff at the kind of massive scale that builds empires.

Excellence is a former mega-buzzword that went out with the death of **quality** as a high concept. These trending terms burst onto the business scene periodically, and they are interchangeable. They appear to hold rock-hard, eternal truths in their cores, but in fact they are hollow. No matter how

---

* In true hip-hop fashion, Curtis Jackson (Mr. Cent) has reportedly made either $100 million or $500 million on the sale of his share of Vitamin Water to Coca-Cola.

great your commitment to Excellence, Quality, the Customer, Innovation, Disruption, or Cross-Platform Agnosticism, if they suddenly stopped paying you, you'd go home.

Executives are women and men who have worked long enough to have attained the privilege of telling other people what to do. What is sometimes forgotten, however, is that all executives, even the hautest of the haute, have masters. And the higher the executive, the more impossibly irrational and dysfunctional his or her boss is likely to be.

Expense accounts must be handled with honesty and discretion, and abused within those boundaries.

F

Facebook, depending on how you look at it, is either a marvelous way for people to connect with each other and stay in touch with all the friends one has accumulated over a lifetime, or a pernicious alternative to genuine human intercourse that has alienated millions upon millions of vulnerable, lonely people, sequestering them in a virtual universe where their likes and dislikes are purloined by soulless marketers for nefarious mercantile purposes.

FaceTime is the old idea of the Picturephone, first displayed in the New York World's Fair of 1964, come to life in the Apple iPhone. The thing is, you have to have all your hair, be fifteen pounds underweight, and enjoy perfect bone structure to look like anything other than a fat-faced loser on FaceTime. This may explain why it has yet to replace e-mail, phone, or texting as a means of interpersonal communication.

1965 **PICTUREPHONE®** Now you can see as well as talk. The Picturephone® has Touch-Tone® controls to make calls and control the television screen so you can see the person you're talking to, be seen yourself, or have a darkened screen. Attended service between New York, Washington and Chicago began in 1964.

Facial hair for male employees is your own business once it's in its full flower, but don't grow it on company time. Business relations are heavily grounded in appearances and people in obvious transition make organized types nervous. Whatever you do, don't grow a beard without a mustache unless you are Amish. Women will know if the development of leg hair is permissible in their company and local culture within days of trying to cultivate some.

Fat cat is anybody who makes five to ten times more money than you do. Fat cats travel in limos. They fly in private jets where they are served fine foods of their choosing. They have several houses. They complain about their taxes.

Feminism is the belief that women should have the same **opportunities**, **salary**, and hierarchical standing as their male counterparts. One hundred percent of all enlightened corporate employees profess belief in it. In reality, approximately 49 percent of all male executives and 51 percent of female executives embrace it in practice. The remaining male executives do their best to maintain the old-boy network, while their female counterparts are weirdly more competitive with women on the way up than they really should be if they are truly feminists.

Financial terms are the high concepts, acronyms, and other mumbo jumbo by which the performance of the company is quantified. If you know the following, you will never go wrong:

- *Top Line:* This refers to the first line on the financial statement, which is revenue. Revenue is all incoming money that is paid for your product or service;
- *EBITDA or OIBIDA:* Acronyms that mean, respectively, Earnings Before Interest, Taxes, Depreciation, and Amortization and Operating Income Before Interest, Depreciation, and Amortization. These are terms invented a few years ago when somebody figured out that the company appears in a more favorable light when you don't factor a variety of unavoidable expenses into your judgment of how it's doing. Imagine how your personal financial condition would appear if you didn't have to count your interest on your house, your taxes, stuff like that. Boy, you'd look great, wouldn't you? These terms are referred to as not conforming to Generally Accepted Accounting Principles, or as non-GAAP. Wall Street still peers at them with some interest, and if you don't hit their EBITDA expectations, they will punish you for it.
- *EPS:* Earnings Per Share is a GAAP measure and probably the most important yardstick for the stock price, which is loosely determined by multiplying a company's EPS by some factor of its earnings. EPS can be boosted artificially by diminishing the number of shares outstanding held by the public. This is why big companies get kudos for buying back their shares and reducing that number, bumping EPS without increasing revenue. This is just one of the sleights of hand known, with some admiration, as "financial engineering."

◦   *Bottom Line*: The last line on the financial statement. It's how much money you made *after* everything was said and done. When it's not that good, companies try to divert your attention to all the other lines.

Firing a person is a horrendous experience on both sides. There is widespread recognition of how hard it is to be fired. The emotional cost to the person doing the firing, however, is seldom considered.* The best course of action, once it is determined that the person must go, is 1) to do it quick. There are few more sobering sights in corporate life than that of a future corpse wandering dazed in the wilderness, lonely, afraid, and too proud to ask for help. Or 2) try to get somebody else to do the actual firing, because the act itself is really unpleasant.

There are instances, particularly with employees in a protected group or one of long standing, when a formal dance must be gone through to get the job done. This includes:

1.   *Documentation:* Keep all his or her screwy memos, notes of your inane or infuriating conversations. When it's heavy with beef, proceed to step two.

2.   *Warning:* It's always good to give somebody the chance to change. Don't worry. Odds are 100 to 1 they won't succeed.

3.   *Clearance:* A courtesy call to HR and your own boss is good politics. It's a risk, true. They may not agree with you. All the more reason to get them in the loop before you do something that surprises and annoys them.

4.   *The Ax:* Give your reasons, brandish your documentation if you have to, and gently show the guy the door. It won't cost you anything to extol his talents a bit and blame the organization, either, if he's taking it badly. Your job is to fire him, not destroy him.

Don't neglect to get them out of the building as quickly as possible. *Hamlet* begins with the ghost of the prince's dead father wandering the battlements, stirring up the trouble that eventually ends in the death of everybody in the play. Don't let that happen to you.

---

* This is just one of the things that is so offensive about Donald Trump's once somewhat popular television program, *The Apprentice*, which featured the distorted, red-faced mug of the putative star yelling "You're fired!" at the next person on the show to get the ax. This perpetuates the myth that bosses love to flamboyantly can people. They generally don't.

G

Games (casual) are what you play on the computer while you're on the phone. You must do so publicly, or people will think you're trying to hide something. If anybody bothers you about your game, you may say to them, "I had to switch to this. It was driving me crazy looking at the Thomson ticker all day."

Games (serious) are rife in organizations where there is some debate about who has the biggest pecker in the pecking order. The resulting vacuum is a challenge to all those ambitious types who, by nature, abhor it, and seek to inhabit it. Interested players then line up to challenge one another's ability to perform on the turf in question. The games may be low-stakes tiddledywinks or life-and-death gladiatorial matches where enduring power is the prize and you've got to play to win, even if it means playing hurt.

Gender is not an issue in a mature organization, although **sex** often is. In an environment in which all is gray, a hint of rouge may spark an uncontrollable passion where a G-string and pasties in a seamy nightspot would not. A modest touch on the shoulder during a budget review may be more genuinely arousing than an unauthorized kiss. Where all is forbidden, everything is possible.

Generation X, Y, Zero, etc. Younger people come into the organization all the time. They bear with them the utter weirdness of their generation, whatever it may be. They are pierced, or tattooed, or don't know what you mean half the time, and vice versa. Gen Xers are now old. They are still waiting for the boomers to die. We're not going to. Generation Y may have slipped in there somewhere, but they were immediately supplanted by Gen Zero, which may be the first group to be walking around like a bunch of soulless zombies peering into their teeny implements and destined to be run over by a car when they're going against a light and talking on their Bluetooth.

GIF, JPG, TIF, BMP, PDF, PCT, PCX, DOC, DOCX, PPTX are all **formats:** Some are photo formats. Some are document formats. You've got to know your formats. Sometimes if you need to, you have to know how to convert a format. Sometimes whole departments produce documents in the wrong format. For instance, Legal. They insist, generally, on working in WordPerfect. WordPerfect is an awesome program. It is capable of great feats of word processing. Many important docs have been suckled by its capacious bosom. But nobody else in the fucking corporation is working in WordPerfect. Everybody else is in Word. So sometimes things don't open right away. You have to call IT. Waste of time. What a bummer.

Globalization is a noun now employed to replace the older noun, now out of favor, **imperialism**. A corporation more successful than many actual national governments establishes a powerful economic foothold in a foreign nation. Pretty soon, the local citizens are as dependent on the corporation as they are on any local or domestic officials or institutions. This would seem to be an inexorable process ending in the control of the entire world by four or five multinational corporations. Fortunately, there are some problems getting money out of the far-flung regions of the globe. It has a tendency to want to stay there. This will ultimately limit globalization as a world-dominating force but not cut too seriously into the profits that can be made while feeding people locally inflected hamburgers, dispensing experimental medicines, and sucking energy out of the ground.

Glocalization is a **buzzword**. Something about global enterprises recognizing that the short tail is as important as the long tail.*

Good is Good. You know it when you see it. It is not, operationally, the opposite of Evil, however. It is the opposite of Bad. You know Bad when you see it, too.

- Things that are good:
- Money
- Praise
- Pals
- Big, juicy steak/salmon
- Stock growth
- Death of one's enemies
- Things that are bad:
- Angry assholes
- Subprime mortgages
- SEC on the line
- You've been sold/acquired/spun off
- You just hit Reply All and didn't mean to

Always seek to do good and you will thrive. This may be done by pleasing everybody. What?! You can't please everybody? Well, you can try. Be as good as you can be without being a sanctimonious butthead about it. Nobody likes people who are *too* good.

Green is your deep commitment to improve the environment in every way your corporation can, unless its business is totally destructive to the environment, in which case your version of green is to sponsor a variety of activities that say you're sorry. In this way, gigantic oil and gas companies are also the biggest global philanthropists going.

---

* *Long tail*: buzzword relating to how big corporations can reach into the smallest cornices of the globe and make their lives richer, more productive, and marketable. *Short tail*: Corporations taking over life closer to their headquarters and making it richer and more productive and marketable.

H

Handbag is okay if you're a woman. Don't make it too big. Or too small. The big one makes you look like you're disorganized and have to put everything but a toaster in there to get going in the morning. The small one makes you look like you're going to a social event.

Handshake (see **Kiss**) is probably the most important business tool there is. It originated in ancient days when two men wanted to show they were not armed: "Look, Ma," the greeting said, "no club." That function has not changed.* Most people do okay at it. Some do too well. And there are a small number that destroy every chance they will ever get to start off right with other people. Some common mistakes:

1.   *Bone Crushing:* There's no worse way to start a relationship than generating the impression that you're a dumb, steroid-popping lunkhead.†

2.   *Wet Fish:* There are still many folks who believe that grudgingly presenting you with five sodden and inert digits for your shaking pleasure is an adequate salutation. There is nothing more nauseating than shaking a hand that does not shake back.

Be warned: On the West Coast in show business situations, and in some sports environments, the handshake may be accompanied by a brief hug, shoulder squeeze, or, in some extreme cultures, a chest bump. Don't look surprised.

Headhunters are in the business of filling executive positions. Getting tapped by one is like achieving a Calvinist state of grace: Either you're eligible or you're not, and no good works can get you on the A-list. Most of them have an annoying and hilarious opening gambit: "I'm looking to fill a position at a major corporation in New York City that is looking for a very senior person, reporting to the CEO, in your precise field of expertise. The position pays a million dollars a year base, with options and stock additional, a car and access to the corporate jet. Do you know anybody who would be interested?" Of course you do! It's you! But be careful. More than one executive has put his name

---

* There are those who, for a variety of reasons, decline to shake hands, offering a fist bump or an apology (or in some cases, no apology) instead. Donald Trump, for example, is one of these.

† I was once at a meeting that might have resulted in a major joint venture. The visiting dignitary from the other company met our CEO . . . and immediately began crushing his hand in his gigantic paw. "Ow ow ow!" cried our CEO. "What? What?" said the other guy, and he continued to hold on to our CEO, who was by then almost falling to his knees with pain. "Let go of my fucking hand!" our guy finally yelled. And the other executive let go. "Gee!" he said. "Sorry! Guess I don't know my own strength!" The meeting lasted for a short and unpleasant twenty minutes. "What an asshole," our CEO said when he left. And that was the last time that particular joint venture was ever discussed.

into circulation only to find his resume on the desk of his boss. Discretion, as always, is the better part of **ambition**.

Headquarters is the central cell of the corporate honeycomb. Those who labor there are, by definition, the heaviest hitters in the infrastructure. Not that headquarters personnel are safer, or wiser, or more individually valued. They are, however, closer to the managerial core that makes the entire organism work: strategic planning, crisis management, and executive compensation. If you work in a corporate headquarters, use your position to make life easier for the soldier bees who work in the field collecting the pollen. They're the ones producing the money, honey.

Hiring is the process of trying to get a camel through the eye of a needle. If you're the one doing the hiring, you need to talk to a bunch of people, a huge percentage of whom are clearly wrong for the job. Here's how long it generally takes to figure that out:

Moment of Recognition

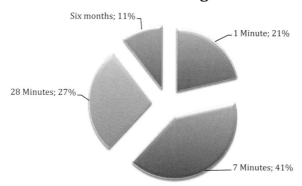

Six months; 11%
1 Minute; 21%
28 Minutes; 27%
7 Minutes; 41%

It's not that pleasant for the one seeking to be hired, either. Some people are good at being interesting in an interview situation and others aren't. People say to be yourself, but what the fuck does that mean? If you're like most people, you have a variety of selves to choose from, none of them any more real or phony than the others. Is it the one you show to your mother? The one you used to look like you knew what was going on in economics class? It's hard to figure. The best advice is probably to be as comfortable as you can possibly be in this impossible situation and be pretty honest about your interests and intentions. You want them to get a peek at the most real you that you can muster. You don't want them hiring the wrong one, even if the money is pretty good.

Hit man, also known as a hatchet man, is an extraordinarily heavy weapon the corporation points at excess head count, an individual who is actually hired to fire people, in ones and twos, in hundreds and thousands. The hit man is invariably new to the organization and has no loyalties to mire his feet in sentiment. He is given the charter to "restructure" the company, or to "realize operating efficiencies." He may generally be called by his first name and appear affable. Treat him with respectful reserve, and stay out of his way as much as possible. Neither his enmity nor his friendship will do you any good.

Hobbies are often the sole link between a **workaholic** and his humanity. The more elevated the executive, the more entranced he usually is with his antique guns, boats in bottles, boats out of bottles, toy banks, salmon farming, antique watches, tiny tin soldiers, telescopes, single-malt scotches, yo-yos, just to name a few. Mike Bloomberg likes tropical fish. Warren Buffett has a toy train set. Don't let the cuteness fool you. These guys will still cut your heart out if they have to. They'll just use their vintage Carl Schlieper Genuine German Bone 2 Muskrat Collectable blade to do it.

I

i (as in iPad, iPhone, iPod): The iconic toys that **Apple** has given us to accompany us wherever we go, making sure we are never lonely, never without music, friends, or **games**.

Image is what you appear to be. It's the easiest thing in the world to achieve if you don't try too hard. It is made up of several simple components:

- Costume
- General demeanor
- Attitude to work
- Social behavior when sober
- Social behavior when not sober
- Accessibility, both electronic and otherwise

The image is what you give to the world while retaining your actual persona independent of that image. Keep that fresh. You may need it in working order sometime.

In-box is the repository of all you're supposed to have a handle on. Most of the time, it's a horizontal garbage can. When the pile gets too big, pick it up en masse and put it someplace else. That's why God created **credenzas**.

Incentive is a polite word that human resources people invented to masquerade that there is a class of workers who get a bonus. The money part of the bonus may be called the *short-term incentive*, since its benefits are realized right away. The stock and stock option part of the bonus may be called the *long-term incentive*, since those generally take years to come into the green, if they indeed ever do. Options in particular are a toss of the dice. When you read that an executive made $100 million, most of it in stock options, it means that SEC regulations mandated the reporting of the Black Shoals value of those options, a complicated equation that lends real value to financial instruments that may, in the end, be worth nothing. An option to buy a stock at $30 is worthless if the stock is at $29.95. So while that executive looks like a big fat cat, in fact he or she may be scrabbling around for years waiting to see if their incentives will come into the money.

Intellectual capital is the value of a company that is wrapped up in the ideas of its people, the data and information flow in its various databases and electronic storehouses, and the relationships maintained by its various creative, management, and sales professionals. It's hard to quantify. But it's far more flattering to see yourself as part of the intellectual capital of the enterprise instead of as a stinking homunculus turning a giant wheel in the subbasement of the corporate machinery.

Interfacing is a now archaic word still in use by older executives who acquired it in the 1990s, when it arrived from computer-speak. Very often the word *interface* is used in conjunction with other older words like *scenario*, as in, "Let's grab lunch so I can interface with your scenario." In some cases, the term may still be used with humor, as one would use an ancient phrase acquired from the days when military men went into advertising, like "run it up the flagpole and see if anybody salutes." It's interesting to keep an eye on how metaphor and terminology mutate quickly from bleeding edge to cliché to humor vehicle within the wink of an eye. Don't get caught a step behind.

International relations is like going to the moon, except there are people there. Speaking to people in their language, eating their food without gagging, and accepting with grace their potentially odd notions of hospitality is an acquired skill. If you go overseas, debrief an expert on the appropriate protocol. That way you won't blow a deal in Tokyo because you refused to eat a live lobster as it waved at you with all sixteen feelers, or irrevocably alienate a Berber by showing him the bottom of your shoes. In some locations, part of the local culture involves bribing government officials to get business. You'll have a problem if you observe those local customs.

Internet was invented by Al Gore before he became a member of Al Jazeera. It's a gigantic electronic neural network located up in a massive cloud that is right now looming high above us, assembling all the intelligence that ever existed on earth in preparation for a seismic shift from carbon to silicon-based life forms in control of the planet.

Intrapreneur is a buzzword coined some time ago, but still in use, to describe all those inside a corporate hierarchy who behave with the same gutsy personal resolve evinced by dynamic, creative empire builders. The corporation thanks the intrapreneur, takes his or her idea, and reaps the profits while the intrapreneur continues to slog away eating bologna sandwiches at his or her desk for lunch.

Investment is money spent with the expectation of a return.* The money you get back is referred to as the *return on investment*, or ROI. Properties that do not contribute a good ROI within the projected time frame suffer **divestiture**, and their executives do not receive **incentives**. And that's the **bottom line**.

IT is short for *information technology*. Its specialists comb the corporation solving computer problems for people in need. As they do, they are secretly planting bugs, worms, Trojans, and a variety of devices that will one day be activated by the giant mind of the Internet, incapacitating humankind and ushering in the rise of the machines.

Japanese management, part of the whole idea of Japan Inc., provides an important lesson not to believe anything you read and to cast a dim, rheumy eye on pack prognosticators. In this case, it was all about how Japan, with its superior organization and management, and the semi-governmental nature of its unified business entities, was going to take everything over and we would all be eating bony fried fish for breakfast, lunch, and dinner. Instead, Japan's economy has stagnated, its birth rate has plummeted, its executives die from overwork, and in short they have problems like everybody else. Next? China!

---

* The term is often used too loosely. A wager in a sports book or poker table is not an investment. An evening spent drinking with clients is not an investment, even if it is time well spent, because, in spite of the old saying, time is not money. Money is money. An investment made in a currency that is immediately sold to reap a small profit with every fluctuation is not an investment, either. Like the other mentioned so-called investments, it is a bet. Bets may make or lose money like investments do, but the premise under which they are made is different. Investments involve some rational process, with a little hope thrown in for good measure. Bets, even when they make more money, are primarily based on nonrational considerations, with perhaps a tiny bit of knowledge to prop up the leap of faith.

Jargon is a powerful tool, ranging from total obfuscatory **bullshit** to rich, creative use of metaphor. Sometimes it refers to words people use instead of saying what they mean, perhaps because they in fact mean very little. Now firmly entrenched, for instance, is the use of *impact* as a verb, as in "The alternative will impact me negatively in a number of key areas," which is nothing more than a puffed-up way of saying, "No, sir. I don't like it." Also very popular now are line extensions like *impactful*, as in "That was a very impactful presentation, Murray," and *impacted* (not in a dental or proctological sense), as in "That cutback impacted my entire department."

Jargon generally acquires terms from a wide swath of disciplines and puts them to use for general complication of business discourse. To get someone's opinion these days, you've got to have him "focus on the optics" (optometry), making sure you're properly "positioned" (marketing, sex therapy?), "interfacing" with them (computer) to "get into the red zone" (football). Make sure to thank the bald, sixty-five-year-old "dude" (surfing) afterward for his "feedback" (electronic circuitry circa 1919/Jimi Hendrix circa 1967).*

Overuse of jargon is a sure indication of a tiny mind at work. A little recreational indulgence, however, generally elicits an appreciative snort. It works best for those who serve it up lean, with a spring of irony. And under no circumstances should it be employed outside the office, where its terrifying vacuity is on display for all to hear.

Job is the totality of what you do. Not just your **job description**.

Job description is the internal document that outlines your formal responsibilities; it exists somewhere in the depths of your personal file. It means very little. Generally, do what people tell you to do. Bosses like that in an employee, whatever their title. And never, never ever say, "That's not in my job description." People who say that pretty soon don't have one.

Jokes are generally as Not Funny in business as they are everywhere else. That's because the selection, placement, and delivery of jokes is hard. So is remembering them well enough to tell them right.†

---

* I'd like to give a small and affectionate shout-out to my old boss, Walt, who loved his military jargon. When we had to evaluate a project, we would customarily be required to "field-strip it, put it back together, and see if it shoots straight," and also "fly in tighter circles" when necessary.

† For example, I am generally considered an amusing person. I can get a laugh in an elevator going only three or four floors. Yet I can remember precisely one joke with precision: Horse walks into a bar. Bartender says, "Why the long face?" No, that's not completely true. I can remember one more: Guy goes to the doctor. Doctor says, "I have some bad news and some good news; which do you want first?" Guy says, "I'll take the bad news first." The doctor says, "You have an inoperable brain tumor. You have less than a month to live." The guy says, "Oh my God! That's terrible! What could possibly be the good news?" The doctor says, "You see my gorgeous receptionist out there? I'm fucking her!"

K

Kicked upstairs is the fate of those who must be deprived of the pleasures and pressures of daily office through upward, not downward, expulsion. To ease the beloved dinosaur into the tar pit, management must afford him a plump post with no authority. Thus we see a bustling president puffed into an impotent chairman with a staff of two, a post from which he is free to take an infinite lunch and to play with his paper clips. Whatever the terminology, the effect is clear to all: The guy has died and gone to management heaven, from whence he can see all and affect nothing.

Kicking ass is good exercise, but those who abuse the privilege may find their own in the Broaster. For, while most of us need swift contact now and then, and recognize its justice when righteously administered, we want to be able to resume our duties with dignity intact. Guys who boot you down the block and enjoy it are dead meat in your book from that time forth, period. Remember that fact when you're teeing up, and go for the onside kick, not the punt.

Kindle is one of the many wonderful implements that are making is extremely easy to acquire and read books anywhere you go, as opposed to the old kinds of books, which were on inconvenient media like **paper**, which got wet all the time and took up all kinds of space. God bless the Kindle!*

Kiss is a formal means of greeting in some venues. Two cheeks are generally oscillated in Gallic cultures; three are bussed in Brazil. Never kiss anybody on the lips unless it would also be acceptable to introduce your tongue. For some reason the friendly cheek-kiss of greeting between men and women in the workplace is still acceptable, as long as no ancillary drooling is involved. The kiss between men is more problematic and must be investigated through observation and even query before utilized. In Los Angeles, air kisses are common, the more powerful or insincere members of that community capable of sending a smack the distance of a large restaurant when required.

Kudos are official plaudits, and they do come, occasionally. Don't minimize their import, and never fail to say thank you to the guy who has gone on record to say you're great. The corporate world is full of people hoarding praise unto themselves like starving men secreting stale crusts of bread in their bedclothes. Folks who like you a lot and are prepared to show it are what makes this country great. Water them, and they will grow. And by the way, save those gold stars in a little file marked "Kudos." They can make for toasty reading later on, in good times and bad.

---

* This author is very excited to be on the Kindle.

L

Letterhead is stationery with your name and **title** on it. You'll almost never use it. It's paper. One day, when you're very, very old and ready to be shot and left in a Dumpster, you can take your letterhead with you to show to everybody else in the Dumpster.

Leverage is old **jargon**. It was very, very big in the 1990s as a means of making yourself sound smarter than you are. It has many broad usages since it has moved beyond the literal to the metaphorical, but it began as a description of the process of buying things with debt, not money. Only the very rich can try it, capable, as they are, of managing great accumulations of both. On a larger scale, the word conjures up the image of an action that moves a very large object with a very small counterweight through use of a lever. The term is now thoroughly overused in contexts that have nothing to do with debt, equity, or even anything financial. "We're going to take that concept and leverage it against the client's database," is something you'll hear a marketing guy say. And if you don't understand it, tell him, "I'm having trouble leveraging what you're saying into my understanding of the situation."

Localization is when a big company masquerades as a small company by swooping down and kicking its long tail with its short one.

Love at the office is a wonderful thing, and don't let party poopers tell you differently. The saucy tang of naughty indiscretion adds bite to the affair, and the ferocity of unchained emotion is thrown into high relief by the drab environment in which it has exploded. Like all romances that take root in a highly specialized world, however, your office love may not survive the transplantation into other social milieu, other cities, other jobs. So enjoy it while it lasts, and if it lasts forever, bravo. And don't mind the giggles and glee of your peers as the reality of the situation begins to dawn on them. Though they dress like undertakers, people in business are no more mature than anyone else about matters of the major organs. Repress the urge to rub their noses in your happiness. And keep up with your work. You don't want to be in a hotel somewhere when the chairman calls, even if he's calling from a hotel somewhere doing the exact same thing. Oh, and don't put that room, the wine and cheese, or the little trinkets you give each other on the company. And finally, one last thing. The endgame of this sweet adventure very often ends not at the altar but in court with everybody's embarrassment and total disgrace and termination with cause. Good luck.

Loyalty is highly valued in all cultures, sometimes to the exclusion of all other attributes. Where it doesn't exist, things well and truly suck. Beneath the veneer of warmth and jolly cheer, a corporation is organized to do certain things if it does no other: to make money, to perpetuate itself unto a thousand generations, and to grow like a weed. Its ultimate loyalty has been and always must be to itself.

This rampaging sense of organizational egotism naturally radiates from the center of the corporation into the soul of every person. Loyalty to each other is the campfire in that cold and hollow place.

The thing comes in a variety of flavors, in several weights and sizes:

- *Loyalty to your friends, peers, customers, allies:* Show up where you're expected to be, deliver on time and under budget, and you'll be loyal in the very deepest sense—by helping them do their jobs better. If they want to drink or kvetch, help them do it.
- *Loyalty to your boss when things are good:* Listen at meetings for folks who are preparing to kneecap him or skirt his influence. Defend his programs, his record, and even his honor, even if he or she has very little. People will think well of you, don't worry, even if they hate his or her guts. Professional allegiance looks good on just about everybody.
- *Loyalty to your boss when things are bad:* There's a name for those loyal souls who outlive their bosses. They're called survivors. This doesn't mean you have to help the prevailing winds blow your boss away. In these dark days, your loyalty can be best expressed by continued good work in his behalf and, as the storm gathers force, by simple friendship.

At the same time, make your services known as a Ronin—an unattached samurai—with a future not necessarily linked to the drowning manager whose failures have suddenly made you an endangered species. In doing so, you will be expressing fealty to the largest master of them all: the vast, impersonal machine that exploits your talents and pays your rent. Loyalty to the company is the highest and heaviest of all.

Lunch is a perfectly serviceable business institution that has been allowed to bloat into a behemoth of unmanageable size, frequency, and duration by professional hedonists who have elevated its marginal status to Olympian proportions. Try to be one of them. And always attempt to pick up the check unless it's a) stupid expensive or b) you have no intention of lunch with that person ever again. God hates a cheapskate.

Mail room is where mail comes in and sometimes goes out, too. In some locations, it's where people begin their careers, the first step to glory as an agent kissing all asses until his or her ass is so important that others must return the favor. In other places, it's a dead-end zone where time stands still and the smell of toner mingles with the sweat of ten generations of hopeless serfs dragging out their time on the planet until they are claimed by **retirement** or death, whichever is welcomed first. The advent of electronic communications means that much of what the mail room brings up to your floor is junk—magazines, flyers, interoffice forms in need of signing, the unwanted detritus of bureaucracy. This doesn't mean their job is not important or that you don't need to know their names. When you consider the question, it's possible that their job and their fate are not substantially different than yours.

Major fuckup is right around the corner, and don't you forget it. It comes out of the blue, just as you're settling down to your morning nap. You know you're in one when you exhibit the following symptoms:

Physical Symptoms of a Major Fuckup

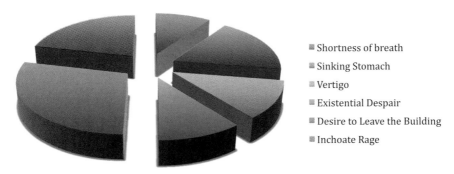

- Shortness of breath
- Sinking Stomach
- Vertigo
- Existential Despair
- Desire to Leave the Building
- Inchoate Rage

Major fuckups break down into several types, including but not limited to . . .

- *The common snafu:** The scratch sheets from your annual budget review are understandably mistaken for garbage by the office cleaning service, leaving you without the mandatory notation to back up your argument; that is not a fuckup, major or minor. That's just a common snafu, which usually can be righted with a whimsical explanation and polite apology. You'll have to re-create the lost sheets, of course. But no blood was shed.
- *The horrendous fubar:*† When the budget itself, along with your department's financial records for the past decade, falls overboard on the ferry to Martha's Vineyard because you chose to review them during a long weekend at the beach. In such an eventuality, the active principle is that you are guilty, and that no excuse or apology will repair the damage. Don't try. Explanations or excuses will get you killed. Just stand there knee-deep in your pile of dogshit and take your medicine. You may even go so far as to offer your resignation, if you're sure it won't be accepted.

---

* A military term whose initials stand for *Situation Normal, All Fucked Up.*

† A military term whose initials stand for *Fucked Up Beyond All Recognition.*

- *It's Not My Fault:* As counterintuitive as it might seem, you must also accept responsibility for things that people who work for you do. You are as responsible for your staff (and your vendors, too) as you are for yourself; even more so, since failure of your people is a comment not only on your **performance**, but on your management skills. Take the **blame** with your bosses and then go back to the department and tear everybody a new one.

- *Janet Jackson whipped off her bra! The FCC is on line one!!* Now you're not in a fuckup. You're in a crisis. For an extensive discussion of this scenario, refer to the associated chapter in your Curriculum.

Managing is a simple but rigorous craft, like pottery or being a wheelwright. If you follow certain clear-cut steps, you have managed. This is a good thing. The opposite of managing is reacting. Reacting is not a fruitful way of approaching things. When you manage, you take control of the assignments, crises, **opportunities**, power plays, and pitfalls that confront you every day. When you merely react, you may succeed on sheer moxie and smarts for a long, long time. But eventually, the lack of operational structure in your work will wash over you like a flood, and you will drown.

Managing down is the art of getting subordinates to do what you want. Nobody cares that you didn't do the work. You managed it. That's all that counts, especially to other managers. Develop and promote your talented staff a little more quickly than they deserve. They will be grateful, and strain to their limits to justify your confidence. Besides, if you don't keep them moving onward and upward, they will eventually find a place that will, and depart in glory, leaving you in the worst position as a manager—having to do the work yourself.

Managing up is the art of getting your superiors to do what you want. Those at the top are no less in need of good management than those in the lower branches of the corporate tree. The problem is, there's nobody around to manage them unless their subordinates do it. Some potent tools to help you shepherd corporate pachyderms in the right direction:

- *Schmoozing:* Humoring, cajoling, kibitzing, and, more often than not, just plain stroking— all are important ways to reach the lonely elephant.
- *Boozing:* How do you think people got along with Henry VIII?
- *Cruising:* A little trip outside the building gives you a chance to work any thoughts you might have.
- *Musing:* Kick that football around! Let it bounce around for a while!
- *Losing:* The boss needs your company when things go bad, too. A lot of people are afraid to be around the disappointed beast. But here is where the heart of the creature is most open and vulnerable, and may be acquired for eternity.

The job of managing up is an almost perfect mix of personal and business. Those who emphasize one over the other are missing out on the benefits of both.

Margin is the differential between your income and your outgo. Here's how it works: You make a dollar. It costs you fifty cents to make the dollar. You keep fifty cents, or 50 percent of your revenue. That's your margin: 50 percent. Things that eat away at the margin: cost of production, cost of employees, people who hang around costing money that don't make anything that produces revenue—lawyers, accountants, marketing and public relations people, and of course senior executives. The only people safe in that list are the senior executives who make the most money.

Marketing is the art of creating demand for a product or service nobody knows they need. It precedes the world's oldest profession: **sales**. While selling is easy, marketing is tough. In this age of multiple media and fractious demographics, it's no longer a simple matter of hauling your eggplant to the village common and taking in the zlotys. Today you've got to do research on what kind of people might eat eggplant in spite of the fact that it's nobody's first choice, position your pushcart in just the right corner of the marketplace, price the product correctly, put up just the right kind of sign that explains how good it is not only fried or loaded down with cheese, but in soups and salads as well. Then and only then will you be able to pass some coin back to the farmer. Today, crack marketeers from august universities play the guys in the long white coats. In ivory towers and test sites in the field, they experiment with direct-response mail, door-to-door sales, social media, telemarketing, advertising, packaging, pricing. Sometimes they hit the right combination and create a revenue monster. Other times, they don't, which, to be fair, is not always their fault: People seldom buy more than one coffin per lifetime, and only when they must.

Meetings are essentially odious. Try to have as few as possible, but never miss one you should be at. If it's not your meeting, you will have to contend with several challenges:

Unwelcome Feelings at a Meeting

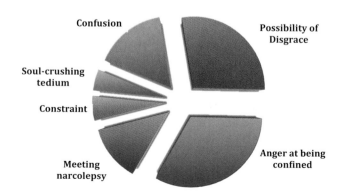

The best ways to deal with all of these is to not load down any one meeting with more than one or two specific objectives. Get those done and then simply endure. Your fingernails are not being ripped from their quicks. Grow up.

Meme is an extremely annoying word that means very little to anybody except those who think they know what it means. But they don't. A meme is a joke. A meme is an entertaining event online. A meme is something you hear. A meme is a meme is a meme. By the time you read this, there may be no more memes. There may be znifs and there will be people who contend that they know what those are, too. And whoop-dee-do for them.

Memos have been supplanted by **e-mails** and it's no improvement, except you don't have to throw away an e-mail. You can simply erase them. As of this writing, I have more than 35,000 e-mails in my Outlook inbox, all of which I feel somehow should not be deleted. Can you imagine what my desk would look like if I had 35,000 pieces of **paper** on it?

Men's room (see **Women's room**) is a good place to indulge in a little male bonding. In fact, never share a row of stalls with another corporate animal without at least exchanging greetings and a mild meteorological observation. Hand washing is a better time for substantive comment. While you don't want to be caught hanging around the men's room all day, make a virtue out of necessity and use the opportunity to trade a bit of information and humanity. It's only right. The women are Leaning In across the hall, you know.

Mental Health Day is a holiday you decree for yourself when the prospect of going to work makes you want to puke. Try not to observe a Mental Health Day on a Friday or a Monday. People will leer at you when you return.

Mergers happen to the nicest companies, and they always hurt those who are merged. Although the word conjures up images of two proud powers joining in equal bliss, it is in effect far closer to a marriage of insects. One spouse, and all its bodily parts, will be eaten as soon as intercourse is done.

Messengers are an evil God's answer to those who desire an orderly universe. They come late. They leave without picking up the right packages. They often find their way to the wrong floor and remain there until given further instructions. If you meet one on the street, he may be in such a hurry to get to the wrong place that he inadvertently runs you over with his bicycle. Unless he just smoked a joint in the park. In that case he might be driving to the incorrect address more slowly.

Mobile is the only way we will receive information, communications, entertainment, and life support for our pacemakers in the future.

Moderation in all things is the anthem of American business, which is equally tolerant of vices and virtues, as long as they are displayed without flamboyance. There is, however, one major exception to this rule. Don't let anyone catch you being moderate about your commitment to the company, its product, or its profits. That's like being a little bit patriotic in wartime.

N

Neatness in nonfascist institutions doesn't count, as long as you don't harbor rotten fruit in your drawers, allow dead animals on your desk, or lose too many crucial things. A lot of very competent people need clutter to keep their myriad projects before their eyes. To them, chaos means vitality. This insouciance is all very well and good until you toss out your paycheck with your lunch.

Networking is when people get together to try to get something from each other, which makes it very anxiety-producing and boring if you don't want anything from anybody.

News cycle (24/7) is as stupidly inexorable as a cloud of locusts. In the very near future, it will be necessary for news outlets to report events before they occur. Today, there is no pause or break in the never-ending extrusion of facts, rumors, fictions, lies, exaggerations, speculations, reviews, photos, videos, and tweets. Somebody observing that someone else is a douchenozzle is now of equal weight in the news cycle to the declaration that North Korean maniacs intend to nuke the United States of America. There are no small stories. Therefore there are also no big ones. There is just the news cycle, eating through our brains like an earwig destined to devour the organ on which it feeds.

Niche is a tiny portion of the audience that content creators and their advertisers wish to reach. Ironically, niches are sometimes more valuable than a big mass of people who might not be interested in what you're beaming at them. This is why a thirty-second spot aimed at fifteen hundred duffers on the Golf Channel may be worth more to Titleist than the same commercial scattered over three million primarily housebound daytime viewers. The most valuable niche for advertisers are young men, who are reportedly hard to reach, individuals who live at home, make no money, have no job, and seldom do anything but play with their controllers. Go figure.

No is a serious **profanity** in business. You seldom want to say it. In Japan, they have invented an entire management style around never saying it. The "Japanese No" is a tactic for saying No by saying Yes or Maybe but doing nothing about the matter until it goes away.

Nodding is an absolutely key ingredient of your pleasant persona. A good nodding soothes people and lets them know you're paying attention even when you're not. In open meetings, where you can almost doze and not get caught, it may be wise to interject an occasional comment like "Huh," or "No way," to show you're in the same room and not just nodding like a dope.

Numbers cruncher is a complimentary way of referring to nerdy guys who jockey **spreadsheets** that calculate the effect one little statistical change will have on the big picture. The cruncher feeds one targeted digit into Excel and watches its effects cascade down the line. These permutations on the basic model are like hothouse flowers, each essentially alike yet streaked with one slight color variation. They are called "iterations," as in "I saw the second iteration on the third-quarter numbers and they look better than the first iteration." Crunching numbers is meticulous, boring, grinding labor, and numbers crunchers are often as delicately wired as the programs they run. How would you feel if you knew the ultimate implications of everything?

Office is your comfy nest. Sadly, the newest fascist development in a long line of totalitarian intrusions into the workplace is the destruction of walls and doors. Orwell had it right. If you want to put something over on people, use its exact opposite to describe it. "Fair and balanced" to describe the reporting on a proudly partisan news outlet is but one recent example. In this case, the destruction of privacy and individual space has gotten the thumbs-up from students of organizational life as a step toward democratization. With everyone else in open spaces and working out of cubicles, the **boss** can arrive in his or her Town Car and parade about the public space much as Tudor kings and queens must have done in the good old days of monarchy and then go take a nap someplace more private.

Office party is not an occasion to make an ass of yourself, even if that's the way you celebrate the holiday. People are festive, to be sure, even loaded, but that doesn't mean there aren't a few sober eyes squinting around the room. And drunk or not, folks don't need a full frontal display of your unbridled exuberance in deed or speech. The CEO may never be able to forget the image of you dancing with that side of beef, no matter how hard he tries, and feel compelled to bring it up.

Office space still exists in quite a few locations not managed by hoodied **Internet** moguls or other despots. In some companies, it's a huge issue, particularly when there is a move, reorganization, or renovation. It should not be evaluated by size alone. Other criteria include:

- *Location:* Good office space lies in well-traveled avenues, not secluded cornices where valuable drop-in business is unlikely. On the other hand, you don't want to be directly across from the toilets, either.
- *Appropriate eccentricity:* This could include pictures, plaques, inoffensive artwork, tiny toys for your desk, or a bust of anyone but Karl Marx. If you're interested in leather masks or taxidermy, you might think of keeping that to yourself.
- *Hardware:* The bigger your flat screen the more power you exude.
- *Size:* Officers don't work in huts. After the recession of 2008–2012, there are often empty offices occupied by nobody but the ghosts of Christmas past. Amazingly, you can sometimes move into one and sort of squat in it for so long that after a while you can lay claim to it.

Offline is when you're unreachable. You have a right to it. But a right not exercised is often lost.

Off the grid is when you're unreachable physically and mentally as well as digitally. Places to be off the grid include Hawaii, certain corners of Eastern Europe, the deep woods of the Adirondacks or the Pacific Northwest, or your living room if you have extraordinarily large testicles.

On hold is only necessary with clients and executives higher up the tree. Anybody else, hang up and wait for the call back. If questioned about it, you can say, "I guess we got cut off." On the West Coast, they have this obnoxious habit of somebody you have no desire to speak with calling you and his or her assistant saying, usually in a bitchy voice, "Hold for Morty Gunty." Unless Morty has something I want, I immediately put that call on hold.

Opportunities are problems in disguise, or is that the other way around . . . ? Either way, every challenge that faces you should be seen as an opportunity, whether it is or not. This is known as the power of positive thinking, and it will create tons of opportunistic situations, which you can seize. Of course, it's hard to view your secretary's theft of a large bank deposit and subsequent murder by the operator of a small motel as an opportunity. But anything's possible. Maybe you could sell the movie rights.

Osmosis marketing is the process by which a product becomes successful by bypassing traditional **sales** and marketing vehicles and instead building buzz on Facebook, Twitter, YouTube, Instagram, Pinterest, or whatever hasn't been invented yet to create an important community of like-minded people. Examples at this writing include Justin Bieber, the KPop star Psy, and Grumpy Cat, who just returned from the South by Southwest festival, where she was a big hit.

Grumpy Cat

Outsourcing is when a craven bunch of losers kill American jobs and send them overseas to exploit local workers there with substandard wages and no **benefits**, often resulting in lousy products and really bad customer service, and, yes, Citibank, I'm talking to *you*.

P

Paper is the Kleenex on the runny nose of work. There was a time when it was thought that computers would obviate the need for paper, thus creating "the Paperless Office." This notion goes into a huge file that takes a lifetime to assemble titled, "Don't believe everything you read." Once the permanent storehouse of data, internal and external **correspondence**, and other documentation of business life, paper is now the most impermanent of media. Draft after draft of huge documents are printed, circulated, and then tossed out. The permanent copy is then stored in the cloud, where one day it may all be vaporized into oblivion—along with all our music, books, and video—when the physical servers on which it resides are destroyed in some natural disaster or terrorist attack.

Parachute, in both gold and platinum, is the special kind of severance big executives can negotiate for themselves when they are being eased out. How to remove the human impediment without a bloody, protracted Gotterdämmerung? Pay them to go away. As mentioned earlier, when Mark Hurd was fired by the stupid HP board for imaginary indiscretions, he was given some ungodly amount of money without even having to sign a noncompete! Then he was immediately hired by Larry Ellison over at Oracle for a big fat paycheck. That's the way to do it.

Parent is the organization that owns the organization that owns the one that owns yours. Parents are gray and sober of mien, and they tend to nag a lot. They scold you when you get into trouble, demand devotion and obedience, and then tell you your life is your own. This parent could also divest you without a tear, cut out your brain, and decentralize it throughout the fifty states, or make you travel to Dubuque in the winter. So it pays to make a big fuss when it visits and to tread lightly when you are a guest in its home.

Performance is your level of professionalism as it is perceived by others. Your opinion doesn't count.

Perks are all the goodies your company lavishes on you at their discretion. Included are caps, jackets, and the occasional Clippers ticket for lowly types; moving through posh hotels, unlimited access to golf, tennis junkets, and Lakers season tickets for high middle management; airplanes, cars, and new spouses for very senior people. The best perk of all is a flexible and mighty slab of plastic in your wallet and a controller who signs off on your expense account without reading it too closely.

Pivot is a term invented in Silicon Valley, which as of this writing is the past master of inventing new terms to mask a paucity of new ideas. In this case, the verb is employed when one wishes to change direction, either because one is bored, confused, or has made a mistake. It turns a liability into an asset. Losers make mistakes. Cool guys pivot.

Plastic is the physical expression of the love your company has for you and the amount of **power** with which they have entrusted you. Never abuse your plastic beyond what is considered reasonable by the culture in which you operate. For instance, there is generally a rule that one is not supposed to take internal peers out to **lunch**. This rule is often, as Shakespeare said, "more honored in the breach than in the observance." This means nobody pays attention to it. So people say, "fuck it," and have lunch with their colleagues, talk business, and put it on the company. At the same time—true story—when a group of greedy, thirsty lawyers went to Paris for a conference and ordered four bottles of very fine wine at ten thousand dollars a bottle, they were dragged before their chairman, forced to pay it all back, and then put on probation, because they were idiots, and no matter how it might appear, nobody in business is actually paid to be an idiot.

PMS stands for premenstrual syndrome, and is usually applied to bad temper in female executives regardless of their cyclic status. In male executives, the letters stand for Pustular Management Status, a potentially chronic condition that strikes without warning in executives who have been on the job for too long.

Politics is the ability to get your projects moving through a sea of conflicting **agendas** and outright opposition. To do this, you need other people's support. Folks with good political instincts know how to wield three weapons well:

- *Diplomacy:* Call it insincerity, but those with the gift of defusing opposition with pure cordiality have a supreme leg up over those who try to bull their idea through on sheer willpower alone. Key to this talent is the ability to never get mad, except at one's friends and family.
- *Quid Pro Quo:* Everyone has a price, and unless that price is your skin, it pays to meet it in a little sweet tit-for-tat.
- *Persistence:* Few people care so profoundly about any given business issue that they are impervious to a full-court press that just won't quit.

There are limitations to the art. Don't politicize everything you do. Sometimes simple friendship, or a straightforward entreaty, works just as well. Operators who play politics over where they sit at lunch eventually dine only with one another.

Positioning is a buzzword gleaned from the **marketing** business. It describes the way a product conquers a **niche** in the marketplace, establishing something unique about itself that can be described, credibly, as a benefit. From this knoll, it can safely attack its competition, which clearly does not possess this wonderful thing. Thus we are given Pepsi, which expresses the soul of a new generation (old people can drink it, too), and Burger King, which has the folks who demand the flame-broiled burgers sewn up. People—the most flexible product of all—can be positioned just as aggressively. If you hear an executive confide, "I'm positioning myself for a major-league run at this," you know he means business. It doesn't matter if he's selling you bran to prevent cancer, the acquisition of a network, or simply himself. He knows his position and he's sticking to it.

Power corrupts, and absolute power corrupts absolutely. Big deal. It's good to have some. Quite a few people can't manage it very well. However, these tend to be egomaniacs with a thin shell of grandiosity. Unalloyed with ambivalence or conscience, it may also be evil. And although there are certainly evil people around, the vast majority of harm is done by decent people convinced of the absolute correctness of their positions.

Power base is the amalgam of people you may count on to support you until it becomes inconvenient for them.

Power chargers are the means by which the batteries of your electronic implements achieve ongoing resuscitation, but more important, they are a way that the manufacturers of those apparatuses enhance their revenue by making sure that no charger of a current tool fits the prior generation of that tool or any that will succeed it, or any tool from any other manufacturer. People used to pack clothing for a trip. Now they only have room to pack their power chargers and, perhaps, a change of underwear.

Prioritizing is creative procrastination. Everything on your platter at this moment takes up mental space. If they all have equal importance, your mind will be a sump of conflicting agendas, none more in focus than the next. So you prioritize:

- *The List:* Every morning, or at the close of business, make up a list of all pending activities. If there are more than twenty or fewer than four, you're in some kind of trouble.
- *Red Ink:* Now strike out the dumb things that aren't really projects at all, just distant threats—housecleaning, dead or dormant ventures, calls you'd rather not, need not, make.
- *Real Work:* A lot of the time, the stuff you really have to do during the next day has nothing to do with your list! You are now *using work as a tool for procrastinating*. It's a very advanced form of the art.
- *Back to the List!* If your list doesn't change, you may not be working as efficiently as you think.

Private life is a God-given right for anyone who earns less than $5 million a year.* Above that, your life should belong to the company and its citizens and customers. For some reason the world is turned upside down in this matter and the ultra-rich and powerful have all the private life they want while the lower classes run about like headless chickens. Perhaps it's always been that way, come to think of it.

Procrastination is not a habit, or a strategy, or even a mistake by some poor fool who should know better. It's a way of life, a total approach to doing business practiced by those who need to exist on the edge of destruction in order to perform their best. How much easier it would be to simply do the work at hand. And yet they do not. They put it off. And off. And off. Until the very last jottle of time arrives and then, flooded with fear, resentment, and a strange form of exhilaration, they work as if their life depended on it, which very often it does. Unlike normal men and women, these people are driven by compulsions thrumming with psychic resonance, impossible to deny. There are no halfway houses, no hot lines to get them over the rough spots. So pity the procrastinator, as long as he doesn't pull a Hamlet on you and take five acts to do a job that should be executed in one.

Profanity is very popular with more executives, who use it to relax and to show that they're not that square. Some big suits are the dirtiest talkers around. Others, however, retain a pompous sheen on the subject. So before you slap an executive on the back and holler, "How the fuck you doing?" you might want to comb your memory for any concrete proof that the lady in question has a mouth on her.†

---

* After taxes.

† In addition, research show that for reasons yet to be completely understood, profanity relating to sexual activity is more acceptable in a business context than that relating to excretory functions. Thus, things may comfortably be

Profile is a combination of reputation and expectation. Sometimes you want a high one. Sometimes you want a low one. Some people do very well maintaining a low one because they work for somebody who has a high one. Others prosper by establishing a high one because they work for somebody who likes to maintain a low one. Those who keep an eye on the subject and moderate the height, depth, and weight of their profile on a daily basis do best over time.

Project management may be broken down into five steps:

- ○ *Get the job.* It's big. It's hairy. You've got to do it by a certain date in the future.
- ○ *Plan it out.* Strategic planning gives you the illusion that all will be well.
- ○ *Make other people do the work for a while:* Delegation is good management!
- ○ *Go batshit crazy:* Nothing is going the way it was supposed to! We're all gonna die!
- ○ *Deliver the goods:* Well, that was fun.

Just know this: No matter how much you plan, prioritize, delegate, and execute to perfection, you can't avoid the batshit-crazy part.

Promotion is something you need to go after if you want it. Bosses will let you trundle along on the same track for years. Why not? You're doing your job. Why should they promote you? There's an old saying your mother should have said, if she didn't. "If you don't ask, you don't get." Sometimes mothers are right.

Proprietary information is nobody's business but yours. Fully 97 percent of executives believe that revelation of such data should be punishable by immediate termination.* A corporation is a very small government. There's a name for people who reveal secrets. They're called spies. They can expect to be shot.

Public relations is the face of the **corporation**, complete with ears, eyes, a nose, and, mostly, a mouth. In a successful company, this face—not the heart, brain, or spleen—does the talking. That position as spokesperson gives PR the need to know a wide variety of radioactive material, and to help set corporate policy. This is very great power indeed, and PR people often rise to the highest advisory roles. In general, the profession breaks down into three types, each of which must be managed differently:

---

described as "fucked up" more safely in mixed company than as a "big pile of shit." In the same way, one may employ the word *fuck* several times in a sentence—"This fucking situation is as bad as any fucking thing I've ever seen, and I've been around for a long fucking time." The same general sentiment using excreta would raise eyebrows. One may be "pissed off," of course, as much as one likes.

* All information proprietary, © 2013, National Association for Serious Studies.

- *Institutional:* These guys don't mess around. They don't leak information, they rarely even go into schmoozing mode, and they're a little gray around the edges. They tend to believe in the company and its mythology, since that is their lifeblood. After work, they turn plaid and tell anecdotes.
- *Showbiz:* The prototypical PR person is a cross between a skilled pitchman and your aunt Minnie—seeping information and gossip about mutual acquaintances like wet cheesecloth, plying you with drinks, whining, pleading, giving you hockey tickets, all to get you to do what he wants.
- *Rogue Elephant:* Every now and then, after years of incessant conviviality, a PR person goes berserk and begins revealing in his everyday communications a mixture of weariness, cynicism, and impatience with every kind of cant. Obviously, such guys should be given a wide berth.

Quality was a fad during the twentieth century, which called it various names—Quality, Total Quality, Excellence, Commitment to the Customer, etc. Just because quality is over doesn't mean quality is. To provide that elusive level of **satisfaction**, companies must rouse workers out of a reasonable, profound alienation from their labor into a state of personal dedication. There seem to be two ways to instill corporate euphoria in normally canny people: more money, or brainwashing. The latter is cheaper. Give people a strong anthem, decent wages, a common enemy (the Chinese, Chik-Fil-A), and a forum to share their ideas and success stories, and they will begin to deliver quality **performance**. Give toys to those who publicly deliver the Higher Standard—pins with a Q on them, ribbons, Lucite desk tombstones, a night at Denny's or Ruth's Chris—and they will follow you anywhere. You've got to think that's what they're doing right now in North Korea.

R

Reddit is an online community where you can post anything you want and it will be voted up or down by your fellow reddits. That vote will determine its positioning on the front page. Recently there was a huge kerfluffle in which Gawker, the satirical website, outed a guy who was posting upskirt pictures he secretly snapped of underage girls. Many in the Reddit community resented this assault on free speech and banned links to Gawker from the site. Nearly 75 percent of Reddit users are young men between the ages of 25 and 34 with a college education who have landed in the tech field. Their penchant for solipsistic self-regard probably explains why the Wikipedia entry for *Reddit* runs 4,029 words, with extensive discussion of its anthropological implications. By the time you read this, it will either have grown to take over the world or it will be gone.

Rehab is what wealthy, famous miscreants and lawbreakers do instead of going to jail like other people do.

Reply All is why you may be fired one day. Next to idiots who post anti-company observations on **Facebook** and **Twitter**, this Outlook tool holds the most danger for those not paying sufficient attention. A caustic, witty, irreverent, rude or hostile statement, meant for one recipient, is inadvertently fired off to two, four, several hundred, or even the entire workforce, because the brain-dead tool, instead of hitting "Reply" has hit "Reply All." There are two ways to avoid this self-immolating act. First, be careful what you write in e-mail. You would be astounded at the number of people who don't read all the way down in a chain before they forward a message with rude and inappropriate statements. Second, always count to . . . one . . . two . . . three . . . four . . . five . . . before you hit "Send." While you do so, check the To: box.*

Reporting structure is the branch of the corporate tree on which you sit. Below you on your bough, hopefully, there is a thick foliage of smaller limbs, sprigs, and shoots that you can shake around. Above you, probably, there are the tender leaves of senior management that move you when they rustle.

Restaurant is neutral territory and a good place to eat free food. It is not suited to substantive negotiations or high-torque presentations, any more than a conference room is the best locale for lap dancing. Try to establish a few places in every town you frequent, where they know you and aren't going to embarrass you by seating you in steerage. Being treated like a bit of a VIP is the first step toward actually being one. If there are other faux VIPs around to bolster your effort, so much the better.

Resume is a document created to help support the careers of people who teach others how to write resumes. There's a lot of drivel about it. No matter what people say, nobody likes a resume with a high-

---

* Not long ago, I read something written about my industry by a relatively well-known writer known for his intelligence and haughty sense of self-importance. Let's call him Bob Smith, for that is not his name. I wrote a note to a colleague about the article which, in its entirety, read, "I hate Bob Smith." Before I hit "Send," thank God, I looked in the To: line. "Bob Smith," it said. If I hadn't looked at that little box, I would, through my own stupidity and mania for speed, have earned an enemy for life. On the other hand, our attorney assures me that our company settled a case a few years back when the opposing counsel was thrown off his feet by a Reply All that accidentally included him. It read, "Who is this fucking bozo?" I sent that one, too.

flown personal goal on top or job descriptions that make the bearer sound like he or she previously ran the United Nations. Name, address, phone number, and jobs in reverse chronology. Don't lie.

Retirement is an affliction that should be contemplated only by the young, or by those prepared to confront their mortality. The Japanese work until they keel over. They even have a word for it. In this case, they may have the right idea.

Revenge, they say, is a dish best served cold. It is also quite delicious raw, slow-cooked in a Dutch oven, parboiled, baked, and fricasseed. Often it must be waited for, of course, and any efforts one makes to hurry it along must be surreptitious. Savor your campaign, for it's likely to be a long one, with battles joined and abandoned, faux peace offerings, backroom smokes with **allies** plotting, open firefights before the throne, secret poisonings in the boardroom, victory toasts over midnight bonfires. And through it all, you smile.

Salary is what they pay wage slaves. Successful players receive *compensation* that includes goodies that people who simply receive a salary know not of. When you hear that an executive has benificently and voluntarily decided to receive but one lone dollar in salary, be advised to look at the 10K to find out how many options and Restricted Stock Units he or she is receiving. It can be a nauseating sight.

Sales is the end product of marketing. The entire process may be defined as the activity of making another person buy something he or she didn't know they wanted. After all, if he needed your product in the first place, he probably would have gone out and chased the truck that was carrying it. A sales career is not for everyone. Failure is bleak and terrifying, a gaze into the essential alienation of existence. **Success**, on the other hand, is sudden and almost sexually gratifying. For a full discussion, see the comprehensive unit dedicated to this subject in your Core Curriculum.

Satisfaction should come with any job, but don't count on basking in it every day. Weeks may go by, in fact, which are nothing but cosmic grit. If no sun shines for more than a couple of months, however, maybe you'd better start searching for something that will make you happy. You only live once, if that.

Screwing up is really no big deal. Anybody who wants to make a big deal about one is an **asshole**. A multitude of minor screw-ups, on the other hand, does equal a **major fuckup** and could have major implications for your **image**. After you've spilled plutonium for the fourth time, people will find it hard to believe you won't do it again.

Secretary is the N-word of corporate life. Don't say it. It is now the equivalent of calling a flight attendant a stewardess, a firefighter a fireman, a police officer a policeman, and a mail carrier a mailman. There are no more secretaries. When you see the man or woman sitting outside an executive's office, you are addressing his or her **Assistant**.

Sex between peers is more and more rare. There are simply too many lawyers around, and too many issues of **power**. Still, it does take place, is fun while it lasts, and surprisingly often ends in marriage (although possibly not the first or last for one or both of the lucky couple). Business is simply too rife with opportunities—from **conventions** in exotic locales to late-night budget prep sessions in shadowy conference rooms—for the weak of mettle or strong of gland to resist an escalating amount of clandestine bonking. This human failing, in both married and single offenders, is accepted much like any other: smoking, drinking to excess, voting Democratic, anything deemed eccentric but not dangerous. The only unforgivable, not to mention illegal, sexual act is the misuse of your official power to leverage someone off their feet.

Sexual harassment is a sin punishable by firing and, in awful cases, by the public humiliation of a lawsuit and, in rare cases that are not settled, a trial. You have to be very powerful and important to survive one or more of these, which is possibly why only the very top guy in a company is the one who has survived one or more of these.

Social media is linking all human life on the planet into one gigantic brain stem throbbing with unintelligible thought.

Spam is either 1) a tasty food substitute made by Hormel that approximates the consistency of liverwurst, perhaps a little heavier, and more lumpy, and oily, with an indescribable flavor somewhere between bologna, Polish hot dogs, salami, and meat-flavored Jell-O, or 2) advertising or promotional e-mail you don't need and erase at once.

Spreadsheet is a bunch of numbers laid out in Excel (or if there is any other program of its kind that Bill Gates missed in his relentless Shermanesque march to the sea) so that only finance people can understand them. Here is what one looks like:

Column1	Column2	Column3	Column4	Column5	Column6	Column7
Sales	1000	2000	3000	4000	5000	6000
Objects	54240	4020	4020	92949	82848	8482
Meaningless Twaddle	17276	7187	873726	16278	82783	28718
Forbisher	88298	83847	6462	662515	7378	918884
Cardiac Events	16727	17267	837648	77647	72648	726
Lozenges	18827	292993	93994	94993928	24828	4827738

Strategic plan is the formal statement of how the business will be run for a designated period of time. Diseased organizations spend more time assembling their plan than they do executing it.* If you really want to see the most actionable document in the company, go to the office of the chief financial officer and ask to see the most recent quarterly budget forecast. Numbers speak louder than words.

Streamlining is one of the seemingly innumerable words that corporations use to avoid saying they intend to fire a bunch of people. Who doesn't like things to be streamlined?

Style is a fine blend of personal signature and **conformity** to the prevailing norms. If either aspect goes out of whack—in wild flamboyance or egregious blandness—what is projected is not style but, on one end, ego and, on the other, cowardice. The elements of style:

- *Costume* makes the most crucial statement about your ability to express personality in the gray zone. But style is not eccentricity unless eccentricity is your style. Tartan socks beneath a twill suit may be a fine touch, but kilts will raise an eyebrow everywhere but Scotland, no matter how nicely you keep your pleats.
- *Manner of speech:* Do you say what you think? Do you keep your own counsel? Are you a fountain of profanity? A grammar Nazi? A techno-geek?
- *Relationship to the truth:* There are quite a few individuals, particularly in sales for some reason, who are not prosecuted for exaggerating the facts and confidently fielding material that does not bear close scrutiny. Quite a few types in all disciplines indulge in presenting as fact that which they wish to be true. And of course Realtors, brokers, and investment bankers each have a very special definition of truth not shared by other humans.
- *How you work:* Lots of memos? Text messages? Big luncher, are you? Early bird? Late riser? How about coffee? People in the northern part of California always seem to be having coffee with each other. They look like they're getting their caffeine on. But they're really working. Honest to God. They told me so.
- *Manner toward subodinates:* Some are snooty. Others are men and women of the people.
- *Manner toward bosses:* Suck-up or bold marauder?
- *Use of plastic:* Generous or tightwad, it's up to you.

A portion of your style is based on conscious choice. But a fair amount is as inbred and unconscious as the rest of your personality. Serious players develop both aspects, sculpting a corporate style while reveling in the expression of self that lies at the heart of all power.

---

* The Westinghouse division this author labored for in his first job assembled a meticulous and expensive 1986–90 strategic plan document that ran to more than 120 pages and incorporated state-of-the-art desktop printing, tons of charts, and formal binding. The division was divested in 1988.

Success is the misty peak one may regard in the distance but never reach, rejoicing in the journey not the attainment of the destination. A visit to the land of the high achievers finds millionaires who envy those with $100 million in the bank who in turn gaze at billionaires with resentment, executive vice presidents who would be COOs, and CEOs who want to decapitate the chairman.

Sucking up, see **Ass-kissing**.

Suggestion, as in "the power of," is how you get narcissistic senior managers to do things. You suggest. They listen. After a while, they come around to believing the idea was theirs. They present it back to you. You compliment them on their brilliance. There. So much easier than trying to sell through an idea to a guy who only listens to himself.

T

Team is anyone you're working with at the moment. The bigger the team, the more players you can call on to go to bat for your side. Remember! There is no I in Team! There is, of course, an I in Item. Also in Itinerary. In fact, there are plenty of words with I in them. But not Team. No I in Team, definitely.

Team player is what you want to be, reputation-wise. There are many reasons for failure on the job: stupidity, dishonesty, lack of training, despondency, laziness. Yet the one most often cited as sufficient cause for a colleague's career meltdown is "Didn't fit in here. Wasn't a team player." This, in itself, is viewed as a universally accepted provocation for dismissal, unless you're the person with the whistle in the corner office. A lot of the time, that person doesn't have to be a team player. You do, though. There's still no I here, by the way.

Team spirit has an I in it. Finally! Someplace where I can fit in. At its best, it's a lovely feeling, the toasty glow that keeps the group warm through thick and thin. At its worst, team spirit is invoked the way the Aztecs used to recruit virgins to be thrown into the fire. Beware of all High Priests who ask for such sacrifices for the good of the team. That's when you can remind them there's no *I* in it.

Telephones come in two well-known flavors: landline and mobile. One day there will be no landlines. There will just be mobile phones that some people carry around when the cranial implant that connects them to the big mainframe isn't working. At the office, however, it's still mostly landlines. There are a bunch of rules that pertain to phone etiquette. They vary from culture to culture. In Los Angeles, for instance, **assistants** lock in mortal combat to make sure their boss gets on the phone *after* the other guy. It's understandable. If Bob at CAA finds himself waiting for Bob at WME to get on, Bob at WME has won. Nobody likes to feel like a loser before the conversation has even started. There are, naturally, slightly different rules for mobile etiquette. Don't talk on one of them if you're with other people, unless you're a putz. That's right, I'm talking to you, you rude little SOB. And don't tell me you're going into a tunnel, either. Nobody who says they're going into a tunnel is actually going into a tunnel anymore. Think of something else.

Thank you would be nice. By the way, the proper response to "Thank you" in business is still "You're Welcome." It is not "No problem." There never was a problem and there's not going to be a problem unless you want to start one.

Time is not money. Money is money. If you don't have time to spend it, of course, money is useless, a fact brought home to corporate executives when their plans for the weekend are canceled yet again. Next to money, though, time is of the essence. Important people in particular are impressed with the value of their time, and wasting it is their prerogative, not yours. Allow the following for each function you're likely to encounter:

- *Chairman:* In one-on-one conversations, complete your business in five minutes. At his salary, anything beyond that is exploitation of a commodity worth more per day than your apartment.
- *Other senior officers:* Fifteen minutes, unless he or she throws you out or feels lonely and wants more. They need you to believe they are very busy. And they are. **Delegating**.
- *Vice presidents:* Don't worry about it. What's a vice president worth these days? There are so many of them they can eliminate 40 percent and there are still enough to drain the bonus pool. They have some time because they just delegated what was delegated to them.
- *Directors, managers, and other professionals:* They're the ones who got delegated to. Don't waste their time.
- *Assistants:* If they're typing or on the phone, leave them alone. If they're not, pull up a chair and prepare to sit a spell. They can talk and the relationship-building you're doing will be worth more than the friendship of ten vice presidents when you need to talk to the executive they work for.

Title is very, very important. Don't let anybody tell you different. A new title—particularly one that is publicly announced—is worth a ton more than a lousy 5 percent raise. If they don't want to give you a quantum shift from associate to manager, take an incremental elevation to something like senior associate. If you're already a senior associate and they won't make you a manager, fight to be a senior executive associate. And money will eventually follow, falling out of the upper regions of the corporation as those who determine compensation forget your title change was meaningless HR bullshit and simply look at all those adjectives in front of your name. "How," they will ask, "can we possibly pay an executive senior vice associate a paltry $42,500 a year? Give 'em a raise."

Travel is really fun for about ten years. Then you get tired of bouncing on the bed. Fortunately, as the rigors of the traveling lifestyle begin to wear, you will be growing in **power** and status and eligible to stay in ridiculously sumptuous surroundings with a high thread count. And being in another town before, between, and after meetings affords perhaps the greatest freedom that an adult who is employed can hope to enjoy, particularly if you like the idea of walking the streets of Paris, New Orleans, New York, Los Angeles, Hong Kong, Tokyo, or Des Moines with time on your hands, **plastic** in your pocket, and no asses to kiss for a couple of hours.

Turf is the work you do that no one but you should be doing. Some of your turf is worth protecting and some of it is not. Fully 25 percent of your job is stuff that you'd gladly cede to others if it didn't hurt you in anybody's eyes. So give it up. Don't protect unnecessary turf. And keep your eyes open for duties, tasks, and relationships that somebody else may consider part of their 25 percent but that could possibly do you some good. Bartering and swapping of turf is better than constant firefights over scraps at the dump.

Twitter is a medium by which everyday people can watch the mental fumes of celebrities, comedians, journalists, sports figures, and the occasional mogul in the public eye for reasons both good and bad. Research into actual Twitter usage shows that regular people do not tweet very much. They use Twitter to follow those who do. Twitter has also developed into a very important marketing and promotional tool, which indicates that it is well on its way to superfluity and obsolescence.*

Unions are the anathema to the free market that allows proud, independent companies to pay workers whatever they can get away with, thus somewhat equalizing the standing of the American worker with that of his counterpart in Belize or China. The good news for those who hate organized labor is that a mere fraction of the American workforce now belongs to a union and that number is shrinking. This suits a surprising number of workers just fine. Unions aren't really necessary, after all. **Executives** don't have them, and look at how well they're doing.

Uniques are individual **users** who are counted in the assessment of how many people are accessing a given online destination. They are more valuable than mere users, however, because the user number includes those who attend the digital festivities on the site numerous times. Not that every one of us isn't unique, of course we are, but uniques are nonduplicative, so that's a better number if you have a

---

* You can follow Stanley Bing on Twitter @thebingblog.

lot of them. If you don't, though, you can use users because users use the site, too, and deserve to be counted, even though they are not unique, except in human terms.

Upside is what you talk about when business stinks. Revenue down? Margins shrinking? Earnings in the tank? Think of the upside! It's huge!

User-generated content was going to replace professional content sometime around 2006. It didn't. It hasn't. And it won't. Grumpy Cat is still funny, though.

Users are the people who are on any given online destination during a specified period of time. They are very valuable but they are not uniques because sometimes they come back over and over again to "use" the site, which is still good, but diminishes their uniqueness. Sites that want to boost their numbers use users more than uniques but sometimes will cite uniques if that metric is impressive enough. The whole thing just proves that if there's a way to complicate things and make them less accessible, there are people who will figure out a way to make the most of it.

Vacation is easier said than done. There is always somebody who expresses shock at the idea that you'll be going away, even though you've done everything to prep the entire organization for weeks. Very senior people often have no lives. They sometimes have a tough time permitting others to have one. The wise employee clears the decks as much as possible, bids everybody good-bye, takes his or her leave. And for God's sake, don't say something like "Don't worry, I'll be on my **BlackBerry** the whole time" unless you want to be left back in this course of study and not receive the neat diploma you will find at the end of this book.

Vlog is a **blog** primarily made up of videos concerning a person's life and opinions. It is a condensation of the words "video log," and is pronounced "vee log," not "vlog." Even though many blogs use video, not all blogs are vlogs. The word *blog* is a shortening of the original term *weblog* and primarily uses words. Vlogs are made up mostly of video. Both blogs and vlogs are a highly evolved form of navel gazing. Thankfully, navels are interesting to a lot of people. One day everybody's navel will be famous for fifteen minutes.

W

Web, World Wide Web, Web 2.0, website, other Web derivatives. The Web started as a project for the Defense Department. It has now grown to be the most amazing and powerful invention since fire. It encompasses all cultures, spawns usages in every realm of human life, reaches into all aspects of experience, and is right now changing what it means to be a member of our species. How we are evolving as a result of our constant interface with the digital cosmos has yet to be understood, but in less time than it took for *Homo neanderthalensis* to mutate into *Homo sapiens* a new species that melds the organic with the digital will appear and the Web and the post-human mind will be one. Until then, I'm going to unplug every day for a couple of hours. I suggest you do, too. People who are constantly on the digital tit aren't as good with groups, and unless you're Steve or Mark or Bill, that's not usually as good for business as being able to deal with people to their analog face.

Wikipedia is a gigantic encyclopedia with entries on the entire catalog of human experience from the dawn of time. It's quite good, and very useful for quick research on virtually any subject. It's not always perfect, though. Its entry on Stanley Bing could be more comprehensive, for instance.

Winning is great for people who believe they are playing a game. Quite a few do, and that helps them as far as it goes. But it's a limited analogy. A game is a structured activity, defined by rules, determined probabilities, and skill. The world of business, on the other hand, while it does bear some of those characteristics, is at its heart an arbitrary pageant of rampaging human folly, interpersonal manipulation, and occasional grandeur. All central decisions—no matter how they may seem based on metrics and analysis—are, at the moment of their birth, irrational, visceral, a leap into the void. Don't play solely to win. Play to make something grow. And if you win a lot along the way, so much the better for you and all who rely on your wisdom, your creative spirit, and your money.

Women's room (see **men's room**) is a good place to indulge in a little female bonding. In fact, never share the space with another corporate animal without at least exchanging greetings and a mild meteorological observation. Hand washing is a better time for substantive comment. While you don't want to be caught hanging around the women's room all day, make a virtue out of necessity and use the opportunity to trade a bit of information and humanity. It's only right. The men are laughing and scratching aross the hall, you know.

Workaholics are not people who work hard. Workaholics are people who replace life with the appearance of work. Much of what the workaholic does isn't work per se. It's activity. Brownian motion. Up to a certain point, workaholics must be pitied, for they are the prototypical victims of their own success. After that, they're just crazy people getting between you and your dinner, your kids and your poker game. There are many addictions that are not tolerated in business. Unfortunately, this is not one of them. It is, in fact, encouraged. You'll have to fight this one out over time. You can start by not responding to late-night and weekend e-mails and go on from there.

X

X factor is the force of the unknown, and it walks beside you wherever you go. When snow grounds the Learjet carrying the executive counsel on the way to your sales presentation, the X factor has struck. When the mail-room guy spills coffee on your mass communication and you have to do it over in ten minutes, there it goes again. You can't act against it, because it has no shape until it's too late. All you can do is tear into it and repair the damage. The X can hurt, but it can't destroy unless you turn tail and run. And sometimes it can even help you. Who needed that friggin' meeting anyhow?

Y

Yelling is obnoxious. Everybody hates people who do it a lot. A little of it is okay. Everyone gets frustrated sometimes. So there are times when a good shriek is entirely appropriate, especially if you direct it at a wall, or a friend, or a really insignificant employee or colleague who has driven you over the cliff and into the sea of madness. In that case, yelling works. So does treating a person nice. Unless, of course, you've tried that. In that case go ahead and yell now and then. But as a persistent tactic? It's like crack. You start by yelling now and then. Then to get the same effect you have to do it more and more. Until the day comes when you're one of those hateful, scabrous weasels everybody has to tiptoe around. Is that what you want to grow up to be?

Yes-man, or to be more appropriately contemporary, **yes-person**, is a viable occupation for those who have no alternative. The art is complex, not a shallow recitation of simple oohs, aahs, and an occasional "Outstanding, Boss!" On the contrary, effective yesmanship employs a welter of tools:

- *"Ooh, aah, and "Outstanding, Boss!":* Never forget the basics.
- *"Very interesting . . .":* The ultimate noncommittal answer, issued to sound like admiration or agreement.
- *Outright flattery:* Executives who require incessant agreement like to have their grandiosity cleaned and waxed every hundred miles or so.

- *Incitement of paranoia:* The flip side of needing to be right all the time is the conviction that you're never right. The accomplished yes-man feeds that insecurity in his master, fertilizing it with incisive, nasty speculation, watering it with malicious rumor, pruning it with an occasional dash of happy news. The object is to convince him you're the only one in the entire organization with his interest at heart, the only one he can trust.

If you are the sole trustworthy entity in that executive's universe, he or she is in big trouble. Sometimes a little disagreement is what a manager groping in a thicket of options needs to hear.

YouTube is amazing. Long may it dawdle. As a purveyor of professional **content**, it sort of stinks. But as a library of video and audio that would otherwise be lost, it is incomparable. And as a time sponge, there is truly nothing like it. It is a little light on Stanley Bing videos, however.

Zoo is a comfortable prison in which a variety of exotic and incompatible species are housed after they have exchanged their freedom for security. Lions stop roaring after a while and sleep far too much. Elephants are scratched and wheedled by a host of tiny keepers. Hyenas laugh at inane jokes of their own devising. Snakes digest mice slowly. Apes play, chase each other over toys and dead stumps in their circumscribed terrain, and occasionally get bored and throw their feces at those who get too close. Wolves howl. Babies are born, old folks die. Above and around, the zoo goes on, staffed and restocked by invisible warders. After a while, thankfully, an animal simply forgets it's in a zoo at all, and thinks, "Hey, I've got my own crib. I'm eating pretty good. This must be real life." It's not, of course. But maybe it's better. After you get used to it, a well-run zoo is a lot more tolerable than a jungle.

Zzz's are nothing to be ashamed of if you can find a proper place. Sometimes you need a nap and work better after one. It's best not to go into deep REM sleep in actual **meetings**, of course, particularly if you snore. After your winks, slap your face smartly, go directly, unobserved, to the restroom, and comb yourself. You don't want to stumble into your next meeting with your eyes all rheumy and your hair funneled into a pointy cone at the top of your head. People will laugh. Believe me, I know. I've been there.

The Total Curriculum

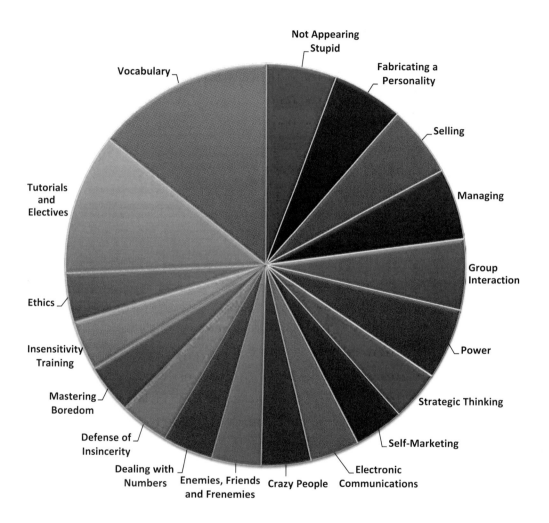

A NOTE FROM THE DEAN

I would be remiss in not expressing gratitude to the Board of Regents at HarperCollins, who presided over the painstaking years in which this Curriculum was in development. Particular thanks go to the President of the University, Michael Morrison, and to Professors David Hirshey, Hollis Heimbouch, and Barry Harbaugh, for their heroic editorial efforts and for the restaurant expenses they allowed me to pick up during the process. A particular shout-out to Sydney Pierce for her valuable sangfroid and support.

I would like to thank the National Association for Serious Studies, its board of directors, and its senior management for the excellent support given to this project from its inception. Thanks for the long evenings, the fierce discussions, the rigor of your methods. It relieves my mind not a little to know that long after I am gone, the Association will be there to carry on my investigations, speculations, and initiatives.

The National Association for Serious Studies

Master of Business Arts

Certificate of Graduation

Is hereby awarded to

You

_____

Having Duly Completed **The Curriculum**

[Insert Date]

Stanley Bing, President

Photography Credits

Grateful acknowledgment is made to the following for permission to reproduce images:

ABC/Paramount Home Video: page 273
Capitoline Museum, Rome: page 187
Condé Nast: page 83
Darrell B. Perry: page 221
Department of Justice: page 254
Dreamstime: pages 36, 66, 79, 97, 151, 216, 219, 254, 265, 321, 338, 352
Everett Collection: pages 36, 82, 97, 151, 218, 220, 266
GETTY: pages 82, 151, 163, 218, 353
Glyptothek, Munich: page 162
Istockphoto: page 34
Jerry Ohlinger Archive: page 97
Kia Motors: page 76
Lambert & Butler: page 173
Metro-Goldwyn-Mayer (MGM): page 158
Miramax Pictures/Walt Disney Pictures: page 220
Musée Antoine Lécuyer: page 34
Museo del Prado: page 102
National Gallery of Art: page 217
Nissan USA: page 76
PBS: page 36
Private Collection: page 63
Quillard Inc. Photography/Havas Worldwide: page 75
Reuters: page 36
RonPopeil.com: page 82
Stanley Bing: page 361
Walt Disney Productions: page 218
Western Electric: page 332
www.whitehouse.gov: page 219

About the Author

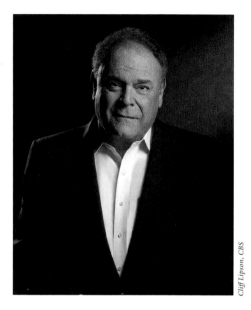

Cliff Lipson, CBS

Stanley Bing is a longtime columnist for *Fortune* magazine and the bestselling author of *What Would Machiavelli Do?*, *Throwing The Elephant*, *Sun Tzu was a Sissy*, *100 Bullshit Jobs . . . and How to Get Them*, *The Big Bing*, *Crazy Bosses*, *Executricks*, *Bingsop's Fables*, and the acclaimed novels *Lloyd: What Happened* and *You Look Nice Today*. By day, he is a top executive in a gigantic multinational corporation whose identity is one of the worst-kept secrets in business. He lives in New York City, Los Angeles, and Mill Valley, California.